The man from

By the same author
A day that changed the world (Inter-Varsity Press)

The man from outside

Gordon Bridger
Rector of Holy Trinity Church, Norwich

Inter-Varsity Press

INTER-VARSITY PRESS
38 De Montfort Street, Leicester LE1 7GP, England

First published 1969
Revised 1978

ISBN 0 85110 406 1

Set in 9/10½pt Plantin 110
Printed in Great Britain by
Wm. Collins Sons & Co. Ltd., Glasgow

*Inter-Varsity Press is the publishing division of
the Universities and Colleges Christian Fellowship
(formerly the Inter-Varsity Fellowship), a student
movement linking Christian Unions in universities
and colleges throughout the British Isles, and a
member movement of the International Fellowship of
Evangelical Students. For information about local
and national activities in Great Britain write to
UCCF, 38 De Montfort Street, Leicester LE1 7GP.*

Contents

Introduction

John's Gospel has been divided into the following small sections for convenience:

Introduction

I had been speaking to some students about the claims of Jesus
Christ and of Christianity. A friend of mine passed on to me afterwards the comment of an interested but uncommitted fellow
student who had heard the talk. It was something like this:
'I wish he hadn't assumed that we all believe the Bible is
true.'

I do not want to assume this in introducing John's Gospel.
There is certainly not space to outline all the reasons for my personal conviction that the Bible is reliable. Some who read this will
already be convinced. Others will not. But I want to suggest some
reasons for believing that in reading this part of the New Testament
we are considering an important and trustworthy source-book of
Christianity. We are looking at a contemporary account of the most
exciting and astonishing events of all time, events that centred on a
unique person, Jesus of Nazareth.

Dorothy Sayers once deplored the fact that so many people
appeared to regard the events and dogmas of the New Testament as
dull. She wrote: 'Here we had a man of divine character walking
and talking among us—and what did we find to do with Him? The
common people, indeed, "heard Him gladly". But our leading
authorities in Church and State considered that He talked too much
and uttered too many disconcerting truths. So we bribed one of
His friends to hand Him over quietly to the police, and we tried
Him on a rather vague charge of creating a disturbance, and had
Him publicly hanged on the common gallows, "thanking God we
were rid of a knave". All this was not very creditable to us, even if
He was (as many people thought and think) only a harmless, crazy
preacher. But if the Church is right about Him, it was more dis-
creditable still, for the Man we hanged was God Almighty . . . This
is the dogma we find so dull—the terrifying drama of which God is

7

the victim and hero. If this is dull, then what in Heaven's name is worthy to be called exciting!'*

This Gospel, then, is the story of the Man from outside—the man from outside our own experience, outside, as we shall see, anything the world had known before. He was very much an outsider, too, with the 'establishment' of his time, so much so that it was the religious leaders who hounded him to death. But before we plunge into the story, we must first clear the ground. How can we be reasonably sure that John gives us a reliable account of these exciting events?

a. The reliability of John's Gospel

1. *Are the documents reliable?* There is much more evidence for the reliability of the New Testament documents than for any other writings of comparable date.† No classical scholar would deny that Thucydides and Tacitus wrote their histories. Yet the earliest manuscripts we have of Thucydides' work is dated well over a thousand years after he wrote; and the manuscript for Tacitus is dated 800 years later. On the other hand, we have two complete New Testaments dated little more than 300 years after the originals;‡ a papyrus copy of about three-quarters of the New Testament about 200 years after the events,§ which includes sections of John's Gospel; the recently-discovered Bodmer papyrus which contains most of John's Gospel (dated about AD 200); and the famous John Rylands fragment, now in Manchester, but found in Egypt, and dated between AD 117 and 138. This must have been circulating within forty years of the writing of John's Gospel.

We may add to the weight of this documentary evidence the frequent quotations from the Gospels in various second-century works. So by comparing the various documents it is possible to arrive at a firm conclusion about the accuracy of copying, and the extent of alterations in the text. On the basis of such evidence a scholar of the standing of the late Sir Frederic Kenyon of the British Museum could say: 'Both the authenticity and the general

*Dorothy Sayers, *Creed and Chaos*, p. 3.
†Read F. F. Bruce, *The New Testament Documents* for a fuller treatment of this subject.
‡Codex Vaticanus and Codex Sinaiticus. The former is in the Vatican Library and the latter in the British Museum.
§Chester Beatty Papyri.

integrity of the books of the New Testament may be regarded as finally established.'*

'Very well,' you will say, 'but even if the documents are reliable, we may still be reading fiction rather than fact. How can we be sure that Jesus was real rather than legendary?'

2. *Is Jesus a historical person?* If we read the Gospels with an open mind, we may decide for ourselves whether there is a self-evident truthfulness about the stories.† Certainly it is hard to imagine why the writers of the New Testament should make up such a story, and in some cases die for it, if they knew it was not true. Furthermore, there is a ring of truth about the story of Jesus in the Gospels which is not echoed in later non-apostolic writings. In the so-called *Gospel of Thomas*, for example, we find this: 'The little child Jesus, when he was five years old, was playing at the ford of a brook. And having made soft clay he fashioned thereof 12 sparrows. And it was the sabbath day when he did these things. And Joseph came to the place and cried out to him saying: "Wherefore doest thou these things on the sabbath which it is not lawful to do?" But Jesus clapped his hands together, and said to them "Go!" And the sparrows took their flight and went away chirping.' The Jesus of the New Testament is not a magician like the apocryphal Jesus.

If, however, the internal evidence of the Gospels themselves does not convince us of the reality of a Jesus of history, there is external evidence to be considered. The Roman historian Tacitus lived between AD 60 and 120. When referring to the fire of Rome and the Neronian persecution, he wrote (*c*. AD 100): 'Nero set up as the culprits and punished with the utmost refinements of cruelty a class hated for their abominations . . . who are commonly called Christians. Christus, from whom their name is derived, was executed at the hands of the procurator Pontius Pilate in the reign of Tiberius.'‡ We might have expected that the execution of a village carpenter, occurring in a completely obscure province, with the minimum of publicity, would have been forgotten in a

*F. G. Kenyon, *The Bible and Archaeology*, p. 288.
†J. B. Phillips, *Ring of Truth* is an interesting testimony of a famous translator of the Bible to this conviction. See also Michael Green, *Runaway World*, especially the first chapter on 'Running away from history'.
‡Tacitus, *Annales*, xv. 44.

week. Yet a generation later Rome is resounding with the news of it.

Another example is that of Suetonius, who refers (c. AD 120) to the expulsion of the Jews from Rome in AD 49 through quarrelling over one 'Chrestus'.* The governor of Bithynia, Pliny the younger, writing around AD 110, refers to the Christians who meet in his province and gather every morning to sing a hymn to Christ as God.†

One further quotation must suffice. The writer was a contemporary of John, but he was not a Christian. 'About this time lived Jesus, a man full of wisdom, if one may call him a man. For he was the doer of incredible things, and the teacher of such as gladly accepted the truth. He thus attracted to himself many Jews and many of the Gentiles. He was the Christ. On the accusation of the leading men of our people, Pilate condemned him to death upon the cross. Nevertheless those who had previously loved him still remained faithful to him. On the third day he again appeared to them living, just as, in addition to a thousand other wonderful things, prophets sent by God had foretold. And at the present day the race of those who called themselves Christians after him has not ceased.'‡ The writer was Josephus, a Jewish historian, writing at the end of the first century AD. We need have no doubt that Jesus really lived.

But this leads to a further question about John's Gospel itself.

3. *Is John's Gospel accurate?* It is not difficult to see that John's Gospel is different from those of Matthew, Mark and Luke (often called the Synoptic Gospels) in a number of ways. If we had only John's Gospel as a record of the life and ministry of Jesus Christ we should be ignorant of such important features as the birth and childhood of Jesus, and the Last Supper. We should know nothing of his teaching by parables, his healing of lepers and demoniacs, or his association with those highly unpopular civil servants, the tax-collectors. We should know nothing of the Lord's Prayer.

On the other hand, John's Gospel alone tells us a great deal that we would not glean from the Synoptics. John alone tells us that Jesus frequently visited Jerusalem, though the Synoptics hint at

*Suetonius, *Life of Claudius*, 25.
†Pliny, *Letters*, x.
‡Josephus, *Antiquities of the Jews*, xviii. 3. 3.

this in the prayer of Jesus for Jerusalem: 'Jerusalem, Jerusalem! You kill the prophets, you stone the messengers God has sent you! *How many times* have I wanted to put my arms round all your people, just as a hen gathers her chicks under her wings, but you would not let me!' (Luke 13:34; Matthew 23:37–39). John alone tells us in any detail about the Judean ministry of Jesus. He alone writes about the wedding reception in Cana, the interviews with Nicodemus and the Samaritan woman, the raising of Lazarus from the dead and certain teaching about the Holy Spirit.

Another difference between John's Gospel and the Synoptics is the different style in the teaching of Jesus. It was fashionable, therefore, some years ago to dismiss John's Gospel as of doubtful historical value. John, it was agreed, was more concerned with theology than with history. Certain terms, such as 'the Word' or 'Logos' (John 1:1), 'children of light' and 'walking in darkness', were supposed to be more suitable for a late-second-century gnostic philosopher than for a first-century fisherman. Furthermore, it was believed that John was hopelessly inaccurate on his topography and knowledge of south Palestinian life, and that some of the places he mentioned were obviously a figment of the author's imagination.

In recent years a number of discoveries and a reconsideration of this Gospel have tended to confirm more and more its historical as well as theological value, and its accuracy. It is now generally believed that John wrote independently of the sources of the Synoptics, though no doubt he had knowledge of them; and it may well be that he wrote deliberately to supplement the teaching of the Synoptics.* He wrote for a definite purpose (see 20:31), and he was selective in his use of material. The style of teaching in his Gospel may well reflect his manner of debate with the rabbis in Jerusalem; for there seems to be little doubt that the rabbis had a style of their own. No doubt the style is 'Radio 3' rather than 'Radio 1' or '2'; but there is no reason to believe that Jesus would not adapt himself to the people to whom he was speaking. We now know, from the discovery of the Dead Sea Scrolls, that phrases used in John's Gospel such as 'children of light', 'life eternal', 'Spirit of truth', 'walking in the light', 'walking in the darkness', 'the light of life',

---

*For a fuller discussion of the relationship between John's Gospel and the Synoptics read the Introduction by R. V. G. Tasker in *The Gospel according to St. John* (*Tyndale New Testament Commentaries*).

do not indicate that the Gospel must have been written in the second century. These phrases can all be found in the Qumran text which is dated *before* the time of Jesus Christ.

Most interesting of all have been the archaeological discoveries that have certainly tended to confirm the accuracy of John's Gospel. The Pool of Bethesda, or Bethzatha, for example, was once thought to be non-existent as there was no trace of it in ancient literature or through archaeological excavations. Now this pool has been discovered, and the name is referred to in one of the Dead Sea Scrolls! Votive inscriptions indicate that the water was believed to possess healing properties. The Pool of Siloam is another exciting archaeological find. Gabbatha, 'the Stone Pavement' (19:13), was once dismissed as unhistorical. In 1934 Père Vincent, excavating in Jerusalem, discovered it some 20 feet below the surface of the city. It is 50 yards square, and was part of the Roman barracks destroyed before AD 70. The pavement can be seen in Jerusalem today.

Again, even the place-names in John's Gospel, and some of the names of people such as Lazarus and Martha, were once thought to be profoundly symbolical and highly fanciful. Some of the names of people have now turned up on ossuary inscriptions at a date which confirms John's use of them. Archaeology has also shown that many of the place-names John uses are far from fictitious and belong to early tradition stemming from the period before the destruction of Jerusalem in AD 70. In John 3:23, for example, John the Baptist is said to have been baptizing 'in Aenon, not far from Salim, because there was plenty of water in that place'. Salim has now been identified with a town of this name south east of Nablus, and Aenon with the neighbouring modern Aenum. This district abounds in springs. One writer,* after a careful reading of John 4:46–54, described his own conviction that John must have been very familiar with the topography of that part of Palestine. 'There is a marked stress on the descent from Cana to Capernaum— the author knew and felt the drop from well above sea-level to well below sea-level, which is so marked a feature of that region then as nowadays.'† The accuracy of John's Gospel continues to be confirmed by modern scholarship.

*R. D. Potter, *Studia Evangelica*, p. 329.
†For further reading on this subject, see R. D. Harrison, *Archaeology of the New Testament*; K. A. Kitchen, *The Bible in its World: The Bible and Archaeology Today*.

b. The authorship and date of John's Gospel

This Gospel has been called the Gospel *according to John* since the second century. The traditional view of the Christian church has been that this John is the apostle John, the son of Zebedee, a Galilean fisherman in partnership with James and Peter (Luke 5:7–10). He was one of the twelve disciples of Jesus, an eyewitness of his life, death and resurrection.

There is considerable external evidence to support John's close association with this Gospel. Irenaeus, who became Bishop of Lyons in AD 177, wrote: 'John, the disciple of the Lord, who also leant upon His heart, himself also published the gospel in Ephesus when he was living in Asia.' Clement of Alexandria wrote (*c.* AD 230): 'Last of all, John, perceiving that the bodily facts had been made plain in the gospel, being urged by his friends composed a spiritual gospel.' Perhaps the most important document is the Muratorian Canon compiled in Rome *c.* AD 170. This manuscript includes this comment: 'At the request of his fellow disciples and of his bishops, John, one of the disciples, said, "Fast with me for three days from this time and whatsoever shall be revealed to each of us, whether it be favourable to my writing or not, let us relate it to one another." On the same night it was revealed to Andrew that John should relate all things, aided by the revision of all.'

According to these traditions and others, John the apostle was certainly the authority behind the Gospel. It is not clear whether he wrote every word himself. He could have dictated it to a disciple or disciples who acted as secretaries.

The possibility that John used an amanuensis or secretary is suggested by a consideration of the Gospel itself. John never mentions his own name; but he does refer on several occasions to 'the disciple whom Jesus loved' (13:23–25; 19:26–27; 20:2; 21:20) who is probably to be identified with John the son of Zebedee. But it is also possible that there is another disciple who is witnessing to the facts he describes (see John 19:34–35; 21:24), and who may be actually writing them down.* Some have thought that it is more likely that another man would describe John as 'the disciple whom Jesus loved' than John himself. Whether we allow an

---

*For a fuller discussion see R. V. G. Tasker, *The Gospel according to St. John.*

13

amanuensis or not, the internal and external evidence is strongly in favour of the apostolic authority of John as the witness to the life of Christ.

It has sometimes been argued that a Gospel of this kind could not have been written by a Galilean fisherman. But as someone once commented: 'This might have been said about Ernest Bevin's speeches as Foreign Secretary, "These couldn't have been written by a barrow-boy in east Bristol." To which of course the answer is that they weren't, they were written by a man who *had been* a barrow-boy in east Bristol.'

If, as we believe, John Zebedee is the authority behind this Gospel, then we may certainly date the Gospel around AD 90 to 100. For it is the last Gospel to be written according to the majority of manuscripts; and we know from a strong tradition that John lived to be a very old man into the reign of Trajan, which began in AD 98.

Indeed, Bishop Robinson* would have us consider an even earlier date, perhaps AD 68, before the fall of Jerusalem in AD 70. For there is no mention of this catastrophic event in the Gospel. Robinson quotes, for example, John's comment (John 5:2): 'There *is* in Jerusalem at the sheep pool a place with five colonnades called in Hebrew, Bethesda.' Robinson adds, 'This was to be obliterated in the demolition of the city only to be uncovered and confirmed recently by the archaeologist's spade. *Yet John says emphatically at the time of writing (and not just of Jesus speaking)* "is" *not* "was".'

Whether Bishop Robinson is right in his interpretation or not, the evidence from the Dead Sea Scrolls and the John Rylands fragment certainly rule out the possibility of a late second century date for this Gospel.

c. The purpose of the Gospel

What then is the purpose of John's Gospel? John clearly expresses it when he writes (20:30–31): 'In his disciples' presence Jesus performed many other miracles which are not written down in this book. But these have been written in order that you may believe that Jesus is the Messiah, the Son of God, and that through your faith in him you may have life.'

*J. A. T. Robinson, *Can we trust the New Testament ?*, p. 86

John undoubtedly writes primarily for those not yet committed to belief in Jesus Christ. One commentator on this Gospel* has written: 'The Gospel could be read intelligently by a person who started with no knowledge of Christianity beyond the minimum that a reasonably well informed member of the public interested in religion might be supposed to have by the close of the first century . . . If he was then led to associate himself with the Church . . . he would be able to re-read the book and find in it vastly more than had been obvious at a first reading . . .'

Probably those who read it first would have been Jews, especially those displaced persons scattered through Asia who were influenced to some extent by Greek thought and culture. So John writes that they may come to believe that Jesus is the Messiah, the Anointed One promised to the Jewish people by God through their prophets, as well as the unique Son of God, or God become man. It is clear too that John is writing for those outside Palestine, without much knowledge of Jewish customs. For he has to explain terms such as purification (2:6), burial (19:40), and even such simple Semitic words as Rabbi (1:38) and Rabboni (20:16). Also, Christians did and do find their faith strengthened as they read this Gospel, and chapters 13 to 17 are perhaps especially relevant for already committed Christians.

The teaching of this Gospel would also be specially relevant in combating certain gnostic heresies which denied, for example, the real humanity of Jesus Christ. The humanity of Jesus is emphasized as well as his deity in this Gospel (see 4:6; 9:6; 11:35; 12:27; 19:28, 34). There are sects today, such as Jehovah's Witnesses, Christian Science and Mormonism, who need a similar corrective concerning the person of Christ.

Primarily, however, this Gospel is written to help an individual to a personal faith in Jesus Christ. I remember once talking to a university professor who said rather wistfully, 'How do you woo faith?' John's answer would be: read this account, consider this evidence, consider Jesus. 'But these have been written *in order that you may believe.*' For this Gospel is written to bring before us certain 'signs' and evidences which John has selected (see 20:30, 31) in order that we may believe in Jesus as the Christ and the Son of God, and that believing we may have life in his name.

*C. H. Dodd, *The Interpretation of the Fourth Gospel.*

There are two further questions that we may be asking, even if we are persuaded that John's Gospel is a reliable historical document, and we ourselves are seekers after truth and 'life'.

1. *Why should we read John's Gospel?* A man once said to me that he wanted to read about all the religions of the world before he could decide whether Christianity was true or not. I suggested that he narrowed his search to consider Jesus Christ first, for Jesus made claims for himself which no other religious leader has ever made.

John's Gospel tells us what those claims are, and gives reasons for believing them. If these claims are false, then we are free to consider the merits of other religions. If they are true, they make such total demands upon us that whatever true things may be found in other religions, Christianity must still be uniquely true, and Jesus Christ the only true way to God. As Jesus himself says, 'I am the way, the truth, and the life; no one goes to the Father, except by me' (John 14:6). That is either intolerant humbug, or one of the most important statements of all time. We should read John's Gospel, therefore, to find out whether these unique claims of Jesus Christ are true or not.

John's Gospel also claims that believing in Jesus leads to '*life* in his name'. 'Eternal life' is much more than 'living for ever'. It clearly refers to a quality of life here and now which, it is claimed, Jesus gives to those who believe in him. According to John's Gospel, 'real life', as compared to 'existence', is found only by those who know God and the Lord Jesus Christ (17:3). Men and women are searching for satisfaction now as they were in the first century. Bertrand Russell once said, 'Life is one long second-best.' A current song-writer expresses the same pessimism when he writes, 'I can't get no satisfaction . . . I've tried and I've tried.' Yet the former England and Sussex cricketer, David Sheppard, can write of his own commitment to Jesus Christ and the cricketing career he relinquished, by saying: 'As with so many things in the Christian life, it has not so much been a case of "giving it up", as "taking up" something else which is infinitely worthwhile.'* What was 'infinitely worthwhile' was the new life in Jesus Christ which has eventually led him and his wife to serve God first in London's dockland and then in the heart of Liverpool. If the reader is

*D. S. Sheppard, *Parson's Pitch*, p. 245.

16

searching for a satisfying and demanding life, as well as a life that continues beyond the grave, then John's Gospel claims to show us how this may become ours. That is why we should read it.

2. *How should we read it?* The story is told of the late Dr. Benjamin Jowett, at one time the Master of Balliol College, Oxford, who was not only a great scholar but also a great wit. At dinner one day a lady tried to draw some clever response from him: 'Dr. Jowett, we would like to know what is your opinion of God?' The Master immediately looked stern, and he said, 'Madam, I should think it a great impertinence were I to express my opinion about God. The only constant anxiety of my life is to know what is God's opinion of me.'

It is because John's Gospel claims to tell us, amongst other things, 'God's opinion' of us, that we would be wise to read it in the following ways.

Honestly and humbly. More than one person has read John's Gospel with the sincere prayer on their lips, 'O God, if there be a God, reveal yourself to me.' According to the Bible God made this promise to the Jewish people: 'You will seek me, and you will find me because you will seek me with all your heart. Yes, I say, you will find me' (Jeremiah 29:13–14). In any subject, if we want to find the truth we have to be honest and wholehearted. This is precisely the same when we seek the truth about God. We shall see in this Gospel that Jesus had nothing to say to triflers. But he once said, 'Seek, and you will find' (Matthew 7:7).

Thoughtfully and regularly. It is possible to read John's Gospel at a sitting, and it is certainly good to do this some time if we can. But this short commentary is designed to encourage you to read about half a chapter a day. *It is hoped that you will read the passage through at least twice, and think about it, before you read the comments.* The commentary is written only to supplement or reinforce what you may have already discovered.

Practically and obediently. A school-teacher once told me how she began to read John's Gospel at a time when she had doubts 'whether there could be a God, and even more doubts as to whether Jesus could be God'. She said that she began to read the Gospel in 'fairly large chunks' at night before sleeping. As she finished the closing chapters she remembers telling herself 'it couldn't be otherwise'. Then she added, 'From that time on I was sure there was a God, *although it was years later that I came to trust Christ with my life.*' When John talks about belief in Jesus Christ he means more than intellectual assent to certain facts about him. He means practical, obedient trust in him. When we discover truth we must do something about it, if we are not to spend years of our life in uncertainty.

It is my prayer that you will discover and act upon the truth of John's words: 'But these have been written in order that you may believe . . ., and that through your faith in him you may have life.'

1 God speaks to man

1:1–18
1 Before the world was created, the Word already existed; he was with God, and he was the same as God. ²From the very beginning the Word was with God. ³Through him God made all things; not one thing in all creation was made without him. ⁴The Word was the source of life, and this life brought light to mankind. ⁵The light shines in the darkness, and the darkness has never put it out.

6 God sent his messenger, a man named John, ⁷who came to tell people about the light, so that all should hear the message and believe. ⁸He himself was not the light; he came to tell about the light. ⁹This was the real light—the light that comes into the world and shines on all mankind.

10 The Word was in the world, and though God made the world through him, yet the world did not recognize him. ¹¹He came to his own country, but his own people did not receive him. ¹²Some, however, did receive him and believed in him; so he gave them the right to become God's children. ¹³They did not become God's children by natural means, that is, by being born as the children of a human father; God himself was their Father.

14 The Word became a human being and, full of grace and truth, lived among us. We saw his glory, the glory which he received as the Father's only Son.

15 John spoke about him. He cried out, 'This is the one I was talking about when I said, "He comes after me, but he is greater than I am, because he existed before I was born." '

16 Out of the fullness of his grace he has blessed us all, giving us one blessing after another. *17God gave the Law through Moses, but grace and truth came through Jesus Christ.* *18No one has ever seen God. The only Son, who is the same as God and is at the Father's side, he has made him known.*

A friend of mine was talking about a mutual acquaintance. 'Mind you,' said my friend, 'he's a difficult person to get to know.' Perhaps we all know some people like that and realize that unless a person is prepared to make themselves known to us, we may never know how they think or feel, or what they want us to know or do. We may never get to know them as friends.

Some people believe that God is a difficult person to know. They think that if he exists at all, he is remote and far removed from them. He is unreal. Someone once said to me, 'I've been seeking God but I've never found him.' John, the writer of this Gospel, has a quite different story to tell us. He tells us that; in fact, God has revealed himself to mankind. That, whether or not men are seeking God, God is seeking men and making himself known to them. He describes this in three ways.

a. God speaks to us through Jesus, who is 'the Word'

From the very beginning, when God was, the Word also was; where God was, the Word was with him; what God was, the Word also was. The Word was there with God from the beginning . . . The Word became a human being and lived among us (verses 1, 2 and 14). John leaves us in no doubt that Jesus, who is here described as 'the Word', was God become man. At this point John does not argue the case, he simply states it. Now in calling Jesus 'the Word', he is telling us that in Jesus, as J. B. Phillips puts it, 'God expressed himself.' God made himself known in human terms that all of us could understand. So God has made it possible for us to know him.

The orthodox Jew, like John, would understand this concept of 'the Word' in a special sense. The Word of God had come to the Jews through the Law and the Prophets. But now, John claimed, God was speaking with love and truth in a supreme and final way in Jesus. The intelligent Greek reader of John's Gospel would have another thought. For him 'the Word' or 'Logos' (the Greek word that John uses) was the Intelligence behind the universe and the marvels of creation. John claims that Jesus, the Word, *was* that Intelligence. He is the Creator and Sustainer of all things (verses 1–3). So, in Jesus, the Creator speaks to us.

I once failed to hear an important party political broadcast. It was not that the Prime Minister failed to speak, but that I failed to tune in. So it is that we sometimes fail to know God, not because he has not spoken, but because we are not tuned in to hear him.

b. God reveals himself through Jesus, who is the light

Another way to describe man's sense of alienation from God is to say that he is walking in the dark. He has lost his way. He doesn't know where to find God, and so he experiences very often a terrible sense of darkness, lostness and aimlessness. A. E. Housman put it like this:

> 'The sun is up and up must I,
> To wash and dress
> And eat and drink
> And look at things
> And talk and think
> And work . . .
> And God knows why.'

But John claims that God has not left man in total darkness to drift aimlessly along.

For God has revealed himself in nature. Jesus is 'the light that comes into the world and shines on all mankind' (verse 9). Even those who have never heard of Christ or read the Bible see something of God in nature. The apostle Paul used the same argument in his letter to the Romans (1:20). Ever since God created the world, his invisible qualities, both his eternal power and his divine nature, have been clearly seen. Men can perceive them in the things that God has made.

God also reveals himself in man. For Jesus is 'the light . . . that shines on all mankind', and all men have an awareness of right and wrong, as well as an appreciation of all that is good, beautiful and true. Men have a conscience, and an awareness of God. The light shines, and has always shone in man even though he walks in the darkness; 'and the darkness has never put it out' (verse 5).*

God uniquely reveals himself in Jesus. This is, as we have already seen, John's most astonishing claim. 'The Word became a human being and, full of grace and truth, lived among us. We saw his glory, the glory which he received as the Father's only Son' (verse 14). This is the light that shines most brightly in the darkness. Not all accepted Jesus or recognized that he was God become man (verse 11). But those who did, saw someone who expressed love and truth and 'glory', the very presence and power of God. In Jesus, as John the Baptist and John the Evangelist believed, the invisible God had become visible to man (verse 18). God had come into focus.

If God seems out of focus, a shadowy, unreal power, an impersonal force, and if John is right in what he says, then the importance of his words can hardly be over-estimated. For John claims that God has revealed himself to men in personal, flesh-and-blood terms in Jesus Christ. Furthermore he offers us, as a gift, the possibility of knowing him for real.

c. God gives through Jesus, who is the life

'The Word was the source of life, and this life brought light to mankind (verse 4) . . . his own people did not receive him. Some, however, did receive him and believed in him; so he *gave* them the right to become God's children (verses 11, 12) . . . Out of the fullness of his grace he has blessed us all' (verse 16). John makes it clear that 'knowing God' means far more than 'knowing about him'.

Few men are interested in theories about God. But many are searching for satisfaction, for 'kicks', for 'experiences', for what John calls 'life'. So John claims, with other Christians (notice the 'we' in verses 14, 16), that it is possible to experience 'life', the life of God, when we receive Christ, become his children (verse 12) and continue to receive his gifts (verse 16). This 'life' is not to be compared with physical life. Neither does it follow automatically

*Cicero once wrote: 'If a man enters a house or a gymnasium of a forum and sees reason, method and discipline reigning there, he cannot suppose that these came about without a cause, but perceives that there is someone there who rules and is obeyed: how much more when he contemplates the motions and revolutions to be seen in the universe (*e.g.* in the heavenly bodies) must he conclude they are all governed by a Conscious Hand.'

upon physical birth. It is not dependent upon heredity (verse 13), nor possible by natural means. This 'life' is given to us by God. It is also by grace (verse 16, 17), which means that he offers us life, not because we deserve it, but because he loves to give it (*cf.* Romans 6:23).

Questions for discussion
1. What place has 'reason' and intellectual argument in a man's search for God?
2. What would you say to someone who says to you, 'I've been seeking God, but I've never found him'? (Base your answer on this passage.)
3. What evidence is there that the person who does not know God is 'in darkness'?
4. What teaching have we in this passage to help us answer the question, 'What will happen to those who have never heard of Jesus Christ?' (See also Romans 1 and 2 and Acts 10 and 14:15–18).
5. What does it mean to 'receive' Jesus (11, 12, 13)?

2 A man gives evidence

1:19–34
19 The Jewish authorities in Jerusalem sent some priests and Levites to John, to ask him, 'Who are you?'

20 John did not refuse to answer, but spoke out openly and clearly, saying: 'I am not the Messiah.'

21 'Who are you, then?' they asked. 'Are you Elijah?'

'No, I am not,' John answered.

'Are you the Prophet?' they asked.

'No,' he replied.

22 'Then tell us who you are,' they said. 'We have to take an answer back to those who sent us. What do you say about yourself?'

23 John answered by quoting the prophet Isaiah:

' "I am the voice of someone shouting in the desert:

Make a straight path for the Lord to travel !" '

24 The messengers, who had been sent by the Pharisees, [25]then asked John, 'If you are not the Messiah nor Elijah nor the Prophet, why do you baptize ?'

26 John answered, 'I baptize with water, but among you stands the one you do not know. [27]He is coming after me, but I am not good enough even to untie his sandals.'

28 All this happened in Bethany on the east side of the River Jordan, where John was baptizing.

29 The next day John saw Jesus coming to him, and said, 'There is the Lamb of God, who takes away the sin of the world ! [30]This is the one I was talking about when I said, "A man is coming after me, but he is greater than I am, because he existed before I was born." [31]I did not know who he would be, but I came baptizing with water in order to make him known to the people of Israel.'

32 And John gave this testimony: 'I saw the Spirit come down like a dove from heaven and stay on him. [33]I still did not know that he was the one, but God, who sent me to baptize with water, had said to me, "You will see the Spirit come down and stay on a man; he is the one who baptizes with the Holy Spirit." [34]I have seen it,' said John, 'and I tell you that he is the Son of God.'

I once saw one of England's greatest footballers, Stanley Matthews, play for England. So when I hear people talking about great footballers, past and present, and his name is mentioned, my words about him carry extra weight. I've not only read about him – I *saw* him in action. I'm an eyewitness to his greatness.

John now introduces a number of eyewitnesses who were contemporaries of Jesus, and *saw* and *heard* him. The first witness is a man we call John the Baptist. The Jewish historian Josephus (born AD 37) has given independent evidence of the existence of this man, and also confirmed the manner of his death described in Luke's Gospel.*

The Gospels tell us that he was the only son of an elderly couple, the priest Zechariah and his wife Elizabeth. His parents believed he was a very special gift from God and that he was a man of destiny. John grew up to be a remarkable preacher. So far as we know he was not trained at any theological college after he had left home. Since the discovery of the Dead Sea Scrolls some have sug-

*Josephus, *Antiquities of the Jews*, xviii. 5. 2.

gested that he might have joined one of the religious communities, such as the Essenes, and received instruction. But his strong individualism and passionate loyalty to the Old Testament Scriptures suggest that he remained in the barren and desolate wilderness of Judea, studying the Old Testament, and preparing for his public ministry alone.

John the Baptist lived simply and ascetically, in marked contrast to many of the religious leaders of his day. He preached courageously, condemning the established order, and calling the regular 'church-goers' to forsake their wickedness and to be baptized, as a way of preparing for the coming of the Messiah (Luke 3:4–6). When crowds began to flock from Jerusalem and the surrounding parts to hear John, it is not surprising that the leaders of the 'establishment' sent a small commission to find out what it was all about. It was in answer to their questions that John the Baptist tells us more about Jesus. He became convinced that Jesus was the Christ, the Messiah. He also recognized Jesus as the 'Lamb of God' and the true Son of God.

a. The Messiah (verses 19–28)

Men have always looked for a Utopia, for a new age, for a brave new world. But their hopes have always been dashed to the ground. Early in this century H. G. Wells, for example, was able to write, 'Can we doubt that presently our race will more than realise our boldest imaginations, that it will achieve unity and peace?'* By 1945 his optimistic hope that man would bring in a new age was shattered. The title of the book which expressed his disillusionment was, fittingly, *Mind at the end of its tether*.

The Jews, however, believed that God had promised a new age which would be ushered in by the coming of God's 'Anointed One', or 'Messiah', or 'Christ'. The Old Testament was full of such promises. So the Jews asked John the Baptist whether he was 'the Christ'. John's answer was clear (verses 20–23). In the East, before a king visited a province, a herald went before him to give men the opportunity to make suitable preparations. In the Baptist's view, Jesus was the Messiah, John was the herald, calling people to make ready for the coming of their king. But already the Baptist understood that this King or Messiah does not come with force but

*H. G. Wells, *A Short History of the World*, p. 289.

in love, for the next day he described Jesus as the 'Lamb of God'.

b. The Lamb of God (verse 29)

As the Baptist spoke perhaps he saw a flock of lambs being led to Jerusalem from the country, for the forthcoming Jewish Passover (John 2:15). The blood of the Passover lamb had once been placed on the door-posts of the homes of believing Jews when they had been slaves in Egypt. It had been a sign that saved them from God's judgment and from death (see Exodus 12:11–13). So when Jesus is described as the Lamb of God, it implies that he would shed his blood to save men from judgment and death.

Certainly John had been thinking about the words of the prophet Isaiah (verse 23). From Isaiah John would know that the Messiah could deliver God's people only through suffering. The 'suffering servant' of Isaiah's prophecies would be led 'like a lamb about to be slaughtered' and would be 'wounded . . . because of our sins . . ., beaten because of the evil we did'. In a remarkable way these words were going to be fulfilled in the death of Jesus Christ, who would die to 'take away the sin of the world'. In the Bible sin means 'missing the mark' or 'breaking the law'. It is because we are all sinners by God's standards that someone is needed to come and 'bear away sin'. But who can forgive sins but one who comes from God and identifies himself with men? The Baptist believed that Jesus did just that, when he called him both 'Lamb of God' and 'Son of God'.

c. The Son of God (verses 30–34)

The brothers of Jesus were cousins of John the Baptist. So probably John and Jesus had met before. But the Baptist tells us that he was not certain that Jesus was the Messiah until a remarkable event took place. Jesus asked to be baptized by John. Although John did not feel worthy to baptize Jesus, he realized that God had a purpose in it. God gave him a sign that day that Jesus was not only the Messiah, but in a unique sense *God's Son* (verse 34). There is no suggestion here that Jesus had sinned, but the significance of Jesus's baptism seems to be that he was identifying himself with sinners.

The Gospel argues that Jesus is uniquely and eternally the Son of God. We have already seen (1:1–18) that John understands by that phrase that in Jesus God became man. We shall need to look carefully at the reasons for such a staggering claim. But Christians believe that because Jesus is both God and man, he is able in a unique way to bring God and man together.

Questions for discussion
1. What impresses you about John's response to the questions put to him about Jesus? (19–21)
2. What do we learn about Jesus in this passage, and about John's attitude to him?
3. What do we think about Jesus in the light of John the Baptist's testimony?

3 Four more witnesses

1:35–51
35 The next day John was standing there again with two of his disciples, [36]*when he saw Jesus walking by. 'There is the Lamb of God!' he said.*

37 The two disciples heard him say this and went with Jesus. [38]*Jesus turned, saw them following him, and asked, 'What are you looking for?'*

They answered, 'Where do you live, Rabbi?' (This word means 'Teacher.')

39 'Come and see,' he answered. (It was then about four o'clock in the afternoon.) So they went with him and saw where he lived, and spent the rest of that day with him.

40 One of them was Andrew, Simon Peter's brother. [41]*At once he found his brother Simon and told him, 'We have found the Messiah.' (This word means 'Christ.')* [42]*Then he took Simon to Jesus.*

Jesus looked at him and said, 'Your name is Simon son of John, but you will be called Cephas.' (This is the same as Peter and means 'a rock.')

43 The next day Jesus decided to go to Galilee. He found Philip and said to him, 'Come with me!' (⁴⁴Philip was from Bethsaida, the town where Andrew and Peter lived.) ⁴⁵Philip found Nathanael and told him, 'We have found the one whom Moses wrote about in the book of the Law and whom the prophets also wrote about. He is Jesus son of Joseph, from Nazareth.'

46 'Can anything good come from Nazareth?' Nathanael asked.

'Come and see,' answered Philip.

47 When Jesus saw Nathanael coming to him, he said about him, 'Here is a real Israelite; there is nothing false in him!'

48 Nathanael asked him, 'How do you know me?'

Jesus answered, 'I saw you when you were under the fig-tree before Philip called you.'

49 'Teacher,' answered Nathanael, 'you are the Son of God! You are the King of Israel!'

50 Jesus said, 'Do you believe just because I told you I saw you when you were under the fig-tree? You will see much greater things than this!' ⁵¹And he said to them, 'I am telling you the truth: you will see heaven open and God's angels going up and coming down on the Son of Man.'

A minister was in a room full of students during a time of mission at a certain university. He was to speak about the Christian faith to a group of men who wanted to make it quite clear that they were not Christians. 'We're all scientists here', they chorused, as if a Christian could not possibly be a scientist as well! I have heard others suggest that only certain 'religious' or 'mystical' or 'inadequate' types could ever become Christians. Such views are quite contrary to the facts. There are many scientists who are also Christians. Jesus Christ does not appeal to certain types of people only. Indeed those who followed him, as described in this chapter, are all very different kinds of people.

It is true that John the Baptist was related to the family of Jesus. He was a preacher, a professional. He had a special relationship to Jesus as a 'fore-runner', a 'herald'. But the next four witnesses could not possibly be accused of bias out of family or 'professional' loyalty. They are not 'sons of the manse' or of the temple. They are working men, tough fishermen. They are practical men of affairs and not starry-eyed idealists; and they are all totally different from one another and from John the Baptist.

Andrew, for example, was a fisherman who had been attracted by the preaching of John the Baptist. He was a humble man who was prepared to play second fiddle to his more extrovert brother, Simon. But quiet and unassuming as he may well have been, *he was prepared to spend time in discovering who Jesus really was* (verses 38–40). Furthermore, once he was sure that Jesus was the Messiah, he could not keep the discovery to himself (verse 41).

Simon (verses 41–42), a real extrovert, was as enthusiastic as he was impulsive, as unreliable as he was on occasions brave. He was as likely to swear violently as passionately to make lofty resolutions. But Jesus realized his potential and recognized that he would one day be a great leader in the church. He would one day live up to his new name, Peter (a rock). The way in which this man's character was moulded is part of the evidence to the unique personality of Jesus, and his influence on men.

Philip (verses 43–44), who came from the same town as Peter and Andrew, was slow and unimpressive. He often lacked faith and vision (John 6:5–7). He was slow to understand spiritual truth (John 14:8–11) and to take initiative (John 12:20–22). But there is a certain down-to-earth, practical side to his character which makes him an important witness. It is encouraging to notice that Jesus does not overlook 'slow and ordinary' people. On the contrary Jesus went to Galilee to find him, and to invite him to become one of his disciples (verse 43).

Nathanael (verses 45–51) was an intellectual. It was a Jewish custom to sit and meditate upon the Scriptures under the shady branches of the fig tree (verse 48). This is what Nathanael loved to do. Because of his knowledge he was at first sceptical of the claim that Jesus was the Messiah (verse 46). His scepticism was not without reason, for Nazareth had already produced a number of fanatics who had falsely called themselves Messiah. But neither was it without prejudice; *and prejudice often hinders a man from discovering the truth.* When Nathanael meets Jesus, however, his prejudices are dispelled. How was this possible? (i) His genuine search for the truth showed there was 'nothing false in him' (verse 47). He was transparently sincere and open to truth. (ii) He was prepared to make the effort to look at the evidence. He was willing to 'come and see' (verse 46). (iii) He was impressed by Jesus' superhuman knowledge (verses 48–49). (iv) He was prepared to acknowledge Jesus as God's Son and Messiah. When we are prepared to go as far as this man in our search, we shall not be far from discovering the truth.

Jesus then promised Nathanael further knowledge about himself (verses 50–52). Perhaps Nathanael had been reading from the book of Genesis the story of Jacob's dream (see Genesis 28:10–17). Jacob was running away from home after tricking and deceiving his father Isaac and his brother Esau. In his dream he saw a ladder stretching from heaven to earth with angels climbing up and down it. This was a sign to him that God was with him. Jesus takes up this theme and tells Nathanael that he will come to recognize that Jesus has come to bring heaven to earth, God to man, man to God. God still reveals this truth to those who seek him sincerely and with all their heart.

Questions for discussion
1. 'Christianity is caught as well as taught.' How far does this passage illustrate this saying? How do we apply this to our own situation?
2. 'Can anything good come from Nazareth?' If this expresses Nathanael's prejudice against Jesus, what are our most frequent prejudices against following him? What convinced Nathanael in the end?

4 The first sign

2:1–11
2 Two days later there was a wedding in the town of Cana in Galilee. Jesus' mother was there, ²and Jesus and his disciples had also been invited to the wedding. ³When the wine had given out, Jesus' mother said to him, 'They have no wine left.'

4 'You must not tell me what to do,' Jesus replied. 'My time has not yet come.'

5 Jesus' mother then told the servants, 'Do whatever he tells you.'

6 The Jews have rules about ritual washing, and for this purpose six stone water jars were there, each one large enough to hold about a hundred litres. [7]*Jesus said to the servants, 'Fill these jars with water.' They filled them to the brim,* [8]*and then he told them, 'Now draw some water out and take it to the man in charge of the feast.' They took him the water,* [9]*which now had turned into wine, and he tasted it. He did not know where this wine had come from (but, of course, the servants who had drawn out the water knew); so he called the bridegroom* [10]*and said to him, 'Everyone else serves the best wine first, and after the guests have had plenty to drink, he serves the ordinary wine. But you have kept the best wine until now!'*

11 Jesus performed this first miracle in Cana in Galilee; there he revealed his glory, and his disciples believed in him.

The writer now describes an incident that would be regarded as a scoop by every Fleet Street reporter. It is a story packed with human interest. A wedding. A crisis in the catering arrangements at the reception. The miraculous turning of water into wine. A happy ending.

It took place in the village of Cana, a few miles north-east of Nazareth. Cana was probably on the site of the modern village of Kefr Kenna, on the dusty road to the Lake of Galilee. We can perhaps imagine its terraced houses with their flat roofs, and the gardens and orchards which, it is said, produced some of the best pomegranates in Palestine. It is possible that Nathanael lived here, and that Jesus and his disciples stayed wtih him before going on to the wedding. Mary, the mother of Jesus, seems to have been an important guest (verses 1, 3).

In Jewish law the wedding of a virgin took place on a Wednesday, and the wedding ceremony itself was held late in the evening after a feast. The festivities then continued for several days, and this of course increased the sense of social disaster that the couple and their parents would have felt when they ran out of wine (verse 3).

The story of the way in which Jesus turned water into wine raises two important questions in our search for truth.

a. Is it reasonable to believe in such a miracle?

Before we dismiss the miraculous as 'unscientific', we would do well to consider three propositions which here can be stated only briefly.

1. *My estimate of miracles will depend on my estimate of Jesus Christ.* If Jesus is no more than a great prophet or teacher, then I would do well to examine his miraculous claims critically. But if, on other grounds, I am persuaded that he is God become man, then I shall not be surprised at the evidence of divine and supernatural power. It would not then be incredible that the God who provides both wine and water should turn the water to wine.

2. *My estimate of miracles must take into account the historical documents of the New Testament.* There is as good documentary evidence for the miracles of Jesus as for his teaching. If we accept the one we must have good reasons for rejecting the other. In this story there are several authentic eyewitness touches which make it very difficult to dismiss the story as make-believe. For example, it was appropriate that the *bridegroom* is addressed by the steward (verse 9). According to Jewish custom the bridegroom paid the bills! It is interesting also that the 'best man' or friend of the bridegroom is not mentioned. The Talmud tells us that in Galilee (but not in Judea: see John 3:29) 'friends of the bridegroom' were not employed. Again, the words of Jesus to his mother, 'You must not tell me what to do, woman . . . My time has not yet come' are hardly the words we would expect to find in a fabricated, make-believe story. They are of course not as harsh as they sound. 'Woman' (Greek: *gunai*) is a word of respect. Jesus addresses his mother in the same way when he is dying on the cross (John 19:26). 'You must not tell me what to do, woman' is an idiomatic expression and probably means 'My way is not your way'. 'My time has not yet come' probably means 'My time is not your time'.*

3. *My estimate of miracles must take into account their meaning and purpose.* It is the meaninglessness of some of the miracles in the apocryphal Gospels which make them incredible. But John rightly calls the miracles of Jesus 'signs' (a better translation than 'mighty works'). Jesus is not a magician but a teacher, and the miracles authenticate his message, reveal his character and the purpose of his coming, and are significant visual aids. If we try to 'explain away' the miracles of Jesus, we shall distrust his teaching. This leads us to the second question.

*For further reading: C. S. Lewis, *Miracles* and F. F. Bruce, *The New Testament Documents*.

b. What is the purpose of this miracle?

John's explanation lies in the phrase 'Jesus . . . revealed his glory, and his disciples believed in him' (verse 11). In other words Jesus let the disciples know a little more about himself and about what he had come to do, when he turned water into wine at that wedding reception at Cana. He showed how he cares about the joyful occasions of life as well as the sad. He showed his concern for domestic as well as ecclesiastical problems. He showed that there is nothing he cannot do in his own time and in his own way, if people will trust him (like Mary, verse 3) and obey him (like the servants, verses 5, 7 and 8).

For the Jews a wedding was very much a religious ceremony, and they would remember that the new age which the Messiah would introduce was sometimes likened to a joyful wedding-feast. Jesus had come to introduce a new age better than the old, even as the new wine was the best at the wedding. As the disciples saw this evidence of his love and power, and this sign that he had every right to be called Messiah, they began to put their faith in him (verse 11).

Questions for discussion
1. What reasons can be given for accepting this miracle of Jesus ?
2. What do I learn about Jesus in this story ?
3. The actions of Jesus in this story are clearly related to other people, *e.g.* the bride and the bridegroom and their families, the disciples, Mary, his brothers, the servants, and the man in charge of the feast. What do we learn from their attitudes and reactions to Jesus ?

5 Jesus the reformer

2:12–25
12 After this, Jesus and his mother, brothers, and disciples went to Capernaum and stayed there for a few days.

13 It was almost time for the Passover Festival, so Jesus went to Jerusalem. ¹⁴There in the Temple he found men selling cattle, sheep, and pigeons, and also the money-changers sitting at their tables. ¹⁵So he made a whip from cords and drove all the animals out of the Temple, both the sheep and the cattle; he overturned the tables of the money-changers and scattered their coins; ¹⁶and he ordered the men who sold the pigeons, 'Take them out of here! Stop making my Father's house a market-place!' ¹⁷His disciples remembered that the scripture says, 'My devotion to your house, O God, burns in me like a fire.'

18 The Jewish authorities replied with a question, 'What miracle can you perform to show us that you have the right to do this?'

19 Jesus answered, 'Tear down this Temple, and in three days I will build it again.'

20 'Are you going to build it again in three days?' they asked him. 'It has taken forty-six years to build this Temple!'

21 But the temple Jesus was speaking about was his body. ²²So when he was raised from death, his disciples remembered that he had said this, and they believed the scripture and what Jesus had said.

23 While Jesus was in Jerusalem during the Passover Festival, many believed in him as they saw the miracles he performed. ²⁴But Jesus did not trust himself to them, because he knew them all. ²⁵There was no need for anyone to tell him about them, because he himself knew what was in their hearts.

For many people the chief barrier to Christian belief is not Jesus Christ but the church. Some people believe the church is irrelevant and unnecessary. A school teacher, for example, wrote, 'I feel that there are so many ways in which we can work for good without going through the church.' She added, 'As people, I quite like the clergy – but I can't stand them when they become religious!' For others, at times the church has seemed to be corrupt.

Jesus Christ had a quite different attitude. The Jewish church of his day was undoubtedly corrupt at the top. There was a great deal that was wrong with 'organized religion' especially in Jerusalem, the centre of it all. But for Jesus the temple was God's house. The Jews were God's people; and the religious leaders were 'shepherds' or leaders accountable to God. Instead, then, of ignoring them, he spoke to them the truth. Instead of avoiding the church of his day, he went in to reform it.

Jerusalem was always busy, especially at Passover time, which by our reckoning would be some time in the middle of April. Crowds thronged the streets; sometimes as many as two and a half million Jews assembled in Jerusalem during the Passover. Travellers bargained in the markets. Sightseers idly gaped at Herod's magnificent temple.

It was, however, within the temple precincts that Jesus saw so much to disturb him. John alone records a 'cleansing of the temple' at the beginning of Jesus' ministry. But it is clear that his purpose in selecting this incident is to show us Jesus as the Messiah at the very start of his public ministry acting not only in love but in righteousness. Jesus saw that the institutional religion of his day was riddled with many evils.

a. Dishonesty (verses 14–17)

The money-changers (verse 14) changed ordinary money into temple currency in order that the pilgrims could pay the temple tax. It has been estimated that the annual revenue from the temple tax was about £200,000 (or roughly $371,000) and that the money-changers made an annual *profit* of £25,000 (or $46,000)!

It is also likely that those who sold oxen, sheep and pigeons charged exorbitant prices. It has been estimated that a pair of doves could cost as little as 20p outside the temple, and as much as £2 inside. Nevertheless, the worshippers would have to pay the higher price because it was very likely that animals bought outside the temple precincts would be rejected as unsuitable for worship by the temple inspectors!

Jesus is passionately concerned about social justice. His action (verses 15, 16) reveals his anger against evil, as well as his love for those who were being exploited.

b. Hypocrisy

It is certain that many who worshipped in the temple were forgetting the true end of worship in using the complicated sacrificial system of the Jews. In the same way, formal religious observance in the church today often has precisely the same effect. 'Take these things away' suggests that Jesus had come to abolish the Jewish system of worship altogether, and to make possible a direct and spiritual worship of God without elaborate ritual and ceremony.

The disciples realized that such zeal for pure and spiritual worship would lead to his death (verse 17). Indeed they understood later that his death and resurrection would be the means of establishing such worship (verses 19–22).

c. Prejudice (verses 18–21)

Men do not like their traditional forms of worship criticized, nor their selfishness and greed shown up. The question 'What miracle can you perform to show us that you have the right to do this?' (verse 18) was the first sign of hostility to the claims and actions of Jesus. Jesus' enigmatic answer, which was later used against him at his trial (Mark 14:58; Matthew 26:61; 27:40), was deliberately obscure, probably because of the prejudice and lack of humility of the questioners. Even the sign of the resurrection failed to convince those who would not humbly seek to know the truth. The disciples realized later, however, that the death and resurrection of Jesus fulfilled the promises of the Old Testament as well as the words of Jesus himself (verse 22).

d. Superficiality (verses 23–35)

Even those who were not hostile to Jesus were superficial in their belief. They were ready to follow a worker of 'miracles', but not always a worker of righteousness. The love of Jesus was attractive. The righteousness of Jesus was demanding. It was easier to accept comfort than to face demands. Jesus knew the difference between sincere and superficial belief, for he knew men's inmost thoughts (verse 25). He knew that true belief would arise out of a genuine need for forgiveness, as well as a conviction that Christ alone, and not animal sacrifices, could provide it. True belief would involve forsaking sin—dishonesty, hypocrisy, hostility to Jesus, superficiality and the rest—as well as following Jesus. The new life could not be received unless the old life was renounced. Jesus knew all this. So he would not commit himself to men, unless they were ready to commit themselves fully to him (verse 24). We cannot follow Jesus without forsaking sin.

Questions for discussion
1. How far does the view that Jesus was 'gentle . . . meek and mild' fit the picture of Jesus that we see here?

2. How far do we identify with the failings of the religious people of Jesus' day?

3. 'My devotion to your house, O God, burns in me like a fire.' How do we apply that attitude to our own approach to the church, and to the worship of God?

4. What is 'spiritual religion'?

6 Jesus meets a sincere churchman

3:1–21

3 There was a Jewish leader named Nicodemus, who belonged to the party of the Pharisees. ²One night he went to Jesus and said to him, 'Rabbi, we know that you are a teacher sent by God. No one could perform the miracles you are doing unless God were with him.'

3 Jesus answered, 'I am telling you the truth: no one can see the Kingdom of God unless he is born again.'

4 'How can a grown man be born again?' Nicodemus asked. 'He certainly cannot enter his mother's womb and be born a second time!'

5 'I am telling you the truth,' replied Jesus. 'No one can enter the Kingdom of God unless he is born of water and the Spirit. ⁶A person is born physically of human parents, but he is born spiritually of the Spirit. ⁷Do not be surprised because I tell you that you must all be born again. ⁸The wind blows wherever it wishes; you hear the sound it makes, but you do not know where it comes from or where it is going. It is like that with everyone who is born of the Spirit.'

9 'How can this be?' asked Nicodemus.

10 Jesus answered, 'You are a great teacher in Israel, and you don't know this? ¹¹I am telling you the truth: we speak of what we know and report what we have seen, yet none of you is willing to accept our message. ¹²You do not believe me when I tell you about the things of this world; how will you ever believe me, then, when I tell you about the things of heaven? ¹³And no one has ever gone up to heaven except the Son of Man, who came down from heaven.'

14 As Moses lifted up the bronze snake on a pole in the desert, in the same way the Son of Man must be lifted up, ¹⁵*so that everyone who believes in him may have eternal life.* ¹⁶*For God loved the world so much that he gave his only Son, so that everyone who believes in him may not die but have eternal life.* ¹⁷*For God did not send his Son into the world to be its judge, but to be its saviour.*

18 Whoever believes in the Son is not judged; but whoever does not believe has already been judged, because he has not believed in God's only Son. ¹⁹*This is how the judgment works: the light has come into the world, but people love the darkness rather than the light, because their deeds are evil.* ²⁰*Anyone who does evil things hates the light and will not come to the light, because he does not want his evil deeds to be shown up.* ²¹*But whoever does what is true comes to the light in order that the light may show that what he did was in obedience to God.*

Some years ago a nurse wrote these words in a letter: 'For several years now, although I've gone to church, read my Bible and really tried to be a true Christian, *I've always felt there was something missing . . .*' It was only later that she found a personal faith. The late Bishop Handley Moule described his religious life as an undergraduate: 'I was aware, as time went on, that my contact with the Lord, whom I saw known and loved before my eyes, was only (if I may put it so) *at second hand.*'* From these examples we see that it is possible to be religious and not Christian, to know about God and not to know him in a first-hand, personal way.

Nicodemus was a religious man like that. As a Pharisee he would have prayed and read the Scriptures and attended a place of worship regularly. He was moreover something of an expert in religion, '*the* teacher of Israel',† and a distinguished member of the Jewish Sanhedrin. It is likely that he was a man of upright character, generosity (giving tithes to the poor) and humility (notice how he addresses Jesus in verse 2). But he needed to know how to enter the kingdom of God, and how to enjoy God's rule and God's life *personally.* He came 'one night' (verse 2) possibly because he preferred that men should not notice his interest in Jesus. It would not be easy for a man in his position to be too closely associated with Jesus of Nazareth. Possibly too he wanted an unhurried time to ask all his questions. In speaking to Nicodemus, Jesus emphasized three truths.

*Harford and MacDonald, *Bishop Handley Moule*, p. 49.
†The definite article is used in the Greek of verse 10.

a. The necessity for the new birth (verses 3–8)

Personal knowledge of God is possible only through spiritual re-birth. A man cannot enjoy physical life unless he is born, and neither can he enjoy spiritual life unless he is born anew (see verse 6). This involves receiving a new life rather than turning over a new leaf. For man cannot save himself. He is spiritually 'dead' until God gives him life. Without the new birth a man can no more appreciate spiritual truths than a dead man can appreciate life or a blind man appreciate the beauties of the sunset (see verses 3, 5).

Nicodemus (verse 4) could not understand such revolutionary teaching, although the Old Testament had spoken of it (see Ezekiel 36:25–27). Like most of us he found it easier to understand material rather than spiritual concepts. Jesus reminds him that it is more important to experience the new birth than to understand it (verses 7, 8). We may not understand how the wind 'works', but we can see its effects as it moves the leaves on the trees. We may not understand the working of God's Spirit in our lives, but once we have experienced this, we shall be able to say 'we speak of what we know' (verse 11). So the new birth is the only way into God's family. It is the gateway to the enjoyment of God's kingdom.

b. The necessity for Christ's death (verses 14–15)

Nicodemus was still puzzled. How could he experience the new birth (verse 9)? Jesus first asserts his authority for speaking with such certainty (verses 11–13). Then he gives Nicodemus an Old Testament illustration (verse 14). It is true that man deserves death, not life. The Israelites had learnt this in the well-known story in Numbers 21:5–9. Because of their grumbling and rebellion against God, God had allowed a plague of poisonous snakes to bring death to many of them as a judgment upon their sin. But when they cried out to God to save them, he ordered Moses to make a serpent of brass and to lift it up on a pole, and God promised that those who looked upon the serpent, and believed his promise, would live.

The lesson is clear. There can be no 'life' without death. Man could not be saved from God's judgment unless Christ was lifted up (like the serpent) and bore the judgment man deserved. That is what Jesus came to do, for, as John comments, 'God loved the world so much that he *gave* his only Son . . .' (verse 16).

c. The necessity for man's response (verses 16–21)

It was only those who believed God's promise, and who looked to the serpent, who lived. So it is only those who believe God's promise and who look to the Lord Jesus Christ as the Son of God (verse 18) and as the one who saves us from the consequences of sin (verse 17) who receive eternal life (verses 15, 16 and 18).

But what happens if I do not believe in Jesus Christ in this way? John tells us that Jesus came into the world primarily to save men, not to judge them (verse 17). But the shining of the sun inevitably brings shadows. To turn our back on the sun is to deepen the shadows. To refuse life is to choose death. To reject salvation is to invite condemnation. An honest seeker (verse 21) will not cover up his failure and sins. He will come to the light and find life. But another, who loves darkness rather than light, will prefer to cover up his sins, and so will be self-condemned (verses 18–20). This is the judgment. It happens every time a man turns his back upon Jesus Christ.

Questions for discussion

1. Jesus makes it clear that everyone (even the religious Nicodemus) must be 'born again' to enter God's kingdom. Does this mean that every Christian will experience the new birth in the same way? (See verses 7 and 8.)
2. How can we be sure that we are 'born again'? (Consider verses 8–17 in particular.)
3. What do we learn here about God's present activity of judgment (verses 17–21)?
4. 'God will surely forgive everyone in the end.' Discuss this in the light of verses 17–21.

7 More evidence about Jesus Christ

3:22–36
22 After this, Jesus and his disciples went to the province of Judaea,

where he spent some time with them and baptized. ²³*John also was baptizing in Aenon, not far from Salim, because there was plenty of water in that place. People were going to him, and he was baptizing them.* (²⁴*This was before John had been put in prison.*)

25 Some of John's disciples began arguing with a Jew about the matter of ritual washing. ²⁶*So they went to John and said, 'Teacher, you remember the man who was with you on the east side of the Jordan, the one you spoke about? Well, he is baptizing now, and everyone is going to him!'*

27 John answered, 'No one can have anything unless God gives it to him. ²⁸*You yourselves are my witnesses that I said, "I am not the Messiah, but I have been sent ahead of him."* ²⁹*The bridegroom is the one to whom the bride belongs; but the bridegroom's friend, who stands by and listens, is glad when he hears the bridegroom's voice. This is how my own happiness is made complete.* ³⁰*He must become more important while I become less important.'*

31 He who comes from above is greater than all. He who is from the earth belongs to the earth and speaks about earthly matters, but he who comes from heaven is above all. ³²*He tells what he has seen and heard, yet no one accepts his message.* ³³*But whoever accepts his message confirms by this that God is truthful.* ³⁴*The one whom God has sent speaks God's words, because God gives him the fullness of his Spirit.* ³⁵*The Father loves his Son and has put everything in his power.* ³⁶*Whoever believes in the Son has eternal life; whoever disobeys the Son will not have life, but will remain under God's punishment.*

How seriously must we take the teaching of Jesus? His words on the necessity for the new birth and the certainty of judgment are serious enough. But are they not the sincere belief of one great prophet amongst others? Is Jesus more than a prophet? Is he unique?

Some of the disciples of John the Baptist were loth to believe that Jesus was greater than their leader. They were sad when they saw that John was taking second place to Jesus. Many more people were going to Jesus to be baptized than to John the Baptist (verses 22–26). We have further evidence here from the Baptist himself.

a. More evidence from John the Baptist (verses 25–30)

John once again makes it clear that it is Jesus who is the Messiah (verses 26, 27). He describes his relationship to Jesus as that of a 'best man' to a bridegroom (verse 29). At an eastern wedding 'the friend of the bridegroom' went ahead of the bride and groom to make all necessary preparations for the wedding festivities. He even guarded the bridal chamber, and would open the door only when he heard and recognized the bridegroom's voice, and could bring the happy couple together. Then he would be glad that his job was done, and that he could fade more and more into the background. So John the Baptist rejoiced that men and women were increasingly coming not to him but to Jesus. It would be absurd for the best man to be jealous of the bridegroom! John's task was to fade into the background. He rightly says, 'He must become more important while I become less important.'

b. The evidence of John the Evangelist (verses 31–36)

These verses are almost certainly the comment of the Evangelist rather than of John the Baptist. They record John's conviction that Jesus is not only the Messiah, but the Son of God (verse 35). It is because Jesus is in this unique relationship to God that his words are authoritative and true and tremendously important. If we wanted to know all about the royal family, our best authority would be someone from that family. If we want to know about God, we need to hear someone from God. It is because Jesus is 'from above' that he is above all other teachers (verse 31). It is because he is 'from heaven' (verse 31) that he can tell us from personal experience about the life of heaven, and the truths of God. It is because God has sent Jesus filled with the Spirit, in a unique sense, that the words of Jesus are the very words of God. For all that we need to know about God and his life has been given to Jesus to reveal to us (verses 34 and 35).

If the words of Jesus are the very words of God (John is sure of this, verse 33; others reject it, verse 32), then they must be taken with extreme seriousness. They become matters of life and death. The issue is this: If a man believes on Christ he receives eternal life. On the other hand to disobey the words of Christ means to disobey God himself, and to face here and now his displeasure (verse 36).

c. The wrath of God (verse 36)

There is one problem in this passage which all must face honestly.

Can we believe that the wrath of God is compatible with the love of God? John, the apostle of love, apparently sees no difficulty. But some modern thinkers are appalled by such a doctrine.

When we speak of God's wrath we are of course using a human term to describe a characteristic of God. It is hard for us to understand how a man can be angry and exercise wrath without vindictiveness and even hatred entering in. This is not so with God. Wrath is the reverse side of his love. It is a way of describing a loving God's hatred of sin and evil and disobedience and all that spoils the lives of those whom he loves. As the light of the sun destroys germs, and the light switched on in a room banishes darkness, so God's sinless and perfect presence banishes sin, and his wrath rests upon the sinner. Jesus has already shown his wrath in taking action against the sin and hypocrisy in the temple at Jerusalem (see chapter 2). The wrath of God teaches us that God does not stand by and condone sin and injustice and evil in the world. He takes action against it. It shows us that there is nothing sentimental about the love of God. It reminds us that we cannot 'get away with' sin.

We have already learnt from the story of the brass serpent that Christ bore God's judgment upon sin when he died on the cross. Jesus had never sinned, but he died in the place of sinners. He was perfectly obedient, but he bore the guilt of the disobedient. That is why it is possible for those who believe on Jesus Christ to be delivered from the wrath of God, and to receive eternal life.

Questions for discussion

1. What is the secret of John the Baptist's humility and lack of jealousy (22–30)?
2. 'Jesus is one of the greatest teachers who ever lived.' What more can we add to that statement in the light of this passage?
3. For some people the wrath of God seems to be incompatible with his love. How, then, would *you* explain verse 36?

8 Jesus speaks to a woman of the world

4:1–30

4 The Pharisees heard that Jesus was winning and baptizing more disciples than John. (²Actually, Jesus himself did not baptize anyone; only his disciples did.) ³So when Jesus heard what was being said, he left Judaea and went back to Galilee; ⁴on his way there he had to go through Samaria.

5 In Samaria he came to a town named Sychar, which was not far from the field that Jacob had given to his son Joseph. ⁶Jacob's well was there, and Jesus, tired out by the journey, sat down by the well. It was about noon.

7 A Samaritan woman came to draw some water, and Jesus said to her, 'Give me a drink of water.' (⁸His disciples had gone into town to buy food.)

9 The woman answered, 'You are a Jew, and I am a Samaritan— so how can you ask me for a drink?' (Jews will not use the same cups and bowls that Samaritans use.)

10 Jesus answered, 'If only you knew what God gives and who it is that is asking you for a drink, you would ask him, and he would give you life-giving water.'

11 'Sir,' the woman said, 'you haven't got a bucket, and the well is deep. Where would you get that life-giving water? ¹²It was our ancestor Jacob who gave us this well; he and his sons and his flocks all drank from it. You don't claim to be greater than Jacob, do you?'

13 Jesus answered, 'Whoever drinks this water will be thirsty again, ¹⁴but whoever drinks the water that I will give him will never be thirsty again. The water that I will give him will become in him a spring which will provide him with life-giving water and give him eternal life.'

15 'Sir,' the woman said, 'give me that water! Then I will never be thirsty again, nor will I have to come here to draw water.'

16 'Go and call your husband,' Jesus told her, 'and come back.'

17 'I haven't got a husband,' she answered.

Jesus replied, 'You are right when you say you haven't got a *husband.* [18]*You have been married to five men, and the man you live with now is not really your husband. You have told me the truth.'*

19 *'I see you are a prophet, sir,' the woman said.* [20]*'My Samaritan ancestors worshipped God on this mountain, but you Jews say that Jerusalem is the place where we should worship God.'*

21 *Jesus said to her, 'Believe me, woman, the time will come when people will not worship the Father either on this mountain or in Jerusalem.* [22]*You Samaritans do not really know whom you worship; but we Jews know whom we worship, because it is from the Jews that salvation comes.* [23]*But the time is coming and is already here, when by the power of God's Spirit people will worship the Father as he really is, offering him the true worship that he wants.* [24]*God is Spirit, and only by the power of his Spirit can people worship him as he really is.'*

25 *The woman said to him, 'I know that the Messiah will come, and when he comes, he will tell us everything.'*

26 *Jesus answered, 'I am he, I who am talking with you.'*

27 *At that moment Jesus' disciples returned, and they were greatly surprised to find him talking with a woman. But none of them said to her, 'What do you want?' or asked him, 'Why are you talking with her?'*

28 *Then the woman left her water jar, went back to the town, and said to the people there,* [29]*'Come and see the man who told me everything I have ever done. Could he be the Messiah?'* [30]*So they left the town and went to Jesus.*

The problem of race relations is not a modern one. When Jesus left Judea and decided to take the short cut to Galilee through Samaria, he entered a country which was still very sensitive about its relationship with the rest of Palestine. The problem began as far back as 720 BC, when the Assyrians conquered the northern kingdom of Samaria, and encouraged widespread immigration from Babylon and other countries (see 2 Kings 17:24). There followed the inevitable intermarrying between Samaritan Jews and immigrants. In the eyes of the orthodox Jew, it was a terrible crime to lose racial purity, and from that time on the Jews and Samaritans hated and despised one another (verse 9). As we know from this story the separation was so deep that the Samaritans had even built their own temple for worship on Mount Gerizim (see verse 21).

It was at the hottest time of day (12 o'clock—for the Jewish day runs from 6 a.m. to 6 p.m.) that Jesus sat down, tired, thirsty and hot, at the well of Sychar (verses 5–6). This well can almost certainly be identified today.

When Jesus first meets the woman from Samaria she is a sharp-tongued, hard and rather cynical woman of the world, who seemed glad to score a few cheap points off an interesting man. By the end of her conversation with Jesus she is so impressed that she forgets why she ever came to the well, leaves her water-pot behind and rushes home to tell her associates all about him (verses 28–29).

If we contrast this story with the interview with Nicodemus (chapter 3), we see that Jesus is concerned about the Samaritan as well as the Jew. He seeks the ignorant as well as the learned. He will talk with the poor as well as the rich. He cares for women as well as men—and remember that the Jews had a prayer which stated 'Blessed art Thou O Lord . . . who hast not made me a woman'! He loved the morally corrupt as well as the morally upright. His love is for all men. His 'life' is offered to all. He came, as the Samaritans said later (4:42), to be 'the Saviour of the world'. Jesus indeed recognized no social, racial or religious barriers which he could not overcome. There are no second-class citizens in his kingdom. An orthodox Jew, who became a Christian, was able to write a few years later: 'So there is no difference between Jews and Gentiles, between slaves and free men, between men and women; you are all one in union with Christ Jesus' (see Paul's letter to the Galatians 3:28).

The rabbis had a saying, 'A man should not salute a woman in a public place, not even his own wife.' No wonder the woman was surprised that Jesus spoke to her—a woman, and a Samaritan (verse 9). We can perhaps imagine her, hands on her hips and a coy look on her face. Jesus, however, was quite prepared to flout convention for the sake of a needy person. As he talks to her we can see that he taught her what her deepest needs were.

a. Spiritual rather than physical (verses 7–15)

At first, when Jesus spoke about 'life-giving water', she thought perhaps of fresh running water from a stream instead of from a well (verse 11). Or maybe she is simply being flippant. Certainly she did not believe that Jesus could improve on Jacob's method of drawing water (notice her sly dig that Jacob was as much the 'ancestor' of the Samaritans as the Jews—verse 12). When Jesus talks about spiritual needs (verses 13–14) she appears deliberately dumb and says in effect, 'If you can save me trouble, then give me this water' (verse 15). But spiritual needs are more important than physical ones. We all have physical needs, but we also have an underlying spiritual thirst that can be satisfied only by Jesus Christ. Water satisfies physical thirst temporarily. The life that Jesus offers to man is permanently satisfying and wells up within man's inmost being like a bubbling spring (verse 14). No doubt this woman thought that sex experience would bring her satisfaction. Jesus taught her that her need was spiritual more than physical.

b. Moral rather than intellectual (verses 16–26)

With a sure touch Jesus puts his finger on her real problem in order to help her to face up to it. 'Go and call your husband, . . . and come back' (verse 16). None of us likes to face up to moral failure in our lives. This woman was no exception and in a short time she was trying to evade the real moral issue with an intellectual red herring on a matter of controversy between the Jews and Samaritans (verses 19–20)—a quick move on her part to get out of an awkward situation. Jesus' answer introduces a further truth. What really matters is not *where* a man worships but *how* he worships. 'God is Spirit', therefore he is not confined to a particular place, or to a particular form of material expression of worship. The time has now come when it is possible to worship God 'in the Spirit' and 'from the heart'. We can now worship God 'in truth', because the only true way to God has been revealed (verses 23–24). In a word, our *moral* and spiritual problems are not dealt with by deciding which church to belong to or by tightening up on our religious duties, or by solving all our controversial, intellectual problems. They can be solved only by the new life in the Spirit which is possible through Jesus Christ.

The woman does not yet fully understand, but Jesus shows himself to her (verse 25) as the Messiah who reveals God in truth and makes possible worship 'by the Spirit'. The mention of the water-pot (verse 28) is surely the mark of an eyewitness account.

Questions for discussion
1. In what ways does Jesus overcome the racial, social and religious barriers that might have kept him from helping this woman and

relating to her? Can we apply this to our own relationships?
2. What were the problems that were keeping this woman from
a deeply satisfying life? Is it true that 'Jesus can solve all our
problems'?
3. If it is true that 'what really matters is not where a man worships
but how he worships', does it matter *at all* where we worship?
And what principles should guide *how* we worship (16–26)?

9 The priorities of Jesus

4:31–54

*31 In the meantime the disciples were begging Jesus, 'Teacher, have
something to eat!'*

*32 But he answered, 'I have food to eat that you know nothing
about.'*

*33 So the disciples started asking among themselves, 'Could some-
body have brought him food?'*

*34 'My food,' Jesus said to them, 'is to obey the will of the one who
sent me and to finish the work he gave me to do. ³⁵You have a saying,
"Four more months and then the harvest." But I tell you, take a good
look at the fields; the crops are now ripe and ready to be harvested!
³⁶The man who reaps the harvest is being paid and gathers the crops
for eternal life; so the man who sows and the man who reaps will be
glad together. ³⁷The saying is true, "One man sows, another man reaps."
³⁸I have sent you to reap a harvest in a field where you did not work;
others worked there, and you profit from their work.'*

*39 Many of the Samaritans in that town believed in Jesus because
the woman had said, 'He told me everything I have ever done.' ⁴⁰So
when the Samaritans came to him, they begged him to stay with them,
and Jesus stayed there two days.*

*41 Many more believed because of his message, ⁴²and they said to
the woman, 'We believe now, not because of what you said, but
because we ourselves have heard him, and we know that he really is the
Saviour of the world.'*

43 After spending two days there, Jesus left and went to Galilee.
⁴⁴For he himself had said, 'A prophet is not respected in his own country.' ⁴⁵When he arrived in Galilee, the people there welcomed him, because they had gone to the Passover Festival in Jerusalem and had seen everything that he had done during the festival.

46 Then Jesus went back to Cana in Galilee, where he had turned the water into wine. A government official was there whose son was ill in Capernaum. ⁴⁷When he heard that Jesus had come from Judaea to Galilee, he went to him and asked him to go to Capernaum and heal his son, who was about to die. ⁴⁸Jesus said to him, 'None of you will ever believe unless you see miracles and wonders.'

49 'Sir,' replied the official, 'come with me before my child dies.'
50 Jesus said to him, 'Go, your son will live !'

The man believed Jesus' words and went. ⁵¹On his way home his servants met him with the news, 'Your boy is going to live !'

52 He asked them what time it was when his son got better, and they answered, 'It was one o'clock yesterday afternoon when the fever left him.' ⁵³Then the father remembered that it was at that very hour when Jesus had told him, 'Your son will live.' So he and all his family believed.

54 This was the second miracle that Jesus performed after coming from Judaea to Galilee.

A young man once found a 5 dollar bill in the street. From that time on, according to an American writer, he never lifted his eyes when walking. In the course of years he accumulated 29,516 buttons, 54,172 pins, 12 cents, a bent back and a measly disposition. He lost the glory of the sunlight, the sheen of the stars, the smiles of friends, tree blossoms in the spring, the blue skies and the entire joy of living! A man's priorities matter!

Now Jesus' emphasis upon the spiritual needs of the woman of Samaria leads to a discussion with his disciples about his own purpose in coming into the world and his own priorities. His description of his mission in the world, and that of his disciples, is very different from the popular view that many people hold. Some people believe that Christianity needs to be reinterpreted entirely in secular terms. Unless the church is feeding the hungry, establishing social justice, housing the homeless, speaking out against war, she has totally failed, we are told. Jesus himself cared both for the bodies and the souls of men, for their physical as well as spiritual needs, for their temporal as well as eternal concerns. He cared for the whole man; and so of course should the Christian church. But Jesus did not 'secularize' religion. He had clear priorities. For him the spiritual was more important than the physical, the eternal than the temporal. In this passage he emphasizes three things about his mission in the world.

a. The importance of obedience (verses 31–34)

The disciples of Jesus are anxious about his physical needs. They know he must be hungry (verse 31). Bound as they are by routine and convention, they no doubt wonder why he spends his time talking to such a woman, when he could be taking refreshment. Jesus' answer shows that it is doing God's will and completing what his Father wants him to do which alone satisfies the inner man (verse 34). It is not only gourmets who are apt to forget that truth. It is through obedience that Jesus fulfils his mission to the world—an obedience which led him to death on the Roman gallows. It is through obedience that we may share in his mission to the world, and discover inner satisfaction.

b. The importance of vision (verses 35–38)

The world is like a field full of crops ready to be reaped. The farmer may say there is four months until harvest. Jesus can say to the disciples that even *now* there are many people ready to be gathered into his kingdom. The disciples seemed blind both to the needs of those around them (such as the Samaritan woman) and to the opportunities of working with Jesus to meet those needs. In an age which can bring the sufferings of the world into our homes through television, many of us seem to be as blind as the disciples in failing to see and to meet man's physical and spiritual problems. However, Jesus promises that if we work with him the rewards and the results of such service will be lasting and joyful. The Christian is not called to 'do good' in the world for his own glory, and for the pleasure it gives him; but rather to work together with others, in obedience to Christ's command and for eternal ends (verses 37–38). Only Jesus Christ can give a man this view of service to the community.

c. The importance of faith (verses 39-54)

The readiness of some people to believe in Jesus at this stage of his ministry is illustrated in the rest of this chapter. How can a person believe?

1. *Through another's testimony* (verses 39–40). 'It was hearing my mates talk about Christ that helped me most,' said a member of a youth club in London. Some of the Samaritans believed in Jesus because of the testimony of the Samaritan woman to what had impressed her about him: 'He told me everything I have ever done' (verse 39). There is real value in listening to the testimony of any ordinary Christian to the reality of Jesus Christ.

2. *Through the words of Jesus* (verses 41–54). The woman's testimony led many in her village to come to listen to Jesus himself. The testimony of others should always lead us to find out more about it for ourselves by studying the words of Jesus, that is, the Bible. It is then that we are able to say: 'We believe now, not because of what you said, but because *we ourselves have heard him*, and we know that he really is the Saviour of the world.' (verse 42).

An illustration of faith (verses 46–54). The story of Jesus' return into Galilee, where John records the second 'sign', illustrates perfectly all we have been saying about the importance of faith resting on the words of Jesus. There must have been many in Galilee who thought of Jesus only as a wonder-worker. Hence Jesus' discouraging words to the official (and the crowd?), 'None of you will ever believe unless you see miracles and wonders' (verse 48). The result of this interview with Jesus is that 'The man *believed Jesus' words* and went' (verse 50).

The official in this story was probably in the court of Herod the Tetrarch, with responsibilities comparable to those of a senior civil servant. He shows the extent of his faith in Jesus in (i) *being humble enough to ask for help*. He was in trouble. His much-loved son who had been ill for some time had taken a turn for the worse. It is common enough for a man to turn to God when in trouble. But this man did more than utter a prayer to God on the grounds that in trouble it is worth trying everything. He came, the courtier, to Jesus, the carpenter. He came humbly and sincerely without caring what others might think or say.

His faith also expressed itself in (ii) *being persistent enough to show he was serious*. Capernaum was almost twenty miles from Cana. It was a long way to come. But he showed he meant business. Jesus' first words to him were not encouraging (verse 48) but he determined to show that he was no trifler. The faith that Jesus rewards is persistent, persevering faith.

Again, this man demonstrated the reality of his faith in Jesus by (iii) *being confident enough to trust his words*. It was a long way to go to return home. But Jesus had promised: 'Go, your son will live!' Faith in Jesus is trusting his words, his promises. 'The man *believed Jesus' words* and went' (verse 50).

Finally, this man proved the genuineness of his faith by (iv) *being willing to share it with others*. Confirmation of the truth of Jesus' words came later (verses 52, 53). His son was healed and he continued to believe in Jesus—and all his family. No doubt it was not easy for him to share his faith with others. But genuine faith in Jesus always leads to this. Like the early Christians (Acts 4:20), Christian believers 'cannot stop speaking of what we ourselves have seen and heard'. If we say we believe, it is worth asking whether we have ever told anyone else.

Questions for discussion
1. What were the priorities of Jesus' life? Can we share them?
2. 'We believe now, not because of what you said, but because we ourselves have heard him' (verse 42). How far can the testimony of others take us in our search for God? What more do we need?
3. What do we learn from this story about the meaning of 'faith' (verses 48–54)?

10 Barriers to belief

5:1–18
5 After this, Jesus went to Jerusalem for a religious festival. ²Near the Sheep Gate in Jerusalem there is a pool with five porches; in Hebrew

it is called Bethzatha. ³*A large crowd of sick people were lying in the porches—the blind, the lame, and the paralysed.* ⁵*A man was there who had been ill for thirty-eight years.* ⁶*Jesus saw him lying there, and he knew that the man had been ill for such a long time; so he asked him, 'Do you want to get well?'*

7 *The sick man answered, 'Sir, I have no one here to put me in the pool when the water is stirred up; while I am trying to get in, somebody else gets there first.'*

8 *Jesus said to him, 'Get up, pick up your mat, and walk.'* ⁹*Immediately the man got well; he picked up his mat and started walking.*

The day this happened was a Sabbath, ¹⁰*so the Jewish authorities told the man who had been healed, 'This is a Sabbath, and it is against our Law for you to carry your mat.'*

11 *He answered, 'The man who made me well told me to pick up my mat and walk.'*

12 *They asked him, 'Who is the man who told you to do this?'*

13 *But the man who had been healed did not know who Jesus was, for there was a crowd in that place, and Jesus had slipped away.*

14 *Afterwards, Jesus found him in the Temple and said, 'Listen, you are well now; so stop sinning or something worse may happen to you.'*

15 *Then the man left and told the Jewish authorities that it was Jesus who had healed him.* ¹⁶*So they began to persecute Jesus, because he had done this healing on a Sabbath.* ¹⁷*Jesus answered them, 'My Father is always working, and I too must work.'*

18 *This saying made the Jewish authorities all the more determined to kill him; not only had he broken the Sabbath law, but he had said that God was his own Father and in this way had made himself equal with God.*

She was a thoughtful enquirer, and we were discussing the claims of Christianity. In the course of the discussion she asked a question which went something like this, 'Why is it', she said, 'that relatively few people in Britain are Christians if Christianity is self-evidently true?'

Part of the answer to that question lies in the next incident which took place near a pool in Jerusalem. For it illustrates how easily we erect our own barriers to belief. Many years ago it was thought impossible that a pool called Bethzatha (or, according to some manuscripts, Bethesda) with five porches or porticoes could have existed in Jerusalem.* However, excavations begun in 1876 near the Church of St. Anne in the north-east of the city revealed an ancient pool divided into two parts. There were four tall, roofed-in porticoes around the two sections of the pool and a fifth in between them. A faded fresco has also been discovered, representing the angel troubling the water, which makes it clear that, according to early Christian tradition, this was the place where our Lord healed the crippled man. A church was built on the spot as early as AD 480. Professor F. F. Bruce says, 'There are few sites in Jerusalem, mentioned in the Gospels, which can be identified so confidently.'†

This incident at Bethzatha, then, provides an example of some common barriers to belief.

a. Personal unwillingness to believe

A man has been a cripple for thirty-eight years. There is a tradition that an angel comes from time to time to stir up the water and to convey healing to those who step into the pool. Year after year he lies near the pool, apparently without friends, and completely paralysed. No-one helps him until Jesus sees him. Jesus does not attack his superstitions but tries positively to help him exercise active faith in himself. He tests his willingness to believe and says, 'Do you *want* to be healed?' This may seem a strange question. Yet it is easy for physical weakness, mental depression, a sense of hopelessness and despair to take away our willingness to *do* anything in such circumstances. We might even be unwilling to believe and obey someone who has the power to heal us completely.

I once asked a research student whether he would be willing to become a Christian if his intellectual objections were answered. He had the honesty to admit that he was *unwilling* to believe for other reasons. Jesus said on another occasion, 'Whoever is *willing* to do what God wants will know whether what I teach comes from God' (John 7:17). Sometimes man's greatest barrier to belief is his unwillingness to believe, however convincing the reasons for belief might be. The man in the story did not understand how Jesus could help him; but when Jesus spoke to him he obeyed and was healed. He had overcome one barrier to belief.

*See Introduction, p. 12.
†F. F. Bruce, *The New Testament Documents*, p. 94.

b. Religious prejudice against belief

The cripple had not yet discovered a complete faith in Jesus. He did not know who Jesus was (verse 13). He had not yet realized that Jesus could save him from his sickness of heart as well as his sickness of body.

Afterwards Jesus found him in the temple and was able to help him further. 'Listen, you are well now; so stop sinning or something worse may happen to you' (verse 14). Jesus implies here that sometimes suffering is a consequence of sin, although elsewhere he makes it clear that this is not always so (see John 9). The man was well on the way to a firm faith in Jesus Christ.

But he had not bargained on the religious prejudice of some of the Jews. Sometimes religious people create serious barriers to belief for would-be disciples. The Jews had become legalistic about the sabbath. The Law had said that the sabbath day must be different from other days, and that on it neither a man nor his servants should work. The Jewish ecclesiastical leaders were not content with broad principles. They set out, for example, thirty-nine different classifications of work. The rabbis solemnly argued that if a man carried a needle in his robe on the sabbath, or wore artificial teeth or a wooden leg, it could be 'work'. Certainly this man who was carrying his bed was working. The actual words were: 'If anyone carries anything from a public place to a private house on the sabbath intentionally, he is punishable by death by stoning.' No wonder the healed man tells the Jews that it is Jesus they want, not him. It looks as if religious men had once again hindered a man from finding and following the truth.

c. Hostility to Jesus

The writer here comments further and gives two reasons for the growing hostility of the religious bodies towards Jesus.

1. Because although Jesus kept the sabbath in principle—he worshipped in the synagogue, he served others, he probably rested from some of the everyday activities—he ignored the petty rules and regulations imposed by the church of his day (verse 18).

2. Because Jesus claimed to be equal with God. When the Bible said that God rested on the seventh day, it meant, said Jesus, that he rested from one form of activity (creation) and continued

in other activity. It did not mean that from that moment he ceased to be active in the affairs of men. 'God is active now,' said Jesus. 'My Father is always working, and I too must work.' To the Jews these words made Jesus a blasphemer who was claiming to be equal with God, and therefore deserving of death (verse 18).

The real question is whether Jesus had a right to say such things. We, for our part, must be willing to obey the truth when we discover it; and we must be ready to distinguish between religious prejudice and religious principle. If we do not we shall find ourselves diverted from the truth or even hostile to it.

Questions for discussion

1. 'Do you *want* to be healed?' Why should this man be *unwilling* to be healed? What makes a man unwilling to be forgiven and 'made whole' by Jesus today?
2. What was wrong with the Jews' attitude to the healing of this man on the sabbath? In what ways may we be guilty of the same kind of attitude and action?
3. Why should the Jews want to persecute Jesus for healing this man on the sabbath? In what ways do men show their hostility to Jesus today?

11 The claims of Jesus

5:19–29

19 So Jesus answered them, 'I am telling you the truth: the Son can do nothing on his own; he does only what he sees his Father doing. What the Father does, the Son also does. 20For the Father loves the Son and shows him all that he himself is doing. He will show him even greater things to do than this, and you will all be amazed. 21Just as the Father raises the dead and gives them life, in the same way the Son gives life to those he wants to. 22Nor does the Father himself judge anyone. He had given his Son the full right to judge, 23so that all will honour the Son in the same way as they honour the Father. Whoever does not honour the Son does not honour the Father who sent him.

24 'I am telling you the truth: whoever hears my words and believes in him who sent me has eternal life. He will not be judged, but has already passed from death to life. ²⁵*I am telling you the truth: the time is coming—the time has already come—when the dead will hear the voice of the Son of God, and those who hear it will come to life.* ²⁶*Just as the Father is himself the source of life, in the same way he has made his Son to be the source of life.* ²⁷*And he has given the Son the right to judge, because he is the Son of Man.* ²⁸*Do not be surprised at this; the time is coming when all the dead will hear his voice* ²⁹*and come out of their graves: those who have done good will rise and live, and those who have done evil will rise and be condemned.*

The majority of people outside the Christian church today probably think of Jesus as little more than a good man, an idealist, and possibly a great teacher and prophet. Certainly 'Jesus Christ Superstar' is not a *divine* figure; and the view of Jesus in the musical of that name may well be a popular one. Indeed even some professional theologians are writing about 'the *myth* of God Incarnate', and casting doubt on the deity of Jesus. So it seems clear that many people today cannot accept the Christian claim that Jesus is divine, any more than many of the Jews could accept it in his own day.

No one needs to pretend that such a claim is easy to understand The late Professor C. S. Lewis once wrote: 'If Christianity was something we were making up, of course we could make it easier. But it isn't. We can't compete, in simplicity, with people who are inventing religions. How could we? We're dealing with fact. Of course anyone can be simple if he has no facts to bother about.' But if we are prepared to grapple with this next passage we shall see how Jesus understands his own unique relationship to his Father, and the extravagance of his claims.

a. Jesus claims that he is dependent on God (verse 19)

The words translated, 'I am telling you the truth' are always used for emphasis in John's Gospel. Jesus wanted to emphasize his dependence upon God in his human life. 'The Son can do nothing on his own; he does only what he sees his father doing.' All who believe in God would want to acknowledge their dependence upon him. But none of us could go on to say, as Jesus did, 'What the Father does, the Son also does.'

Jesus' dependence upon God is a perfect dependence. Expressed positively, he explained it in his own words when he said, 'I always do what pleases him (the Father)' (John 8:29). Is he mad, bad or God to make such a claim?

b. Jesus claims that he is equal with God (verses 20–29)

For (see verse 19 again) 'What the Father does, the Son also does.' Jesus claims equality with God by announcing that he shares the rights and powers of God himself.

1. *By doing the works of God* (verse 20). When Nicodemus met Jesus (see John 3) he said to him, 'No one could perform the miracles you are doing unless God were with him.' Jesus goes further than this: 'For the Father loves the Son and shows him all that he himself is doing. He will show him even greater things to do than this.' Jesus not only knows that God is working *with* him. He knows perfectly all that the Father is doing in the world through him. Jesus speaks here of a uniquely close relationship with God, the heavenly Father.

2. *By giving eternal life* (verse 21). Surely only God has the power to give eternal life, and to raise men from the dead? God alone is the source of life. Jesus claims these rights.

3. *By judging men* (verse 22). The Jew believed that God alone is the judge of all men. God alone knows our hearts and motives. The Jew believed that there would be a climax to history, and that God would judge all men. This authority to judge, Jesus claims for himself. 'Nor does the Father himself judge anyone. He has given his Son the full right to judge.' Who is this peasant preacher who can make such a claim?

4. *By accepting man's honour* (verse 23). Humility is a virtue that we expect to find in great saints and religious leaders. This claim of Jesus to have an equal right with God to receive the honour of men is utter conceit, unless Jesus was indeed equal with God. Jesus claims that to honour him is to honour God, and to dishonour him is to dishonour God. When a man says I believe in God, but I cannot accept Jesus, he is, according to Jesus, dishonouring and ignoring God himself. Is this conceit or sober truth?

5. *By settling man's destiny* (verses 24–29). No mere man,

however great, would claim to settle the eternal destiny of another unless he was suffering from delusions or megalomania. But Jesus claims with great emphasis that a man's attitude to his own words, as well as his faith in God, settles his present enjoyment of spiritual life now (the Greek tense suggests that a believer in Jesus *already has* eternal life), as well as his destiny in the future (verse 24).

Jesus goes on to use two titles to describe himself. He is the unique *Son of God*. Those who hear his voice *now* and respond to him will live. They will come alive spiritually. They will recognize that God is speaking to them. He also claims to be the *Son of man*. In the Old Testament book of Daniel the prophet sees a vision of a divine figure, called the Son of man, coming in the clouds in judgment (see Daniel 7:13–14). Jesus claims to be the Son of man. He will execute judgment. If Jesus is merely a man, a prophet, an outstanding teacher, then we need not take this claim seriously. Indeed any man who claims to do the works of God, to give eternal life, to judge sinners, to accept honour due to God and to settle a man's destiny, must be either deluded or divine. The one thing he cannot be is just a good man. No mere man in his senses could make claims like this. Only God himself has the right to make such claims. If Jesus is God, then these words are serious indeed. It is God who has come to tell us that there are two possible destinies for each of us—the resurrection to life or the resurrection to judgment (verses 28–29). *Who, then, is Jesus Christ?* Is he deluded or divine?

Questions for discussion
1. When Buddha was dying he was asked how people could best remember him. He urged his followers not to bother with that question. What mattered, he said, was his teaching and not his person. In what way is the attitude of Jesus different from Buddha in this matter? Give examples from this passage.
2. How does Jesus' claim to judge men (verse 23), help us to accept the fact of judgment, and to prepare for the final judgment (verses 24–29)?
3. What does Jesus teach here about our final destiny and about eternal life?

12 The authority of Jesus

5:30–47

30 'I can do nothing on my own authority; I judge only as God tells me, so my judgment is right, because I am not trying to do what I want, but only what he who sent me wants.

31 'If I testify on my own behalf, what I say is not to be accepted as real proof. ³²But there is someone else who testifies on my behalf, and I know that what he says about me is true. ³³John is the one to whom you sent your messengers, and he spoke on behalf of the truth. ³⁴It is not that I must have a man's witness; I say this only in order that you may be saved. ³⁵John was like a lamp, burning and shining, and you were willing for a while to enjoy his light. ³⁶But I have a witness on my behalf which is even greater than the witness that John gave: what I do, that is, the deeds my Father gave me to do, these speak on my behalf and show that the Father has sent me. ³⁷And the Father, who sent me, also testifies on my behalf. You have never heard his voice or seen his face, ³⁸and you do not keep his message in your hearts, for you do not believe in the one whom he sent. ³⁹You study the Scriptures, because you think that in them you will find eternal life. And these very Scriptures speak about me! ⁴⁰Yet you are not willing to come to me in order to have life.

41 'I am not looking for human praise. ⁴²But I know what kind of people you are, and I know that you have no love for God in your hearts. ⁴³I have come with my Father's authority, but you have not received me; when, however, someone comes with his own authority, you will receive him. ⁴⁴You like to receive praise from one another, but you do not try to win praise from the one who alone is God; how, then, can you believe me? ⁴⁵Do not think, however, that I am the one who will accuse you to my Father. Moses, in whom you have put your hope, is the very one who will accuse you. ⁴⁶If you had really believed Moses, you would have believed me, because he wrote about me. ⁴⁷But since you do not believe what he wrote, how can you believe what I say?'

If my car has gone wrong and I want to know how it might be mended, I don't ask my wife what to do (although she may well know more about it than I do!). I go to my garage where I hope to find someone who is an authority on cars. In practical matters of that kind I find it best to go to someone who is an expert, and who can speak with authority.

In matters of religion it is also important that we are able to go to someone who can speak with authority. It is this that Jesus claims to be able to do, since he claimed equality with God, and therefore the authority of God for all that he says. The vital question is, 'On what authority does he make such claims?' or to put it another way, 'In what ways does he substantiate such stupendous statements about himself?'

Jesus makes it clear in his teaching that he is not 'another God'. He is not independent of his heavenly Father (verse 30). So, as he argues with the critical Jewish leaders about his own authority, he brings forward his witnesses.

a. The witness of his Father (verse 32)

'But there is someone else who testifies on my behalf, and I know that what he says about me is true.' The true witness of the Father to Jesus' unique Sonship to which Jesus refers here seems to be the occasion of Jesus' baptism (John 1:29–34). But the Jewish leaders, unwilling to be baptized by John the Baptist, failed to hear or see God's witness to Jesus on that occasion (verse 37). For those who were looking for the Messiah, and longing for his coming, God had not been silent in witnessing to the truth about Jesus.

b. The witness of John the Baptist (verses 33–35)

He too witnessed to the truth about Christ. John the Baptist was admired by the Jews for his single-mindedness and courage. Here was a man who spoke the truth even at risk to his life. He was a great personality and 'a lamp burning and shining', and could easily have taken away a large following of disciples for himself. But he always pointed to Jesus as the Messiah, and acknowledged that Jesus was the Son of God (John 1:34). If the Jews had only listened to John the Baptist they would have acknowledged Jesus and would have been saved from the inevitable judgment that would follow their rejection of the Messiah (verse 34).

c. The witness of the work of Jesus

The Jews ought to have recognized that the 'works' or 'miracles' which Jesus did were 'signs' to them that God's Messiah had come. The Old Testament prophets had looked forward to a day when the Messiah, who was to be the agent of all God's purposes in the world, would come to his people. He was described significantly as Emmanuel, *God with us* (Isaiah 7:14). He would be called 'Wonderful Counsellor, *Mighty God*, Eternal Father, Prince of Peace' (Isaiah 9:6). One sign of his coming would be that he would preach good news to the poor, bind up the broken-hearted, proclaim release to the captives and recovering of sight to the blind, and set at liberty those who are oppressed (see Isaiah 61:1–2; Luke 4:16–21). There was a time when John the Baptist in a fit of depression almost lost his faith in Jesus. Jesus reminded John of the 'works' he was doing, in fulfilment of the Old Testament, as an answer to the question John's followers brought, 'Are you the one John said was going to come, or should we expect someone else?' (Luke 7:18–22). The Jewish leaders ought to have seen in the 'works' of Jesus his authority, that he was indeed from God.

d. The witness of the Scriptures (verse 39)

We have noticed already how the Old Testament Scriptures pointed to Jesus. 'These very Scriptures speak about me!' When Jesus spoke with the disciples on the Emmaus road after the resurrection (Luke 24) he 'explained to them what was said about himself in all the Scriptures' (that is the Old Testament as we know it) (verse 27). The Jews did well to search the Scriptures, for in them they might indeed find eternal life. But the Scriptures are a sign-post that points to Jesus Christ. They are not Christ himself. It is possible for us to make the same mistake as the Jews. We can read about the Christ of the Bible, but never come to the Christ of the Bible. The Bible 'speaks about me', says Jesus 'yet you are not willing to *come to me* in order to have life.' It is not enough to read the Bible. We must obey the Bible and come to Jesus Christ himself. In him alone is eternal life.

e. The witnesses rejected

Why did so many of the Jews refuse this witness to Jesus Christ? Jesus gave these answers.

1. *Their love for God was formal* (verses 41–42). They said they loved God, but their hearts were unmoved. Religion to many of them was only a form, an outward façade.

2. *Their consideration of Christ was superficial* (verse 43). They accepted the claims of other men sometimes with no evidence as to their genuineness. But they would not consider the witness of God to the claims of Jesus. I am always amazed at the way men will accept, say, the arguments for Mormonism, or flying saucers, or re-incarnation, on the slenderest of evidence and never consider the weighty evidence for the deity of Christ.

3. *Their acknowledgment of God was hypocritical* (verse 44). They pretended that they wanted God to be honoured in their lives. In reality they wanted the praise and honour of their friends. They regarded man's honour as more important than God's praise. Many a man has turned his back upon God because of his fear that he would lose the good opinion of men.

4. *Their knowledge of the Scriptures was theoretical* (verses 46–47). They said they believed in the writings of Moses. They set their hope on him. They memorized many of his words. They even taught others what he said. But they did not act on what he said. They showed therefore that they did not really take the Old Testament seriously. If they claimed to believe Moses in theory, but failed in practice, how unlikely it would be that they would act on the words of Jesus, when they would not believe his claims. Christian belief is more than theoretical assent to certain propositions in the Bible. It is practical experimental trust in the living Jesus Christ to whom the Scriptures witness.

Christ's authority rests on God himself. God has vouched for that divine authority through men (*e.g.* John the Baptist), through miracles and through the Scriptures. However, *a person will never be convinced of his authority until he is willing to submit to it, and humbly come to Jesus.*

Questions for discussion

1. In what ways does Jesus claim to be equal with God in this passage? Why should we believe this claim?

2. Why is the Bible's witness to Christ insufficient on its own to bring us to faith in Jesus as God?

3. How far do the opinions of others affect our attitude to Jesus Christ (verses 41–47)?

4. Do we need to believe in the authority of the Bible to become Christians and to live the Christian life?

13   The power of Jesus

6:1–24

6 After this, Jesus went across Lake Galilee (or, Lake Tiberias, as it is also called). ²A large crowd followed him, because they had seen his miracles of healing those who were ill. ³Jesus went up a hill and sat down with his disciples. ⁴The time for the Passover Festival was near. ⁵Jesus looked round and saw that a large crowd was coming to him, so he asked Philip, 'Where can we buy enough food to feed all these people?' (⁶He said this to test Philip; actually he already knew what he would do.)

7 Philip answered, 'For everyone to have even a little, it would take more than two hundred silver coins to buy enough bread.'

8 Another of his disciples, Andrew, who was Simon Peter's brother, said, ⁹'There is a boy here who has five loaves of barley bread and two fish. But they will certainly not be enough for all these people.'

10 'Make the people sit down,' Jesus told them. (There was a lot of grass there.) So all the people sat down; there were about five thousand men. ¹¹Jesus took the bread, gave thanks to God, and distributed it to the people who were sitting there. He did the same with the fish, and they all had as much as they wanted. ¹²When they were all full, he said to his disciples, 'Gather the pieces left over; let us not waste any.'

13 So they gathered them all up and filled twelve baskets with the pieces left over from the five barley loaves which the people had eaten.

14 Seeing this miracle that Jesus had performed, the people there said, 'Surely this is the Prophet who was to come into the world!' ¹⁵Jesus knew that they were about to come and seize him in order to make him king by force; so he went off again to the hills by himself.

16 When evening came, Jesus' disciples went down to the lake, ¹⁷got into a boat, and went back across the lake towards Capernaum. Night came on, and Jesus still had not come to them. ¹⁸By then a strong wind was blowing and stirring up the water. ¹⁹The disciples had rowed about five or six kilometres when they saw Jesus walking on the water, coming near the boat, and they were terrified. ²⁰'Don't be afraid,' Jesus told them, 'It is I !' ²¹Then they willingly took him into the boat, and immediately the boat reached land at the place they were heading for.

22 Next day the crowd which had stayed on the other side of the lake realized that there had been only one boat there. They knew that Jesus had not gone in it with his disciples, but that they had left without him. ²³Other boats, which were from Tiberias, came to shore near the place where the crowd had eaten the bread after the Lord had given thanks. ²⁴When the crowd saw that Jesus was not there, nor his disciples, they got into those boats and went to Capernaum, looking for him.

Down the years there have always been some men who have made great claims for themselves: pharaohs, Roman emperors, modern dictators and even the boxer Muhammed Ali! But how many have lived up to their claims? The two incidents in this passage show us that Jesus not only made great claims but lived up to them. He practised what he preached. So it was not only in what he said (his claims) but in what he did (his works) that we understand and appreciate his power and deity.

a. The feeding of the five thousand (verses 1–15)

The narrative describes an act of superhuman power. Five loaves and two fishes taken into the hands of Jesus, then broken and distributed, feed about five thousand people. Twelve baskets are then filled with the scraps that are left over. Someone has said that the example of the boy handing over his picnic lunch to Jesus led all the others to bring out their food too and to share it so that there was enough for all. That is very ingenious, but it is not what the writer describes. Here again an estimate of Jesus Christ himself will determine our view of the likelihood of such a miracle (see note on John 2).

We could add to this argument the fact that early non-Christian writers who refer to Jesus at any length do not dispute that he performed miracles. Josephus called him a 'wonder-worker'. Other Jewish rabbis attribute his miracles to sorcery. Celsus, the second-century critic of Christianity, also attributed them to the power of sorcery, but these writers do not deny that they happened!* We ought to remember too that the apostles in the early church refer to the miracles of Jesus as facts which no one would dispute (Acts 2:22) and some of the early Christian apologists refer to them as events beyond dispute by the critics of Christianity.†

Jesus had no doubt welcomed the escape with his disciples to the solitude of the hills after the hectic days in Galilee. But it was not long before the crowds, including some of the pilgrims who were on their way to the Passover festival, heard where he was and came swarming up the hillside to see him (verses 1–5).

Jesus' question to Philip was partly a sign of his concern for the people, and partly a way of testing Philip's faith: 'Where can we buy enough food to feed all these people?' (verses 5–7). Did Philip know Jesus well enough to believe he could do something about this situation? Philip was down to earth, practical and unimaginative as ever. A quick reckoning showed him that it would take more than six months' wages to buy enough food to feed this crowd! (A denarius was the standard day's wage for a working man.) It was just not an economic proposition. I sometimes wonder how often the church of Jesus Christ has failed to see the power of Christ at work for the same reasons.

Andrew's suggestion is also half-hearted, and he probably felt slightly ridiculous in making it. 'There is a boy here who has five loaves of barley bread and two fish. But they will certainly not be enough for all these people.' But it is precisely with the picnic lunch of a young lad, willingly given, that Jesus demonstrates his power to satisfy the needs of the crowd. Small things, small gifts, in the hands of Jesus can often be a source of power and help to others. Furthermore, Jesus never does things in half measures (see verse 13).

When the people saw the sign which he had done they said, 'Surely this is *the* Prophet who was to come into the world!' (verse

*Origen, *Against Celsus*, i. 38; ii. 48.
†*E.g.* Quadratus, in his Apologies addressed to the Emperor Hadrian in AD 133 (Eusebius, *Ecclesiastical History*, iv. 3).

14). They recognized this amazing miracle as a sign that Jesus was the long-expected Messiah, or King (verse 15). The crowd did not yet understand the kind of King he would be, so that Jesus had to slip away quietly (verse 15). But they were beginning to see that you cannot explain Jesus completely by saying 'He is just a good man'.

b. Jesus walking on the lake (verses 16–21)
(*cf*. Matthew 14:22–27; Mark 6:45–51)

Jesus now gives the disciples further opportunity to understand who he is and to exercise faith in him. One of the sudden storms that often descend on the lake causes the disciples great distress as, without Jesus, they row across the sea to Capernaum. They toss about on the waves. For three or four miles they row desperately. Although they are experienced sailors, they begin to be terrified. Suddenly Jesus appears, walking on the water. He is not only Lord of the harvest, but Lord of the elements as well. To some Jewish minds the water in a lake is the place of evil spirits. The deity of Jesus assures us that he is Lord and Sovereign over all. As the Negro spiritual has it: 'He's got the whole world in his hands.' So Jesus can say 'Don't be afraid . . . it is I!'

In Mark's account (Mark 6:45–51) we are told that when Jesus got into the boat with them, 'The wind died down. The disciples were completely amazed, *because they had not understood the real meaning of the feeding of the five thousand*; their minds could not grasp it.' This must have been their first reaction. We find it hard to believe at first that Jesus is as powerful as this, especially when we have just discovered our own weakness and inadequacy in a situation in which we are supposed to be experts. The disciples were *skilled* fishermen! Jesus often comes to us even when we fail in our strong points, and says, 'Don't be afraid . . . It is I!' We may at first harden our hearts, like the disciples. However, we learn from Matthew's Gospel (Matthew 14:22–32) that those in the boat later worshipped him, saying, 'Truly you are the Son of God!' They were beginning to understand, by considering his works, who Jesus really was.

Many people are discouraged because they *feel* they have so little faith, especially in times of failure and fear. The New Testament encourages us to believe that it is not the *amount* of faith that

66

matters most but the *direction* of it. My faith may be as small as a grain of mustard seed, but if it is centred on Jesus Christ and a growing understanding of who he is, it will become living and strong. The Christian believes that Jesus Christ is in control of all things. So he is not afraid.

Questions for discussion

1. It has been said that the miracles of Jesus are always 'signs' and not merely 'wonders' or 'acts of magic'. What purpose do we see in the two miracles described here?
2. What does the story of the feeding of the five thousand tell us about Jesus' concern for people?
3. In what way should we be involved in caring for people, and how should we go about it, in the light of this story?
4. Of what is modern man most afraid? How do these stories of Jesus help?

14 Jesus and the seeker

6:25–40
25 When the people found Jesus on the other side of the lake, they said to him, 'Teacher, when did you get here?'

26 Jesus answered, 'I am telling you the truth: you are looking for me because you ate the bread and had all you wanted, not because you understood my miracles. ²⁷*Do not work for food that goes bad; instead, work for food that lasts for eternal life. This is the food which the Son of Man will give you, because God, the Father, has put his mark of approval on him.'*

28 So they asked him, 'What can we do in order to do what God wants us to do?'

29 Jesus answered, 'What God wants you to do is to believe in the one he sent.'

30 They replied, 'What miracle will you perform so that we may see it and believe you? What will you do? ³¹*Our ancestors ate manna in* *the desert, just as the scripture says, "He gave them bread from heaven to eat."'*

32 'I am telling you the truth,' Jesus said. 'What Moses gave you was not the bread from heaven; it is my Father who gives you the real bread from heaven. ³³For the bread that God gives is he who comes down from heaven and gives life to the world.'

34 'Sir,' they asked him, 'give us this bread always.'

35 'I am the bread of life,' Jesus told them. 'He who comes to me will never be hungry; he who believes in me will never be thirsty. ³⁶Now, I told you that you have seen me but will not believe. ³⁷Everyone whom my Father gives me will come to me. I will never turn away anyone who comes to me, ³⁸because I have come down from heaven to do not my own will but the will of him who sent me. ³⁹And it is the will of him who sent me that I should not lose any of all those he has given me, but that I should raise them all to life on the last day. ⁴⁰For what my Father wants is that all who see the Son and believe in him should have eternal life. And I will raise them to life on the last day.'

A self-confessed agnostic once wrote, 'Christians do not need miracles to sustain their beliefs. Christ himself was the miracle.' So although many people do not acknowledge the deity of Jesus, or his claims upon their lives, there are few who have not been drawn in some way by the attractiveness of Jesus.

Charles Lamb, the writer, once said: 'If Shakespeare was to come into the room, we should all rise up to meet him; but if that Person (Jesus) was to come into it, we should all fall down and try to kiss the hem of His garment.'* Here in this story in John's Gospel we find crowds of ordinary people, not really understanding who Jesus is, or what he came to do, 'looking for him' (verse 24), attracted by him.

However, this narrative makes it clear that if we are to find the satisfaction and life that Jesus can give us, we must come to him with some understanding of who he is and what he comes to do, and what he offers and demands. The answers Jesus gives to certain questions that are put to him help us to understand how we may approach him.

---

*Quoted by P. Carnegie Simpson in *The Fact of Christ*, p. 22.

a. The questions of the crowd

1. *'Teacher, when did you get here?'* (verses 25–27). Jesus saw this as a polite opening gambit. He does not answer this unimportant question, but speaks instead of *why they had come to him*. Our motives for seeking Jesus are important. These men came to Jesus for what they could get out of him. They came hoping for material gain and physical satisfaction. They saw Jesus possibly as the answer to their economic problems, and as one who would raise their standard of living. Jesus does not promise us material prosperity if we follow him, or physical and material comforts, nor should we expect advance in social status. We may well find the opposite is true. But he does not turn us away if we seek him at first with false or mixed motives. He merely helps us to see that spiritual satisfaction is more important than physical (though his feeding of the five thousand shows that he is not unconcerned about man's physical need, and the starving millions). Our greatest effort should be given to discovering that spiritual food which leads to eternal life. This food is to be found in Jesus Christ. For God himself, in giving him power to feed 5,000, has set his seal on him, and marked him out as God's answer to man's need.

2. *'What can we do in order to do what God wants us to do?'* (verse 28). This question again uncovers the way that most of us first approach God's offer of life and satisfaction in Jesus Christ. 'What can we *do*?' 'What works must we perform?' Does Jesus require more prayers, more church-going, more deeds of mercy, more kind actions? In our hearts we all think like the Jews here, 'What can we *do*?' There is of course something to do. But it is nothing we can achieve. It is nothing that earns us the right to new life in Jesus Christ. Jesus said, 'What God wants you to do is *to believe* in the one he sent!' It is not achieving anything that saves me, but believing, trusting in Jesus.

3. *'What miracle will you perform so that we may see it and believe you? What will you do?'* (verse 30). Men say, 'Seeing is believing.' The Jews said, 'We must have proof. Moses was a great leader because he provided food for the Israelites in the wilderness. What proof do you give us that you are greater than he is?' It was a natural question. This Gospel goes on to show us that a deeper faith can say 'believing is seeing'. But the answer Jesus gives provides sufficient grounds for a firm belief.

(i) He corrects their argument. Moses had not given bread (or manna, as it was called) to the Israelites. *God* had provided it, and met the physical needs of the Jews at that time. This bread saved their lives.

(ii) God likewise has provided the true bread from heaven, because Jesus has come from heaven into the world. In Jesus all men may find their spiritual needs met. He gives life to all.

(iii) In answer to their request 'Sir . . . give us this bread always', Jesus explains more exactly what he means. He says, 'I am the bread of life.' Bread is the staff of life; without it we cannot live. Jesus is the source of spiritual life; without him we cannot live. Bread satisfies for a time. Jesus will satisfy always. Those who are hungry and thirsty of heart will find complete satisfaction in Jesus Christ.

b. The mystery of God's actions (verses 36–40)

Why is it that some men do not come to Jesus even when they know something about him (verse 36)? Jesus' answer uncovers a mystery which the finite mind of man has never fully understood. For when a man comes to Christ two complementary truths can be recognized in his experience.

1. *God the Father gives the man to Christ.* 'Everyone whom my Father gives me will come to me. I will never turn away anyone who comes to me' (verse 37). Every Christian knows that he is a Christian only because of the working of God the Father in his life. God took the initiative. God was in control of the circumstances. God laid hold on us before we laid hold on him. God spoke to us before we spoke to God. He loved us before we began to love him. Furthermore, once God has given us to Christ, we know that it is God's will to keep us and to raise us up on the last day. 'For what my Father wants is that all who see the Son and believe in him should have eternal life; and I will raise them to life on the last day' (verse 40). Once God has given me to Jesus Christ, I am eternally secure in him.

2. *A man must come to God the Son and believe.* The previous truth about God's sovereignty does not lessen the importance of man's responsibility. It is 'anyone who *comes* to me', says Jesus, 'I will never turn away' (verse 37). It is '*all* who see the Son *and believe* in him' who have eternal life (verse 40). Moreover, it is

possible to see who he is and to understand what he came to do with the eye of faith.

The late Professor C. S. Lewis has described this paradoxical and existential experience in his own inimitable way. 'The odd thing was that before God closed in on me, I was in fact offered what now appears a moment of wholly free choice. In a sense I was going up Headington Hill on the top of a bus. Without words and (I think) almost without images, a fact about myself was somehow presented to me. I became aware that I was holding something at bay, or shutting something out. Or if you like that I was wearing some stiff clothing, like corsets, or even a suit of armour, as if I were a lobster. I felt myself being, there and then, given a free choice. I could open the door or keep it shut. I could unbuckle the armour or keep it on. Neither choice was presented as a duty: no threat or promise was attached to either, though I knew that to open the door or to take off the corset meant the incalculable. The choice appeared to be momentous but it was also strongly unemotional. I was moved by no desires or fears. In a sense I was not moved by anything. I chose to open, to unbuckle, to loosen the rein. I chose, yet it did not really seem possible to do the opposite.'*

God never forces a man to be a Christian. He has given us the precious gift of free will. He respects that gift. We must come to him and believe. But when we have come we know it is the work of God. When we have believed we know it is the gift of God.

Questions for discussion
1. What motives caused these people to seek for Jesus (verses 22–35)? What motivates your interest in Jesus Christ?
2. What place has 'good works' in the religion of Jesus (see verses 25–35)?
3. How secure is the person who has 'come to Jesus' and 'believed on him?' Can he ever be finally 'lost'? If not, why not? (See verses 32–40.)

*C. S. Lewis, *Surprised by Joy*, p. 211.

15   The challenge of personal faith

6:41–71

41 The people started grumbling about him, because he said, 'I am the bread that came down from heaven.' 42So they said, 'This man is Jesus son of Joseph, isn't he? We know his father and mother. How then, does he now say he came down from heaven?'

43 Jesus answered, 'Stop grumbling among yourselves. 44No one can come to me unless the Father who sent me draws him to me; and I will raise him to life on the last day. 45The prophets wrote, "Everyone will be taught by God." Anyone who hears the Father and learns from him comes to me. 46This does not mean that anyone has seen the Father; he who is from God is the only one who has seen the Father. 47I am telling you the truth: he who believes has eternal life. 48I am the bread of life. 49Your ancestors ate manna in the desert, but they died. 50But the bread that comes down from heaven is of such a kind that whoever eats it will not die. 51I am the living bread that came down from heaven. If anyone eats this bread, he will live for ever. The bread that I will give him is my flesh, which I give so that the world may live.'

52 This started an angry argument among them. 'How can this man give us his flesh to eat?' they asked.

53 Jesus said to them, 'I am telling you the truth: if you do not eat the flesh of the Son of Man and drink his blood, you will not have life in yourselves. 54Whoever eats my flesh and drinks my blood has eternal life, and I will raise him to life on the last day. 55For my flesh is the real food; and my blood is the real drink. 56Whoever eats my flesh and drinks my blood lives in me, and I live in him. 57The living Father sent me, and because of him I live also. In the same way whoever eats me will live because of me. 58This, then, is the bread that came down from heaven; it is not like the bread that your ancestors ate, but then later died. The one who eats this bread will live for ever.'

59 Jesus said this as he taught in the synagogue in Capernaum.

60 Many of his followers heard this and said, 'This teaching is too hard. Who can listen to it?'

61 Without being told, Jesus knew that they were grumbling about this, so he said to them, 'Does this make you want to give up?' [62]*Suppose, then, that you should see the Son of Man go back up to the place where he was before?* [63]*What gives life is God's Spirit; man's power is of no use at all. The words I have spoken to you bring God's life-giving Spirit.* [64]*Yet some of you do not believe.'* (*Jesus knew from the very beginning who were the ones that would not believe and which one would betray him.*) [65]*And he added, 'This is the very reason I told you that no one can come to me unless the Father makes it possible for him to do so.'*

[66]*Because of this, many of Jesus' followers turned back and would not go with him any more.* [67]*So he asked the twelve disciples, 'And you—would you also like to leave?'*

[68]*Simon Peter answered him, 'Lord, to whom would we go? You have the words that give eternal life.* [69]*And now we believe and know that you are the Holy One who has come from God.'*

[70]*Jesus replied, 'I chose the twelve of you, didn't I? Yet one of you is a devil!'* [71]*He was talking about Judas, the son of Simon Iscariot. For Judas, even though he was one of the twelve disciples, was going to betray him.*

Many people prefer to keep their religion undemanding and impersonal. C. S. Lewis expressed it like this:*

'An "impersonal God"—well and good. A subjective God of beauty, truth and goodness, inside our own heads—better still. A formless life-force surging through us, a vast power which we can top—best of all. But God himself, alive, pulling at the other end of the cord, perhaps approaching at an infinite speed, the hunter, king, husband—that is quite another matter. There comes a moment when the children who have been playing burglars hush suddenly: was that a *real* footstep in the hall? There comes a moment when people who have been dabbling in religion (Man's search for God!) suddenly draw back. Supposing we really found Him? We never meant it to come to *that*! Worse still, supposing He had found us?'

Jews in Jesus' day were a bit like that. As soon as they were confronted with God in the person of Jesus, they began to evade him, and even to fight against him. For Jesus to say 'Come to me' or 'Believe in me!' was too personal and too demanding.

*C. S. Lewis, *Miracles*

So, they began to deny the claims that Jesus made, just as many people, even religious people, do today.

a. They denied his claim to be divine (verses 41–51)

They sneered at his earthly home. The Jews disagreed with Jesus' claim to be 'the bread that came down from heaven'. They recognized this as a claim to deity. Jesus was not simply born into the world: *he came from heaven.* But, his critics said, we know this man's parents, Joseph and Mary. He comes from a carpenter's home, and from Nazareth, of all disreputable places! Would God come from such humble stock, and in such a humble manner?

Jesus' answer points out that their very objection shows how little they know God, for all their boasting to be religious. If they knew the voice of God, they would acknowledge the words of Christ (verse 45). He also reiterates the point that unless the Father draws them they will not come to him (verse 44). However, Jesus does not deny their charge, but simply restates his own claim, (see verses 44, 45, 46, 47, 50, 51). We are already familiar with his claims to raise up believers at the last day, to give eternal life and satisfaction. But Jesus now includes a deeper truth. 'The bread that I will give him is my flesh, which I give so that the world may live' (verse 51). Jesus now teaches that eternal life and satisfaction are made possible only by his death—by giving his flesh, or by laying down his life for the world.

b. They denied his teaching about death (verses 52–58)

They sneered at its crudity. There is no denying that the words of Jesus concerning the giving of his own body in death are crude and difficult to understand. There is something even more crude and terrible about the crucifixion of Jesus Christ which the writer of this Gospel sees as 'the hour', the great moment, of the ministry of Jesus. Jesus did not die on a beautiful gilded cross such as we see in some churches; but on a rough-hewn tree, knocked into the shape of a cross.

Quite apart from the crudity of the idea, what did Jesus mean by *'eating his flesh and drinking his blood'*? Even his disciples found this hard to understand and offensive to their ears (verses 60–61). Jesus explained this in a sermon in the synagogue at

Capernaum (verses 52–59), and possibly privately to his disciples as well (verses 60–71). The two main points stand out.

1. *The importance of a personal appropriation of Christ himself.* If you gave a starving man a lecture on the chemical properties of bread, or held up a poster depicting the satisfying nature of a whole-meal loaf, it would not help to satisfy the poor man at all. A hungry man needs to take food and eat it. He cannot live unless he eats.

So it is not enough to hear about Jesus Christ, or to analyse his nature, or to believe certain facts about him, or simply to read about him. Spiritual satisfaction and life is given only when we take him and personally appropriate or receive him for ourselves. We take him as God become man (the bread from heaven). We take him as the Saviour of sinners (flesh and blood *given* for the life of the world, verse 51). When we receive Jesus as Son of God and Saviour of sinners personally into our lives, we may be said to eat his flesh and drink his blood. He then lives in us, and we in him, in close union and friendship (verse 56). He then continues to sustain us spiritually as we continue to believe on him, and draw strength and life from him (see John 15). A friend of mine, a research graduate from Ceylon, wrote this about his search for the truth in the Gospels. 'As I read the Gospels there was a growing awareness in my mind that a Person stood out of the pages, and He seemed alive. The historical Jesus became very immediate. I knelt and prayed, perhaps for the first time sincerely, and asked Jesus to forgive my sins and come into my life. I can say quite honestly that moment proved to be very decisive in my life . . . From that day onwards the Lord Jesus Christ has proved to be my Saviour, Friend and Companion through all walks of life.' He had received Jesus personally by faith.

2. *The importance of a right interpretation of Christ's teaching.* The disciples who found this teaching of Jesus offensive had failed to understand the spiritual significance of what Jesus was saying. They failed to understand that Jesus often spoke of spiritual truths in material terms. Clearly Jesus did not mean that they must literally eat his actual flesh and blood if they were to know eternal life. As Jesus said, 'It is the spirit that gives life, the flesh is of no avail; *the words that I have spoken to you are spirit and life* (verse 63, RSV). Those who use these words to endorse the view of some Christians that at the Holy Communion service the bread and wine is changed into the actual body and blood of Christ are surely

75

making the same mistake as the disciples here. When Jesus speaks of the Son of Man ascending to heaven (verse 62), perhaps he is suggesting that when this happens they will understand better the spiritual significance of these words (*cf.* John 16:7). It is as the Spirit of God applies the words of Christ to us that we are able spiritually to feed on Christ in our hearts by faith.

Men often find it easier to worship God in a material form than in a spiritual manner. Idolatry in the Old Testament was an example of this. Priestcraft and ritual in all religions endorse this view. Even Judas, the disciple who later betrayed Jesus, found the material advantage of betraying Jesus (thirty pieces of silver) at first more satisfying than the spiritual gain of following him. If spiritual life is possible only through the physical death of Jesus, then what sort of Messiah, what sort of King was he? What sort of life was he offering them? We are not surprised to find that 'because of this, many of Jesus' followers turned back and would not go with him any more' (verse 66). Would his special followers, the twelve disciples, also leave him at this point in his mission? Simon Peter's answer to the question, 'And you—would you also like to leave?' is a good one to turn over in our minds (see verses 68–69).

Questions for discussion
1. 'Many people prefer to keep their religion undemanding and impersonal.' Is that true? If so, why?
2. Is the teaching here about the deity and the death of Jesus essential to Christianity? If it is, why is it?
3. 'Whoever eats my flesh and drinks my blood lives in me, and I live in him.' What does this mean? How would it help someone who asks how to become a Christian?
4. Why did many of the followers of Jesus turn back and go with him no more (verses 66–71)?
5. Why was the teaching of Jesus (as in this passage) offensive to many of the people? Are people offended in the same way and for the same reasons today?

16 Growing opposition

7:1–31

7 After this, Jesus travelled in Galilee; he did not want to travel in Judaea, because the Jewish authorities there were wanting to kill him. ²The time for the Festival of Shelters was near, ³so Jesus' brothers said to him, 'Leave this place and go to Judaea, so that your followers will see the things that you are doing. ⁴No one hides what he is doing if he wants to be well known. Since you are doing these things, let the whole world know about you!' (⁵Not even his brothers believed in him.)

6 Jesus said to them, 'The right time for me has not yet come. Any time is right for you. ⁷The world cannot hate you, but it hates me, because I keep telling it that its ways are bad. ⁸You go on to the festival. I am not going to this festival, because the right time has not come for me.' ⁹He said this, and then stayed on in Galilee.

10 After his brothers had gone to the festival, Jesus also went; however, he did not go openly, but secretly. ¹¹The Jewish authorities were looking for him at the festival. 'Where is he?' they asked.

12 There was much whispering about him in the crowd. 'He is a good man,' some people said. 'No,' others said, 'he is misleading the people.' ¹³But no one talked about him openly, because they were afraid of the Jewish authorities.

14 The festival was nearly half over when Jesus went to the Temple and began teaching. ¹⁵The Jewish authorities were greatly surprised and said, 'How does this man know so much when he has never had any training?'

16 Jesus answered, 'What I teach is not my own teaching, but it comes from God, who sent me. ¹⁷Whoever is willing to do what God wants will know whether what I teach comes from God or whether I speak on my own authority. ¹⁸A person who speaks on his own authority is trying to gain glory for himself. But he who wants glory for the one who sent him is honest, and there is nothing false in him. ¹⁹Moses gave you the Law, didn't he? But not one of you obeys the Law. Why are you trying to kill me?'

20 'You have a demon in you !' the crowd answered. 'Who is trying to kill you ?'

21 Jesus answered, 'I performed one miracle, and you were all surprised. *22*Moses ordered you to circumcise your sons (although it was not Moses but your ancestors who started it), and so you circumcise a boy on the Sabbath. *23*If a boy is circumcised on the Sabbath so that Moses' Law is not broken, why are you angry with me because I made a man completely well on the Sabbath? *24*Stop judging by external standards, and judge by true standards.'

25 Some of the people of Jerusalem said, 'Isn't this the man the authorities are trying to kill? *26*Look! He is talking in public, and they say nothing against him! Can it be that they really know that he is the Messiah? *27*But when the Messiah comes, no one will know where he is from. And we all know where this man comes from.'

28 As Jesus taught in the Temple, he said in a loud voice, 'Do you really know me and know where I am from? I have not come on my own authority. He who sent me, however, is truthful. You do not know him, *29*but I know him, because I come from him and he sent me.'

30 Then they tried to seize him, but no one laid a hand on him, because his hour had not yet come. *31*But many in the crowd believed in him and said, 'When the Messiah comes, will he perform more miracles than this man has?'

Recently I watched a programme on television where Mrs Mary Whitehouse was ruthlessly criticized by a well-known television interviewer. A few weeks later Malcolm Muggeridge was caricatured and parodied on another programme. 'Why', I asked myself, 'do some TV personalities use their invective on those who speak up for God and purity (like Whitehouse and Muggeridge) while at the same time they go out of their way to defend those who advocate that violence, immorality and explicit sex should be freely shown on television?' There must be something about 'good' people that draws the hostility of others.

This was certainly true for Jesus. Opposition to him was now becoming stronger (verse 1) and the tension between belief and unbelief greater. As people began to take sides for or against Jesus it is instructive to note the reasons men gave for their unbelief and opposition.

a. The brothers of Jesus—criticized his methods (verses 1–9)

It is clear that Jesus is working to a timetable—God's timetable. It is not yet the best time for him to go publicly to Jerusalem (verse 6), so he remains quietly in Galilee. The Jewish Festival of Tabernacles lasted for eight days (end of September and beginning of October). Jesus arrived some time in the middle of the festivities, not at the start, as his brothers had suggested. His brothers cannot understand his reticence. They probably argued: 'Jesus has supernatural power. We have seen evidence of that. Why does he not work some spectacular miracle in Jerusalem, so that all may see without doubt that he is what he claims to be—God's Son and God's Messiah?' The only miracle attributed to Jesus in Jerusalem was the curing of the impotent man at the pool (John 5). You can almost hear the impatience and perhaps cynicism in their tone of voice when they say, 'Since you are doing these things, let the whole world know about you!' (verse 4). Would not this prove to all that Jesus was no phoney? Why will he not demonstrate his power in the strategic city of Jerusalem? It could not have been easy for Jesus to be misunderstood by his own family.

Perhaps the brothers could not understand either why Jesus was so hated by the religious leaders of the day. Men prefer to support popular causes. Jesus seems to them to have thrown away his chance of being a popular success. Jesus' answer is revealing: 'The world . . . hates me, because I keep telling it that its ways are bad' (verse 7). None of us likes to be shown up by a good man.

We reject Jesus sometimes for the same reason as his brothers. We criticize his methods. We prefer not to talk about his death. We wonder why he led a minority movement, and why the church has always been like this. We sometimes blame the church in the same way. We accuse it for its lack of the spectacular, for its minority size. God's ways are not our ways. We must accept Jesus on his own terms or not at all. We must expect the church to be a minority movement, and sometimes a persecuted and hated minority, for, like Jesus, it lives in a world whose works are evil.

b. Many of the Jews in Jerusalem—criticized his character (verses 10–31)

When Jesus eventually visited Jerusalem for the Jewish Feast of the Tabernacles, he discovered that there was a good deal of gossip about him. Men were taking sides. No-one spoke openly because they were afraid of the reaction of officialdom. It is strange that even today in some church circles the mention of the name of Jesus in conversation can sometimes be followed by an embarrassing silence. Some could not avoid the conclusion that Jesus was a *good man* (verse 12). Those who criticized his character and took an opposite view could only make the following charges.

1. '*He is misleading the people*' (verse 12). No-one defines in what way Jesus is doing this. No-one can give an example of any-one who has been led to corruption, or disloyalty to church or state. On one occasion Jesus said to his critics, 'Which one of you can prove that I am guilty of sin'? (John 8:46), and they could not answer one word. The sinlessness of Jesus, the blamelessness of his character, is one of the reasons for believing that he was divine.

2. '*You have a demon in you*' (verses 14–24). There were many in Jerusalem who were astonished at the authoritative teaching of Jesus, even though he had had no official theological and academic training in the schools of the Jewish rabbis (verse 15). On another occasion the people had marvelled at his teaching because he spoke with authority, and 'wasn't like the teachers of the Law' (Matthew 7:28). Jesus explained that his teaching was authoritative because it was God's teaching. What God says, Jesus says; and anyone *willing to do what God wants* would know this truth for certain. If we are willing to do God's will as he reveals it, we shall know that what Jesus says is God's truth (verse 17). Unfortunately, many of the Jews were not willing to do God's will. They had failed to obey the spirit of God's law (hence their criticism of Jesus for healing a man on the sabbath), they had judged Jesus superficially and falsely, and now they tried to blacken his character (verse 20) and to get rid of him. It is a sign of weakness to abuse your opponent. Some-times opposition to Christianity can too easily become like this.

The shallow thinking of the Jewish ecclesiastics is well shown up in this controversy about the sabbath and circumcision (verses 22–24). Circumcision, given to every male Jewish baby when eight days old as a sign of God's covenant or agreement with him and the family, involved a slight mutilation of the body. Jesus points out that if it is lawful to carry out an operation on the sabbath day which mutilates the flesh (circumcision), surely it cannot be un-lawful to carry out an operation which makes the body whole (a healing miracle). Legalists often forget that people matter more than things, principles more than hard-and-fast rules.

3. '*We all know where this man comes from*' (verses 25–32). Some of the people in Jerusalem began to accept the claims of Jesus, and wondered whether the authorities' delay in failing to forbid his teaching was a sign of their own conviction that he really was the Messiah (verses 25–26).

Others thought they knew better, and doubted the honesty and integrity of Jesus' teaching. A little knowledge is sometimes a dangerous thing. They believed they knew the Scriptures better than Jesus. They dismissed his claims on the grounds that, whereas they all knew where Jesus came from, no-one would know where the Messiah would appear.*

Jesus, as ever (verse 28), affirms that the Jews do not know where Jesus comes from. For he comes from God, and they continually reveal the fact that they do not know God by their attitude to himself. Yet again this stirs up the enemies of Jesus, but they cannot touch him until God's time has come. Furthermore, many believed, as they weighed up the evidence, and considered the works of Jesus that so clearly authenticated his claims to be the Messiah.

It is right that we should consider carefully the methods, character, teaching and claims of Jesus Christ. This passage shows us the danger of criticism without reason, and accusation without evidence.

Questions for discussion
1. What do you think was behind the criticism of Jesus' family? How much does the opinion of our family and friends affect our attitude to Jesus and his ways? (See 1–10 and 25–31.)
2. 'Stop judging by external standards, and judge by true standards' (verse 24). By what standards do we judge Christ and the followers of Christ? What are 'true standards' (verses 10–24)?

*The common belief was that the Messiah would *appear* suddenly, and no-one would know where he had come from. The Jews had a saying: 'Three things come wholly unexpectedly, the Messiah, a godsend, and a scorpion.'

17 The conflict continues

7:32–52

32 The Pharisees heard the crowds whispering these things about Jesus, so they and the chief priests sent some guards to arrest him. [33]Jesus said, 'I shall be with you a little longer, and then I shall go away to him who sent me. [34]You will look for me, but you will not find me, because you cannot go where I will be.'

35 The Jewish authorities said among themselves, 'Where is he about to go so that we shall not find him? Will he go to the Greek cities where our people live, and teach the Greeks? [36]He says that we will look for him but will not find him, and that we cannot go where he will be. What does he mean?'

37 On the last and most important day of the festival Jesus stood up and said in a loud voice, 'Whoever is thirsty should come to me and drink. [38]As the scripture says, "Whoever believes in me, streams of life-giving water will pour out from his heart." ' [39]Jesus said this about the Spirit, which those who believed in him were going to receive. At that time the Spirit had not yet been given, because Jesus had not been raised to glory.

40 Some of the people in the crowd heard him say this and said, 'This man is really the Prophet!'

41 Others said, 'He is the Messiah!'

But others said, 'The Messiah will not come from Galilee! [42]The scriptures says that the Messiah will be a descendant of King David and will be born in Bethlehem, the town where David lived.' [43]So there was a division in the crowd because of Jesus. [44]Some wanted to seize him, but no one laid a hand on him.

45 When the guards went back, the chief priests and Pharisees asked them, 'Why did you not bring him?'

46 The guards answered, 'Nobody has ever talked like this man!'

47 'Did he fool you, too?' the Pharisees asked them. [48]'Have you ever known one of the authorities or one Pharisee to believe in him? [49]This crowd does not know the Law of Moses, so they are under God's curse!'

50 One of the Pharisees there was Nicodemus, the man who had gone to see Jesus before. He said to the others, 51 'According to our Law we cannot condemn a man before hearing him and finding out what he has done.'

52 'Well,' they answered, 'are you also from Galilee? Study the Scriptures and you will learn that no prophet ever comes from Galilee.'

If you have ever seen dark, brooding clouds gather together threateningly before a storm, you will have a picture of the drama and tenseness that is now becoming part of John's story of Jesus. The religious leaders in Jerusalem are determined to get rid of Jesus (verse 32).

Who were these leaders? Some of them belonged to a group in Judaism called the *Pharisees*. They were the separatists or Puritans of the Jewish religion. Their name is derived from the word *parash*, 'to separate', and their aim was to withdraw from all evil associations and to obey in detail every precept of the oral and written law.*

Many Pharisees became excessively self-righteous: others like Nicodemus (see chapter 3 and 7:50) set a high moral and spiritual standard. It is interesting to note that of all the sects of Judaism, Pharisaism has alone survived. It has become the modern orthodox Judaism of today which follows a Pharisaic pattern of morality, ceremonialism and legalism.

Another group opposed to Jesus was the chief priests, who at this time were almost certainly *Sadducees*. The *Sadducees* was the title of the priestly party in the time of Christ. They were a political party and collaborators with their Roman masters. They differed from the Pharisees in many of their beliefs, as they acknowledged as authoritative only the first five books of the Bible, and they denied the supernatural—especially the existence of angels and spirits (Acts 23:8) and the resurrection after death. They did not want a Messiah, as this would interfere with their own vested interests under the Romans.

There is no doubt that the teaching of Jesus was a threat to the privilege and position of the Sadducees and many of the Pharisees. Some of the hardest things that Jesus said were said in rebuke of

*For an interesting list of seven types of Pharisees, see Merrill C. Tenney, *New Testament Survey*, p. 110.

the hypocrisy and self-righteousness of these religious leaders (see Matthew 23). Furthermore, some of these ecclesiastics no doubt believed that it was important to keep on the right side of the Roman authorities. Palestine was an occupied country, and if the followers of Jesus started an unwise uprising, they would bring trouble down on the Pharisees themselves. Again, Jesus had claimed to be God. There was no question of examining whether or not Jesus had a right to such a claim. In their eyes it was blasphemy. That was sufficient.

So at last, hearing of the constant mutterings of the crowds in Jerusalem, the chief priests and Pharisees sent officers to arrest Jesus. I think we must imagine that Jesus is speaking to the temple police, with the scribes and the Pharisees and the rest of the people standing around and listening intently. In the dialogue that follows the arrival of the police, we cannot fail to notice certain points concerning Jesus.

a. His complete control of the situation (verses 32–36)

Jesus is completely unafraid of the threats of men, and shows that he is quietly and voluntarily moving towards the end of his earthly ministry, when he will return to his heavenly Father (verse 33). The Jews show how little they have listened to his teaching or understood it. Yet Jesus implies that their rejection of it will one day exclude them from the presence of God. 'I shall go away to him who sent me . . . *you cannot go where I will be*' (verses 33–34). Man cannot do whatever he likes with Jesus. Nor can man choose his own time. It is Jesus Christ who is in control of circumstances, and life and death itself. It is possible to reject Jesus Christ so often that we no longer *want* to listen to him.

b. His simple offer of life (verses 37–39)

These words were spoken on the last (eighth) day of the Festival of Tabernacles. This feast was compulsory for all adult male Jews who lived within twenty miles of Jerusalem. The purpose of the feast was to remind the Jews of their wanderings in the wilderness before they reached the promised land: 'so that your descendants may know that the Lord made the people of Israel live in simple shelters when he led them out of Egypt' (Leviticus 23:40–43). The festival was also a harvest thanksgiving, sometimes called 'the Festival of Shelters' (Exodus 23:16) to be celebrated 'in the autumn'. Indeed, it included thanksgiving for all God's gifts. Josephus called it 'the holiest and the greatest Festival among the Jews'.*

It was on this last day of the feast that Jesus directed the thoughts of all the worshippers once again to himself. He turned their thoughts away from the water that refreshed their bodies to that water which refreshes the soul. Jesus could provide refreshment of spirit which would not only bubble up inside a man but overflow to the refreshment of others. He suggests that as we cannot live physically, without water, so we cannot live, spiritually, without Christ. Men would find this true if only they would come to him and receive the 'life' he was offering them. Once more Jesus insists that he is offering a new inner quality of life and satisfaction which must be received by faith. John adds the comment (verse 39) that the truth of these words was experienced after the death, resurrection and ascension of Jesus, when the disciples received the gift of God's Holy Spirit (see also John 14:16).

c. His challenge to faith (verses 40–52)

Once again a simple and personal challenge to come to him creates a division among the people. There were many different reactions to Jesus Christ then, as there are today.

1. *Some believed that Jesus was 'the Prophet'* (verse 40). Yet a prophet's authority is derived. A prophet says 'the Lord says'. Surely Jesus is more than a prophet. He says, 'But now *I* tell you . . .'. He says, 'Come to *me* . . . learn from *me*' (Matthew 11:28, 29).

2. *Some believed that he was 'the Christ'* (verse 41). At least, they gave intellectual assent to this claim. But Christian belief involves more than intellectual assent (see John 6).

3. *Some were agnostic*, for they did not know sufficient about him to make a decision (verse 42). Quite rightly they searched the Scriptures to check his claims. They had not discovered that Jesus was indeed descended from David and born in Bethlehem. Or were they keeping Jesus at arm's length by engaging in a theological argument for its own sake?

*Josephus, *Antiquities of the Jews*, iii. 10. 4.

4. *Some were antagonistic*, possibly out of jealousy, or fear, or guilty conscience, or unwillingness to change their lives, and they wanted to remove the challenge of Jesus' life and teaching by getting him out of the way (verse 44). Like the man mentioned in the Psalms, they hated him 'for no reason' (Psalm 35:19).

5. *Some were interested.* The temple police, for example, are intrigued, impressed and almost believing. 'Nobody has ever talked like this man!' (verse 46). They go out to silence the man. They come back amazed and deeply moved. The only answer the Pharisees can give them is: 'This is not the official teaching of the church. None of the church leaders believes in him.' This pre-supposes of course that only the scholars and ecclesiastics can understand the truths of God, an impression that some church pronouncements of our own day do little to avoid. This was religious, intellectual and social snobbery of the worst kind. It is still true today that some reject Jesus for the same reasons. They think themselves too clever or too respectable to become enthusiasts for Jesus Christ. They stop at religion without Christ. They are religious but not Christian.*

6. *Some wanted more time to think.* Like Nicodemus, they wanted more time to weigh up the evidence. In a typically cautious and scholarly way he voices his hesitation to the other members of the Jewish Cabinet, or Sanhedrin, 'According to our law we cannot condemn a man before hearing him and finding out what he has done' (verse 51). For Nicodemus, it was not only a question of justice, it was also a concern for truth. The suggestion that Nicodemus spoke for justice only because of some supposed local Galilean loyalty shows how desperate these men were for arguments. If they had bothered to ask a few more questions, and had really wanted to know the truth, they would have soon discovered that Jesus had not been born in Galilee anyway (verse 52). Nicodemus was slow, and still sitting on the fence, but his basic attitude was honest and good. The pressure of circumstances and honest seeking was one day to lead him to open and unashamed allegiance to Jesus (see John 19).

---

*The word 'Christian' was first a nickname, probably a word of abuse, given to the early followers of Jesus Christ, because of their enthusiasm and whole-heartedness in following him in the face of persecution and death (Acts 11:26).

Questions for discussion

1. What do we learn in these verses about the reaction of Jesus to hostility and adverse circumstances? How could it apply to us and our circumstances?

2. 'Whoever believes in me, streams of life-giving water will pour out from his heart' (verse 38). What does this tell us about the life Jesus offers to those who follow him?

3. 'There was a division in the crowd because of Jesus' (verse 43). What divisions does Jesus create today amongst those he challenges? Where do we stand?

18 Jesus' attitude to immorality

8:1–11

8 Then everyone went home, but Jesus went to the Mount of Olives. *²Early the next morning he went back to the Temple. All the people gathered round him, and he sat down and began to teach them.* *³The teachers of the Law and the Pharisees brought in a woman who had been caught committing adultery, and they made her stand before them all.* *⁴"Teacher,' they said to Jesus, 'this woman was caught in the very act of committing adultery.* *⁵In our Law Moses commanded that such a woman must be stoned to death. Now, what do you say?'* *⁶They said this to trap Jesus, so that they could accuse him. But he bent over and wrote on the ground with his finger.*

7 As they stood there asking him questions, he straightened himself up and said to them, 'Whichever one of you has committed no sin may throw the first stone at her.' *⁸Then he bent over again and wrote on the ground.* *⁹When they heard this, they all left, one by one, the older ones first. Jesus was left alone, with the woman still standing there.* *¹⁰He straightened himself up and said to her, 'Where are they? Is there no one left to condemn you?'*

11 'No one, sir,' she answered.

'Well, then,' Jesus said, 'I do not condemn you either. Go, but do not sin again.'

The story is told of a former archbishop who was once asked what he thought about sin. Unhesitatingly the archbishop replied, 'I'm against it!'

In this next moving little story in John's Gospel, we see the attitude of Jesus to the sins of hypocrisy and adultery. Some manuscripts place this incident at the end of John's Gospel or after Luke 21:38. We are not concerned in this commentary to go into the details of textual criticism. It is sufficient to say that there is little reason to doubt the authenticity of this story, whether or not this is the best chronological position for it.

In the time of Jesus, difficult legal and moral questions were taken to a rabbi for a decision. Hence the seemingly polite request of the scribes and Pharisees, 'Teacher, this woman was caught in the very act of committing adultery. In our Law Moses commanded that such a woman must be stoned to death. Now, what do you say?' The action of these men was, of course, an appalling one, especially as they realized that whatever answer Jesus gave they could turn it against him (verse 6). The law of Moses laid down that 'If a man commits adultery with the wife of a fellow Israelite, both he and the woman shall be put to death' (Leviticus 20:10). In Deuteronomy 22:13–24 it is determined that death shall be by stoning. So if Jesus pardoned the woman, the scribes and Pharisees would condemn Jesus for disregarding the law of Moses. If Jesus said she ought to be stoned, he would not only be accused of being unmerciful and harsh, but he would probably come up against the Roman authorities as well, for the Jews had no power to pass or carry out the death sentence on anyone.

Before Jesus answers, he bends down and writes with his finger on the ground. Whether he did this to gain time before he answered such a vile question, or because he was overcome with a terrible sense of shame, so that he could not look upon a scene that showed up so clearly the hypocrisy and cruelty of the Pharisees, we do not know. Some commentators suggest that he was writing in the dust the sins of the very men who were accusing the woman. The normal Greek word for 'to write' is *graphein*: here the word is *katagraphein* which can mean 'to write down a record against someone'. Whatever the reason for this strange action, the men continue to press their question avidly upon him.

The answer that Jesus gives not only turns the tables on his critics, but lays down principles that help us to discover a right attitude to immorality in our own day.

a. We are all sinners

Many people today define sin in terms of the kind of things we read about in the newspapers—rape, adultery, murder, crime, and so on. The scribes and Pharisees of Jesus' day were inclined to think in a similar way. To sin was to break the law. But even someone deliberately hunting out and persecuting Christians, like Saul of Tarsus, could claim that 'As far as keeping the Jewish Law is concerned . . . I was without fault', for to him keeping the law was a matter of avoiding sins such as adultery, murder and stealing.

Jesus defined sin more clearly. Sin was indeed 'breaking God's law', but man could do this by loving money more than God, by nourishing the lustful thought as well as committing the act of adultery, by hating a man as well as killing him, by failing to do positive good as well as avoiding evil. Indeed, according to Jesus Christ, we sin and break the greatest commandment of all when we fail to love God with all our heart, mind, soul and strength and our neighbour as ourself (see Matthew 5:21, 22, 27, 28; 22:37–40). No wonder Saul of Tarsus could write, after he had become a Christian and understood the perfect standard of God's law, 'For there is no distinction; since all have sinned and fall short of the glory of God' (Romans 3:23, RSV).

Sin is defined in the New Testament as 'missing the mark' and 'breaking the law', and if we offend in one point only we are still guilty (see James 2:10). It is not only the Pharisees who are rebuked at the convicting words of Jesus, 'Whichever one of you has committed *no sin* may throw the first stone at her' (verse 7). When they heard it they slunk away (verse 9). If we understand 'sin' as breaking God's standards in thought, as well as word and deed, we too shall be ashamed before the purity and sinlessness of Jesus Christ.

b. Sin is always condemned

'Jesus was left alone, with the woman still standing there.' No doubt her eyes were on the ground, her clothes dishevelled, her face a mixture of sullenness, shame and hope. 'Is there no one left

89

to condemn you?' 'No one, sir,' she answered. 'Well, then' Jesus said, 'I do not condemn you either. Go, but do not sin again.'

What is clear in this story is that Jesus does not condemn her act of adultery more than the Pharisees' act of cruelty and hypocrisy. In Jesus' eyes we may well believe that adultery is no better or worse than hypocrisy. Both the woman and her accusers have *sinned*. They have broken God's law. They deserve God's judgment. 'Go, but do not *sin* again.' Sin matters to Jesus. It mattered so much to Jesus that he was prepared to die on a cross to bear its judgment and its shame.

Those writers who argue that Jesus displaced law by love have failed to notice that Jesus does not hesitate to call the woman's act of adultery *sin*. For Jesus, love would be blind without the law to guide it. 'If you love me,' said Jesus on another occasion, *'you will obey my commandments'* (John 14:15).

c. Jesus is altogether merciful

Jesus condemns sins, but loves the sinner. If we slink away from Jesus like the Pharisees we may never receive his mercy and forgiveness. The woman stayed in the presence of Jesus and heard his words of mercy and hope, 'I do not condemn you either. Go, but do not sin again.' There is no-one outside the love and mercy of Jesus.

In Camus' novel, *The Fall*, Jean-Baptiste Clemence, a once successful Paris barrister who had fallen into debauchery and immorality, becomes terribly aware of his own guilt, and believes that religion can no longer help him. 'I am inclined to see religion . . . as a huge laundering venture—as it was once, but briefly, for exactly three years, and it wasn't called religion. Since then soap has been lacking, our faces are dirty, and we wipe one another's nose.'* It is true that religion cannot make us clean from sin. But Jesus can. What Camus failed to realize was that Jesus is alive today to offer complete forgiveness and mercy to those who come to him. He does not condone sin. He went to the cross to bear its consequences. But because of his death for sin he offers to those who turn from their sin and trust in him complete forgiveness and the prospect of a new life—'Go, but do not sin again.'

*Albert Camus, *The Fall*, p. 82.

Questions for discussion
1. It is said of Jesus that 'He hated sin and loved the sinner.' How does this help us to have a right attitude to those who have sinned, like the Pharisees and the woman in this story?
2. Jesus taught in the Sermon on the Mount that 'the righteousness' of his followers should exceed that of the scribes and Pharisees. How does this story help us to understand what he meant by these words?
3. What is wrong with the attitudes of the Pharisees in this story? What modern examples of 'Pharisaism' of this kind can you give?
4. In the light of this incident, what can we say to the person who says to us, 'I'm too bad, God will never forgive me'?

19   Jesus, the light of the world

8:12–30
12 Jesus spoke to the Pharisees again. 'I am the light of the world,' he said. 'Whoever follows me will have the light of life and will never walk in darkness.'

13 The Pharisees said to him, 'Now you are testifying on your own behalf; what you say proves nothing.'

14 'No,' Jesus answered, 'even though I do testify on my own behalf, what I say is true, because I know where I came from and where I am going. You do not know where I came from or where I am going. 15You make judgments in a purely human way; I pass judgment on no one. 16But if I were to do so, my judgment would be true, because I am not alone in this; the Father who sent me is with me. 17It is written in your Law that when two witnesses agree, what they say is true. 18I testify on my own behalf, and the Father who sent me also testifies on my behalf.'

19 'Where is your father?' they asked him.

'You know neither me nor my Father,' Jesus answered. 'If you knew me, you would know my Father also.'

20 Jesus said all this as he taught in the Temple, in the room where the offering boxes were placed. And no one arrested him, because his hour had not come.

21 Again Jesus said to them, 'I will go away; you will look for me, but you will die in your sins. You cannot go where I am going.'

22 So the Jewish authorities said, 'He says that we cannot go where he is going. Does this mean that he will kill himself?'

23 Jesus answered, 'You belong to this world here below, but I come from above. You are from this world, but I am not from this world. ²⁴*That is why I told you that you will die in your sins. And you will die in your sins if you do not believe that "I Am Who I Am".'*

25 'Who are you?' they asked him.

Jesus answered, 'What I have told you from the very beginning. ²⁶*I have much to say about you, much to condemn you for. The one who sent me, however, is truthful, and I tell the world only what I have heard from him.'*

27 They did not understand that Jesus was talking to them about the Father. ²⁸*So he said to them, 'When you lift up the Son of Man, you will know that "I Am Who I Am"; then you will know that I do nothing on my own authority, but I say only what the Father has instructed me to say.* ²⁹*And he who sent me is with me; he has not left me alone, because I always do what pleases him.'*

30 Many who heard Jesus say these things believed in him.

If the writers and dramatists of today reflect the attitude of the majority of ordinary people, then most of us are aware of the darkness and uncertainty of living in the twentieth century. In Samuel Beckett's play, *Waiting for Godot*, the main characters are two tramps who in utter boredom wait for Godot to turn up. They don't know who Godot is, and at the end of the play, when he has failed to appear, one tramp says to the other, 'Well, shall we go?' The reply comes, 'Yes, let's go.' But the final stage direction says simply 'they do not move'. There have been many interpretations of this play, but there is little doubt that it reflects the twentieth-century mood. We are waiting for something, maybe for someone, to turn up. Some light to shine in the darkness.

So were the Jews in the days of Jesus. At this same Feast of Tabernacles (see John 7) a ceremony had begun called 'the illumination of the temple'. Hundreds of Jews were gathered in the temple waiting for God's help and guidance in their lives, knowing the darkness of ignorance and moral failure. Their hope lay in a Messiah who would come as a light in the darkness. As dusk began to fall upon the temple courtyard, the four great golden candelabra were lit, and sent out a blaze of light which flooded every courtyard, and, as some said, shone all over Jerusalem. Some pious Jews began to dance and to sing Hebrew chants. 'The Lord is my light,' they cried. 'By his light I walked through darkness.'

It was on this day that some of the crowd heard Jesus say, 'I am the light of the world . . . Whoever follows me will have the light of life and will never walk in darkness.' Was Jesus the Messiah, they asked? Was he claiming to be God who alone is 'the light'? The Pharisees of course again accused him of lying. They tried to support their contention by quoting the Jewish law, that if a statement was to be regarded as true, it must be supported by at least two witnesses. For example, in the book of Deuteronomy we read, 'He may be put to death only if two or more witnesses testify against him (Deuteronomy 17:6). When it was convenient to them, of course, they quietly forgot this law (see John 18:19–24).

Jesus answers their point by claiming that his own unique relationship to God dispenses with the necessity for any further witness to himself (verse 14); but in fact if they knew God themselves they would have seen that God the Father had also witnessed to the truth of Jesus' claims (verse 18). The answer Jesus gives enables us to consider again some of his claims.

a. Jesus claimed a unique relationship with God

No ordinary man could have made the claims that Jesus made about himself without being deluded, or suffering megalomania. We have only to imagine a popular preacher today standing up and saying some of these things to realize how astonishing these claims are. The words of verse 14 might sound ambiguous to some of the crowd; but they seem to mean that Jesus knew his future destiny as clearly as his pre-existent state. As he said later on (verse 23), 'You belong to this world here below, but I come from above. You are from this world, but I am not from this world.' Jesus did not begin to exist when he was born as a baby at Bethlehem. He claims that he existed before that, and that he came from the presence of God (verses 23, 26). Because of this unique relationship with God always, he claims the authority to judge with the same perfect judgment as God (verses 15–16).

Furthermore, if his opponents really knew God they would know him also. Jesus' relationship with his Father was so close that he could imply that to know him was to know God, and to listen to him was to listen to God (verses 26–28). Strangely enough, Jesus predicts that the Jews would not recognize him as divine* until they had lifted him up on a cross to die (verse 28). The almighty God was to reveal himself most clearly to men when his Son Jesus Christ was crucified in weakness.

b. Jesus claimed to be perfect like God (verse 29)

'I always do what pleases him.' Many great saints have been able to say 'God is with me; he has not left me alone' (verse 29); but no good man would say 'I *always* do what pleases him' unless he was perfect; and God alone is absolutely pure and absolutely good. Down the ages the greatest saints have always been those who have been humbly aware of their failings and short-comings. Paul, towards the end of his life, found it appropriate to call himself 'the worst of sinners' (see 1 Timothy 1:15). One of the well-known Christian hymns expresses it in the words:

> 'And they who fain would serve Thee best
> Are conscious most of wrong within.'

The nearer we get to the light of God's purity, the darker our own lives are seen to be.

Yet Jesus, here and elsewhere, assumes this purity and sinless-ness of character. He never apologizes or confesses sin. He says to his enemies on another occasion, 'Which of you can prove that I am guilty of sin?' (John 8:46) and no-one answers. Furthermore, his closest friends, in spite of their honesty about one another's failures, speak of Jesus as one who was like a lamb 'without defect or flaw' (1 Peter 1:19) and one who 'committed no sin; no one ever heard a lie come from his lips' (1 Peter 2:22). 'There is no sin' said John 'in him' (1 John 3:5). Even today when men criticize the church, and the clergy, and other Christians, they very rarely criticize Jesus Christ. He is the one perfectly good and sinless man. But as Jesus himself once said to a young man who was seeking the truth, 'No one is good except God alone' (Mark 10:18).

*'I Am Who I Am' was the same word in Hebrew as one of the divine names of God which the Jew never spoke out of reverence for God. Jesus may well be deliberately using it here as a claim to be God.

Was Jesus then deluded or divine?

A megalomaniac can make extravagant claims. But as C. S. Lewis once wrote: 'The discrepancy between the depth and sanity, and (let me add) shrewdness of his moral teaching, and the rampant megalomania which must lie behind his theological teaching unless he is indeed God, has never been satisfactorily got over.'* Furthermore, those who talk 'big' usually act 'big'. Hitler made great claims for himself and acted arrogantly and brutally. Jesus uttered self-centred claims, but acted selflessly and sacrificially. Is selflessness and love a characteristic of God or of a madman? If we believe that Jesus is divine, God become man, then the tension between his self-centred claims and his selfless life is resolved. For if he is God, he has a right to make such claims, and at the same time he will act with selflessness and love.

It would have been remarkable, if not impossible, for many to have believed in Jesus after he had spoken these words (verse 30) unless his life had backed up his words. But with Jesus his life endorsed his claims.

Questions for discussion

1. If modern man is 'waiting for something, or someone, to turn up', what is he really looking for? Describe the 'darkness' you feel in modern society today.
2. In what sense can Jesus be *the light* of the world?
3. What do we learn here about the authority of Jesus as a teacher?
4. 'I always do what pleases him' . . . Discuss some of the things this attitude to God the Father involves for Jesus, and how it might apply to us.

20 The marks of a genuine disciple

8:31–59
31 So Jesus said to those who believed in him, 'If you obey my
*C. S. Lewis, Miracles.

teaching, you are really my disciples; ³²*you will know the truth, and the truth will set you free.'*

33 *'We are the descendants of Abraham,' they answered, 'and we have never been anybody's slaves. What do you mean, then, by saying, "You will be free"?'*

34 *Jesus said to them, 'I am telling you the truth: everyone who sins is a slave of sin.* ³⁵*A slave does not belong to a family permanently, but a son belongs there for ever.* ³⁶*If the Son sets you free, then you will be really free.* ³⁷*I know you are Abraham's descendants. Yet you are trying to kill me, because you will not accept my teaching.* ³⁸*I talk about what my Father has shown me, but you do what your father has told you.'*

39 *They answered him, 'Our father is Abraham.'*

'If you really were Abraham's children,' Jesus replied, 'you would do the same things that he did. ⁴⁰*All I have ever done is to tell you the truth I heard from God, yet you are trying to kill me. Abraham did nothing like this!* ⁴¹*You are doing what your father did.'*

'God himself is the only Father we have,' they answered, 'and we are his true sons.'

42 *Jesus said to them, 'If God really were your Father, you would love me, because I came from God and now I am here. I did not come on my own authority, but he sent me.* ⁴³*Why do you not understand what I say? It is because you cannot bear to listen to my message.* ⁴⁴*You are the children of your father, the Devil, and you want to follow your father's desires. From the very beginning he was a murderer and has never been on the side of truth, because there is no truth in him. When he tells a lie, he is only doing what is natural to him, because he is a liar and the father of all lies.* ⁴⁵*But I tell the truth, and that is why you do not believe me.* ⁴⁶*Which one of you can prove that I am guilty of sin? If I tell the truth, then why do you not believe me?* ⁴⁷*He who comes from God listens to God's words. You, however, are not from God, and that is why you will not listen.'*

48 *They asked Jesus, 'Were we not right in saying that you are a Samaritan and have a demon in you?'*

49 *'I have no demon,' Jesus answered. 'I honour my Father, but you dishonour me.* ⁵⁰*I am not seeking honour for myself. But there is one who is seeking it and who judges in my favour.* ⁵¹*I am telling you the truth: whoever obeys my teaching will never die.'*

52 *They said to him, 'Now we are certain that you have a demon! Abraham died, and the prophets died, yet you say that whoever obeys*

your teaching will never die. ⁵³*Our father Abraham died; you do not claim to be greater than Abraham, do you? And the prophets also died. Who do you think you are?'*

54 *Jesus answered, 'If I were to honour myself, that honour would be worth nothing. The one who honours me is my Father—the very one you say is your God.* ⁵⁵*You have never known him, but I know him. If I were to say that I do not know him, I would be a liar like you. But I do know him, and I obey his word.* ⁵⁶*Your father Abraham rejoiced that he was to see the time of my coming; he saw it and was glad.'*

57 *They said to him, 'You are not even fifty years old—and you have seen Abraham?'*

58 *'I am telling you the truth,' Jesus replied. 'Before Abraham was born, "I Am".'*

59 *Then they picked up stones to throw at him, but Jesus hid himself and left the Temple.*

When one of our daughters was very young, we taught her how to recognize a genuine silver spoon from one that was silver plated. One day, when visiting her grandparents, she carefully examined one of their spoons looking for the hall-mark. Imagine our embarassment when she suddenly announced to all present, with an air of surprise, that one of their spoons was not real silver at all. It was only silver plated! It may matter little whether a spoon is silver or not, but it could matter a great deal whether or not our belief in Jesus is genuine.

So, what is the hall-mark of genuine discipleship? How do we tell a genuine believer from someone who merely professes to believe? We know that these Jews 'believed' in Jesus (verse 31); but we're not sure how genuine that belief was. Jesus teaches us here some of the ways in which we can recognize those who are genuinely his disciples.

a. A genuine disciple continues and does not give up (verses 31-33)

'If you obey my teaching (RSV 'continue in my word') you are really my disciples.' Jesus said on another occasion, 'The person who holds out to the end will be saved' (Mark 13:13). It is possible to *say* we believe and to make some 'decision' for Christ. But the only sure evidence for the genuineness of our faith is that we are still obeying the words of Jesus Christ, knowing the truth and enjoying its freedom.

b. A genuine disciple enjoys freedom and not slavery (verses 34–38)

Real freedom is not to be found in resisting the claims of Jesus Christ, or in trusting in religious privileges. Religion does not make us free, for it cannot free us from sinful habits and self-centred thinking. 'Everyone who sins is a slave of sin.' It is easy to see how this is true for a drunkard, or a sex pervert, or a drug addict. But it is also true of the person who is a slave to men's opinions, or the world's fashions, or that thing 'which everyone does', or 'keeping up with the Jones's'. Even religious people can become slaves to ecclesiastical practices or jargon, or prejudices or conventions. Jesus promises to set us free if we continue to obey his word and know the truth in him. For it is the truth that sets us free.

c. A genuine disciple behaves like a child of God, not a child of the devil (verses 39–47)

The Jews claimed to be the children of Abraham, and they were such by physical descent; but they were certainly not the children of God, or they would not be seeking to kill Jesus. Nor would a child of God make suggestive remarks about the illegitimacy of Jesus' birth (verse 41). These men, suggests Jesus, have never become God's children, because they clearly do not exhibit God's nature. They have not the hallmark of love. They do not love Jesus although he has 'come from God' (verse 42). If they were God's children they would understand the teaching of Jesus, instead of hating to hear it (verse 43). They would tell the truth instead of lies. They would acknowledge the truth instead of denying it. For although they can find no fault in Jesus (verse 46), yet they are prepared to slander him (verse 48). These men have a family likeness to the father of lies, the devil, rather than God the heavenly Father. 'He who comes from God listens to God's words. You, however, are not from God, and that is why you will not listen.'

d. A genuine disciple honours Jesus Christ and does not dishonour him (verses 48–59)

'You dishonour me,' Jesus said. In spite of their religious professions these men were prepared to insult Jesus (verse 48), to reject his claims (verse 52) and to put him to death (verse 59). Jesus patiently continues to reiterate his own claims and motives. He seeks only to honour God (verses 49–50). His words are a matter of life and death: 'Whoever obeys my teaching will never die' (verse 51). He obeys God and God honours him—to say anything else would be a lie. Even Abraham longed for the day when Jesus would come to this earth, for, said Jesus, 'Before Abraham was born, "I am".' This is perhaps the clearest direct claim to be God that Jesus uttered. He makes it with great emphasis: 'I am telling you the truth' (RSV 'truly, truly'). He includes the thought of his own previous existence before he was born on earth. But there is no mistaking his claim to be God when he takes upon his own lips the title 'I am'. Hundreds of years before, according to the Old Testament, God had spoken to Moses and said, 'This is what you must say to them: "The one who is called I AM has sent me to you"' (Exodus 3:14). This title 'I AM' speaks of God's eternal, timeless existence. Jesus had used this phrase before in the same discussion (verses 24, 28). We know that the Jews clearly believed he was claiming to be God, for they took up stones to stone him. The Jewish penalty for blasphemy was death by stoning. Jesus escaped from the angry mob, but knew that the issues of belief and unbelief were becoming clearer.

The genuine disciple is glad to honour Jesus as God. He can say, as Thomas did later, 'My Lord and my God!' (John 20:28).

Questions for discussion

1. How is it possible to 'believe in Jesus' and yet not be a genuine disciple?

2. In what way are men 'enslaved' by sin? Is the freedom Jesus offers freedom to 'do what we like'? What kind of freedom does he offer?

3. How does this teaching here help the person who has 'made a decision for Christ', but later says 'it hasn't worked'?

4. In what ways can we honour God most, according to this passage?

21 The problem of suffering

9:1–12

9 As Jesus was walking along, he saw a man who had been born blind. ²His disciples asked him, 'Teacher, whose sin caused him to be born blind? Was it his own or his parents' sin?'

3 Jesus answered, 'His blindness has nothing to do with his sins or his parents' sins. He is blind so that God's power might be seen at work in him. ⁴As long as it is day, we must keep on doing the work of him who sent me; night is coming when no one can work. ⁵While I am in the world, I am the light for the world.'

6 After he said this, Jesus spat on the ground and made some mud with the spittle; he rubbed the mud on the man's eyes ⁷and said, 'Go and wash your face in the Pool of Siloam.' (This name means 'Sent.') So the man went, washed his face, and came back seeing.

8 His neighbours, then, and the people who had seen him begging before this, asked, 'Isn't this the man who used to sit and beg?'

9 Some said, 'He is the one,' but others said, 'No he isn't; he just looks like him.'

So the man himself said, 'I am the man.'

10 'How is it that you can now see?' they asked him.

11 He answered, 'The man called Jesus made some mud, rubbed it on my eyes, and told me to go to Siloam and wash my face. So I went, and as soon as I washed, I could see.'

12 'Where is he?' they asked.

'I don't know,' he answered.

Most of us have felt at some time the sentiments of the young man faced by human suffering in one of Hugh Walpole's novels. 'You know there can't be a God, Vanessa. In your heart you must know it. You are a wise woman. You read and think. Well, then, ask yourself. How *can* there be a God, and life be as it is? If there is one He ought to be ashamed of Himself, that's all I can say!'

The problem of suffering in a world made by a good and loving God is one of the commonest barriers to belief. We may be sure there are no slick answers. But in this story, the healing of a scruffy blind beggar sitting in rags at the side of a dusty road, Jesus sheds some light.

The disciples were worried by this problem. Knowing that the beggar had been blind from birth they said, 'Teacher, whose sin caused him to be born blind?' The disciples assumed that *suffering was the result of sin*. In one sense they were right. According to the Bible, when God made the world in the beginning it was perfect: or, in the words recorded in Genesis, it was 'very good'. There was in the beginning no sin, no suffering, no disease, no pain. Man enjoyed perfect friendship with God. But God had not made man an automaton, but a person who was able to exercise choice. As a result of man's disobedience and rebellion against God's will, that is, his 'fall', man's original innocence was lost (see Genesis 3). Sin, suffering, disease and disorder entered into God's world. This is the Bible's explanation of man's basic self-centredness. Because of the unity of the human race, all men have fallen and disobeyed 'in Adam', and man has inherited a selfish, sinful nature. This is the cause of much suffering today. As the apostle James wrote: 'Where do all the fights and quarrels among you come from? They come from your desires for pleasure. You want things, but you cannot have them, so you are ready to kill; you strongly desire things, but you cannot get them, so you quarrel and fight' (James 4:1-2).

Man's sinful human nature, and the reality of evil in the world, go a long way to help us to understand the cause of human suffering. The humanist's philosophy of the essential goodness of human nature is hopelessly unrealistic in comparison and many modern writers have now discarded it. The novelist, William Golding, for example, expresses the purpose of his novels as trying 'to trace the defects of society back to the defects of human nature'.* The French novelist, Camus, who was very concerned about the whole problem of human suffering and rejected the Christian explanation, was not so foolish as to imagine that man was innocent. In the words of Jean-Baptiste Clemence in *The Fall* he believed that 'we cannot assert the innocence of anyone, whereas we can state with certainty the guilt of all'.†

In general, then, all human suffering is the consequence of the fall (see Genesis 3:16-19). God is not the author of suffering. In

*Quoted in Stuart Babbage, *The Mark of Cain*, p. 25.
†Albert Camus, *The Fall*, p. 81.

many particular instances suffering is caused by man's inhumanity to man. But still there is the question raised by this story, why is a man *born* blind? Is it the direct result of his own sin or the sin of his parents? Jesus does more than give a straight answer to this one question. He throws some shafts of light upon the whole problem of suffering. The light Jesus gives is enough to help us to face up to human suffering, even though we may not fully understand it or escape it in this life.

a. Suffering is not always a direct result of sin

Some of the rabbis believed that suffering was always the direct result of sin. It is difficult for us to understand how a man *born* blind could be responsible for this blindness. But some of the Jewish theologians had the strange idea that a baby could begin to sin while he was still in his mother's womb, or even in a preexistent state before he was conceived. The other possibility was that this man's blindness was due to his parents' sin. This is sometimes possible. Recently we have read of babies who have been born with all the symptoms of drug-addiction, because their mothers were addicts. None of us lives to himself. But in this case Jesus makes it quite clear that suffering is not always the direct result of a man's own sin or the sin of his parents. Some of the greatest saints have been some of the greatest sufferers.

b. Suffering is not part of the direct will of God

'It's God's will, I suppose,' mutters a heroic sufferer. The Bible makes clear that sin and suffering is not part of God's direct will for the world. But it can be part of his permissive will. God allowed this blind man to suffer for a purpose: 'His blindness has nothing to do with his sin or his parents' sin. He is blind so that God's power might be seen at work in him' (verse 3). So this man's suffering was overruled by God *for his benefit*. Through his blindness and need he had an encounter with Jesus Christ which changed his life. A man once said to me, 'I thank God for polio.' I knew what he meant. It was not that polio is good, or God's will for his world. But for this man, this illness which afflicted two members of his family was the means of leading him to a personal faith in Jesus Christ.

Again, suffering can be *for God's glory*. The sufferings of Jesus are the supreme example. In this story, too, other men learnt of God's plan for their spiritual sight and healing through the healing of this blind man, and so God was glorified. I once visited a seriously ill girl in hospital whose courage and gaiety and Christian witness made a profound impression upon the hospital staff. God was honoured by her courageous suffering. God strengthened her in it. God may sometimes allow suffering for man's good and for his own glory. We can realize this when we remember that many virtues such as patience, courage, humility, pity and compassion grow most strongly in the garden of suffering. We could add to this the fact that pain is a necessary protection for man against injury, and essential to man's physical survival.

c. Suffering is not inconsistent with the love of God

Jesus is the light of the world. He came to men in the darkness of suffering and sin to bring healing to their bodies as well as illumination to their minds. He showed that he loves men by many acts of healing and compassion. And we know that he calls us to relieve suffering where we find it. In this story he moves quickly from theological discussion to active love—much more quickly than we do! (verses 3–6). He tests the man's faith and obedience. It is the man's faith and obedience which are the conditions of healing. The blind man sees (verse 7).

If God is revealed in Jesus in the way that the writer asserts (see John 1), then in this story we have further evidence of God's love and concern for human sufferers. Further evidence may be seen in the sufferings of Jesus himself (see John 19). Furthermore, the Christian believes that by the death and resurrection of Jesus Christ, sin and evil were defeated, and the gateway to heaven opened. In heaven, according to the author of the book of Revelation, followers of Jesus Christ can look forward to this experience: God 'will wipe away all tears from their eyes. There will be no more death, no more grief or crying or pain. The old things have disappeared' (Revelation 21:4). Then God's perfect will shall be done, and all suffering banished.*

*For further reading on this subject see C. S. Lewis, *The Problem of Pain.*

Questions for discussion

1. How far, and in what way, does man's sin explain the fact of suffering in the world?

2. In what way was this man's blindness 'for the glory of God'? How do we find purpose and meaning in suffering?

3. Jesus healed this blind man. How do we expect him to heal today? What can we learn from the way the blind man responded to Jesus?

(Other passages for reference include: The Book of Job, Romans 5 and 8, 1 Peter 1, James 1, Hebrews 12:1–13 and 2 Corinthians 4:7 – 5:10)

22 The problem of spiritual blindness

9:13–41

13 Then they took to the Pharisees the man who had been blind.
¹⁴The day that Jesus made the mud and cured him of his blindness was a Sabbath. ¹⁵The Pharisees, then, asked the man again how he had received his sight. He told them, 'He put some mud on my eyes; I washed my face, and now I can see.'

16 Some of the Pharisees said, 'The man who did this cannot be from God for he does not obey the Sabbath law.'

Others, however, said, 'How could a man who is a sinner perform such miracles as these?' And there was a division among them.

17 So the Pharisees asked the man once more, 'You say he cured you of your blindness—well, what do you say about him?'

'He is a prophet,' the man answered.

18 The Jewish authorities, however, were not willing to believe that he had been blind and could now see, until they called his parents ¹⁹and asked them, 'Is this your son? You say that he was born blind; how is it, then, that he can now see?'

20 His parents answered, 'We know that he is our son, and we know that he was born blind. ²¹But we do not know how it is that he is now able to see, nor do we know who cured him of his blindness. Ask him;

he is old enough, and he can answer for himself!' ²²His parents said this because they were afraid of the Jewish authorities, who had already agreed that anyone who said he believed that Jesus was the Messiah would be expelled from the synagogue. ²³That is why his parents said, 'He is old enough; ask him!'

24 A second time they called back the man who had been born blind, and said to him, 'Promise before God that you will tell the truth! We know that this man who cured you is a sinner.'

25 'I do not know if he is a sinner or not,' the man replied. 'One thing I do know: I was blind, and now I see.'

26 'What did he do to you?' they asked. 'How did he cure you of your blindness?'

27 'I have already told you,' he answered, 'and you would not listen. Why do you want to hear it again? Maybe you, too, would like to be his disciples?'

28 They cursed him and said, 'You are that fellow's disciple; but we are Moses' disciples. ²⁹We know that God spoke to Moses; as for that fellow, however, we do not even know where he comes from!'

30 The man answered, 'What a strange thing that is! You do not know where he comes from, but he cured me of my blindness! ³¹We know that God does not listen to sinners; he does listen to people who respect him and do what he wants them to do. ³²Since the beginning of the world nobody has ever heard of anyone giving sight to a blind person. ³³Unless this man came from God, he would not be able to do a thing.'

34 They answered, 'You were born and brought up in sin—and you are trying to teach us?' And they expelled him from the synagogue.

35 When Jesus heard what had happened, he found the man and asked him, 'Do you believe in the Son of Man?'

36 The man answered, 'Tell me who he is, sir, so that I can believe in him!'

37 Jesus said to him, 'You have already seen him, and he is the one who is talking with you now.'

38 'I believe, Lord!' the man said, and knelt down before Jesus.

39 Jesus said, 'I came to this world to judge, so that the blind should see and those who see should become blind.'

40 Some Pharisees who were there with him heard him say this and asked him, 'Surely you don't mean that we are blind, too?'

41 Jesus answered, 'If you were blind, then you would not be guilty;

but since you claim that you can see, this means that you are still guilty.'

A young ballet student, who had recently come to faith in Jesus Christ, once asked me rather sadly, 'Why are there not more Christians in the world?' We might well ask why so few people believed in Jesus in spite of his claims, his miracles, and the obvious attractiveness of his life. Part of the answer may be found in this chapter where John describes the clash between the blind beggar who has been healed by Jesus, and the Jewish leaders.

Physical blindness is a great tragedy. This story shows us that spiritual blindness is a greater one. Jesus comes to give light and sight to all who want it. But many people remain spiritually blind. Here are some of the marks of the spiritually blind.

a. They put prejudice before facts

The evidence was strong that this man had been healed by Jesus. Some of his neighbours recognized him (verse 8). He himself repeatedly stated that he was the man (verses 9b, 11, 15, 25, 30), in spite of the fact that his insistence led to excommunication (verse 34), and he had nothing to gain in sticking to his story if it was not true. The parents of the man also confirmed the fact that this man had been born blind and was indeed their son. It is astonishing that in the light of these facts the Pharisees were still prepared to deny that Jesus had given this man sight.

The reason is plain—and it is true of many people today. Men are prejudiced against facts when they are not convenient to them. The Jews were also prejudiced against Jesus. Jesus did not interpret the laws of the sabbath as they did (verse 16). He was not a follower of Moses, as they were (verse 28), nor did he have theological qualifications or the right social background (verse 29). They implied, without evidence, that he was morally suspect (verse 16). They were jealous of his influence upon the people (verse 22). They had no arguments to offer against the evidence of the man himself, and so resorted, not to reason, but to slander (verse 16), dangerous assertion (verse 24) and blustering anger (verse 34). It is a dangerous thing to put prejudice before facts. It is a mark of spiritual blindness. The case for Christianity does not rest on prejudice but on facts.

b. They put half-truths before the whole truth

As we have noticed before (John 6), the Jews had taken away from the real value of the sabbath, as a day of rest and worship and service, by the absurdity of their traditions. 'The day that Jesus made the mud and cured him of his blindness was a Sabbath' (verse 14). Respect for the sabbath was important. It was part of God's law. 'The sabbath was made for man'—for his benefit. The Pharisees had half the truth in desiring to keep the sabbath as a different day; but a half-truth is often dangerous. The whole truth is that the sabbath is made for man. To heal a man kept the spirit of it completely. This the Pharisees failed to see. Sometimes a man fails to follow Jesus Christ today by saying 'religion is a personal matter', and so refusing to discuss it with anyone else. This is half the truth. Christianity is personal, but not secret. We need to beware of half-truths. They can sometimes keep us from seeing and believing in Jesus Christ.

c. They put argument before action

These men were constantly arguing and never coming to a decision (verses 24–38). They were always asking questions, but never *wanting* to find the answer. When the man asked the shrewd question, 'Maybe you, too, would *like* to be his disciples?', he hit the nail on the head. It is possible to engage in religious discussion with no intention of finding the truth. This man of course spoke from experience and not from theory. He could say, 'I was blind and now I see.' Indeed, this story makes plain that because this man wanted to know the truth about Christ, and because he was willing to believe and follow up such truth as he knew, his eyes were opened more and more to see who Jesus really was. First he spoke of Jesus as 'the man called Jesus' (verse 11), then 'a prophet' (verse 17). Then when Jesus asked him outright, 'Do you believe in the Son of Man?' his willingness to follow the truth wherever it might lead is clear: ' "Tell me who he is, sir, so that I can believe in him!" Jesus said to him, "You have already seen him, and he is the one who is talking with you now." "*I believe, Lord!*" *the man said, and knelt down before Jesus.*' In contrast, many of the Jews found it easier to argue than to act. It is easier to discuss than to decide to follow Christ. But the easy way is the way of spiritual blindness.

d. They put pride before humility

Pride is the basic cause of spiritual blindness. When a man stands before Jesus there is judgment on his pride (verse 39). Jesus came to give sight to the blind. The man who had been born with physical blindness discovered physical and spiritual sight in trusting and obeying Jesus Christ. Those who had physical sight in this story became even more spiritually blind by their repeated rejection of the facts, and especially of Jesus himself. Their blindness was no accident. It could not be blamed on their environment. Although they too were blind from birth in a spiritual sense, in that they inherited a sinful human nature, they were also blind because of their deliberate self-righteousness and pride. 'But since you claim that *you can see*, this means that you are still guilty.' If we would see Jesus and know him to be all he claims to be, we must first of all humbly acknowledge our blindness and pride. To say that 'all is well' when I am blind to the truth of Jesus Christ is a mark of spiritual blindness.

Questions for discussion
1. 'The case of Christianity does not rest on prejudice but on facts.' What prejudices have we about Jesus Christ and the Christian church?
2. What are the most common 'half-truths' that people believe about God and Christianity?
3. According to this story how far is spiritual blindness *my* responsibility? What do I learn from the blind man about searching for truth?

23 Jesus the good shepherd

10:1–21
10 Jesus said, 'I am telling you the truth: the man who does not enter the sheepfold by the gate, but climbs in some other way, is a thief and

a robber. ²*The man who goes in through the gate is the shepherd of the sheep.* ³*The gatekeeper opens the gate for him; the sheep hear his voice as he calls his own sheep by name, and he leads them out.* ⁴*When he has brought them out, he goes ahead of them, and the sheep follow him, because they know his voice.* ⁵*They will not follow someone else; instead, they will run away from such a person, because they do not know his voice.'*

6 *Jesus told them this parable, but they did not understand what he meant.*

7 *So Jesus said again, 'I am telling you the truth: I am the gate for the sheep.* ⁸*All others who came before me are thieves and robbers, but the sheep did not listen to them.* ⁹*I am the gate. Whoever comes in by me will be saved; he will come in and go out and find pasture.* ¹⁰*The thief comes only in order to steal, kill, and destroy. I have come in order that you might have life—life in all its fullness.*

11 *'I am the good shepherd, who is willing to die for the sheep.* ¹²*When the hired man, who is not a shepherd and does not own the sheep, sees a wolf coming, he leaves the sheep and runs away; so the wolf snatches the sheep and scatters them.* ¹³*The hired man runs away because he is only a hired man and does not care about the sheep.* ¹⁴⁻¹⁵*I am the good shepherd. As the Father knows me and I know the Father, in the same way I know my sheep and they know me. And I am willing to die for them.* ¹⁶*There are other sheep which belong to me that are not in this sheepfold. I must bring them, too; they will listen to my voice, and they will become one flock with one shepherd.*

17 *'The Father loves me because I am willing to give up my life, in order that I may receive it back again.* ¹⁸*No one takes my life away from me. I give it up of my own free will. I have the right to give it up, and I have the right to take it back. This is what my Father has commanded me to do.'*

19 *Again there was a division among the people because of these words.* ²⁰*Many of them were saying, 'He has a demon! He is mad! Why do you listen to him?'*

21 *But others were saying, 'A man with a demon could not talk like this! How could a demon give sight to blind people?'*

'The world is looking for a leader.' That is a common saying today. It could be argued that much of the unrest in the modern world is due to there being a lack of leadership or having the wrong kind of leader.

It was much the same in the days of Jesus. Many of the Jews who listened to him were longing for a leader to guide and protect them. Jesus once described their need by saying of the crowds that 'they were like sheep without a shepherd' (Mark 6:34). For in the pastoral environment of Judea, the shepherd was a title often used of a leader. Jeremiah, for example, spoke of the unfaithful leaders of Israel as shepherds (Jeremiah 23:14).

However, in the Old Testament, God was sometimes described as the Shepherd of his people (see Psalm 80:1). Jesus knew that when he said 'I am the good shepherd'. Was this another claim to deity?

Why did Jesus call himself the *good* shepherd? Probably he is contrasting himself with the unfaithful leaders of Israel. But there is a further thought for us. 'Good' here means literally 'attractive' (Greek, *kalos*). There is nothing weak and feeble and anaemic about this picture of Jesus. This is not the 'pale Galilean' or the 'gentle Jesus, meek and mild' of the sentimentalist.

In Dr. William Barclays' commentary on John's Gospel,* he quotes Sir George Adam Smith's words about the shepherds of Palestine. 'On some high moor, across which at night the hyenas howl, when you meet him (the shepherd) sleepless, far-sighted, weather-beaten, leaning on his staff, and looking out over his scattered sheep, every one of them on his heart, you understand why the shepherd of Judaea sprang to the front in his people's history; why they gave his name to their king, and made him the symbol of providence; why Christ took him as the type of self-sacrifice.'

A good shepherd was someone who was watchful, resourceful and courageous, and yet loving, patient and sacrificial too. We shall see the force of this description still more if we remember two further factors. First, Palestine sheep were mostly kept for their wool, whereas today they are often kept for their meat as well. Eastern shepherds, therefore, would stay longer with their sheep and a close relationship between shepherd and sheep often developed. The shepherd knew his sheep by name (verse 3), and sheep were able to distinguish between the voice of the shepherd and the stranger (verses 3–5).

Second, in Palestine the shepherd leads his sheep from one sheep-fold to another over difficult and dangerous country. He does not drive them and chivvy them as elsewhere. In some

*W. Barclay, *Daily Bible Readings: The Gospel of John*, vol. 2, p. 61.

villages, the shepherd might be able to leave his sheep for the night in a well-built communal sheep-fold which would have a door and even a door-keeper (see verses 1–4). But usually, as he led his sheep over the rough ground on the Judean plateau, the only sheep-fold for the night was a roughly-made wall, and the shepherd himself was the door (verse 7), lying down across the narrow opening to the fold, ready to defend his flock (verses 8–15).

So when Jesus said to the crowd, 'I am the good shepherd', he was offering to be their leader, and amongst other things to provide them with security, satisfaction and unity.

a. Security

'I am the gate', said Jesus. 'Whoever comes in by me will be saved.' Sheep need the security of the sheep-fold. Many of the Jews had no sense of security. Politically, they were an occupied country. Religiously, their leaders were like the hired shepherds, who were more interested in their pay packet than the well-being of their flock (verse 11). The 'thieves and robbers' (verse 8) may refer to the false messiahs and false prophets who were trying to steal away their people from a true relationship with God. There is no security in religious leaders who have not come to Christ (verses 7–8) and who destroy a man's relationship to Jesus Christ by destructive teaching and inconsistent lives. Nor is there security in those 'false messiahs' who promise a new age, or an exciting life apart from Jesus Christ. Men make many such promises today in the name of Communism, Humanism, Mormonism, or some other philosophy of life. Jesus teaches us that there is no security apart from him. When we belong to Jesus Christ we shall hear his voice, and he will speak to us personally (verse 3), and lead us and go before us (verse 4), and we shall know his voice, and know when others would draw us away (verse 5). This security and safety in Jesus Christ is possible only because the good shepherd 'is willing to die for the sheep'.

b. Satisfaction

It is well known that those who attack Christianity will often do so on the grounds that it is narrow and that if a person becomes a Christian they will forfeit their enjoyment of life.

111

Jesus says the opposite is true. Those who try to draw us away from him are those who come 'to steal, kill, and destroy' (verse 10). A girl persuaded against her better judgment to commit immorality does not thereby enter into a fully satisfying new life. Indeed the experience of those who have fallen in this particular way is that something good has been 'lost, killed and destroyed'. Those who come to Jesus, on the other hand, are promised the security of being saved or delivered from spiritual death (verse 9), and satisfaction from being able to 'come in and go out and find pasture'. 'I have come', said Jesus, 'in order that you might have life—life in all its fullness' (verse 10). A member of our church congregation wrote: 'Having been brought up on the philosophy "eat, drink and be merry, for tomorrow we die" I was determined to get the most out of life. I joined clubs, went to all-night parties and lived in a constant whirl of social activity. To my friends I really seemed to be "living", but deep down inside I knew it wasn't true. I became more and more dissatisfied and life seemed pointless. Then I heard about the new life that Christ offered. Somehow I knew this was what I needed and so I asked Him into my life to renew it and redirect it. Since then I have known increasing satisfaction and fulfilment more than I had ever known before.' As we follow the Shepherd, however hard the way, he will lead us on to find more and more satisfaction in him.

c. Unity

Jesus was not only concerned about those already in the Jewish fold. He was concerned about those who were outside organized religion—the Gentiles. 'There are other sheep which belong to me that are not in this sheepfold. I must bring them, too; they will listen to my voice, and they will become one flock with one shepherd' (verse 16).

Jesus lived in a divided world even as we do. The Jew hated and despised the Gentile. But Jesus came to bring men together by bringing them, first, not into the same 'fold', but into the same flock—that is, in relationship to himself, the good Shepherd. In giving up his life for all men (verse 18) he was to break down barriers that divide men from one another. But the same Christ who unites those who believe in him, divides those who cannot make up their minds about him. Again, is he deluded or divine (verses 19–21)?

112

Questions for discussion

1. In this description of Jesus as the 'good shepherd', what marks of good leadership do we find? How do these characteristics apply to leaders we know, or to ourselves?

2. In the light of this passage what can we say to those who accuse Christians of being 'narrow-minded kill-joys' whose life will be spoilt if they follow Jesus? What truth is there in the accusation?

3. What answer can be given to those who say they cannot become Christians because the church is divided (see verse 16 especially)?

4. What does this picture of the good shepherd tell us about God's dealings with those who follow him?

24 A time of national thanksgiving

10:22–42

22 It was winter, and the Festival of the Dedication of the Temple was being celebrated in Jerusalem, 23Jesus was walking in Solomon's Porch in the Temple, 24when the people gathered round him and asked, 'How long are you going to keep us in suspense? Tell us the plain truth: are you the Messiah?'

25 Jesus answered, 'I have already told you, but you would not believe me. The things I do by my Father's authority speak on my behalf; 26but you will not believe, for you are not my sheep. 27My sheep listen to my voice; I know them, and they follow me. 28I give them eternal life, and they shall never die. No one can snatch them away from me. 29What my Father has given me is greater than everything, and no one can snatch them away from the Father's care. 30The Father and I are one.'

31 Then the people again picked up stones to throw at him. 32Jesus said to them, 'I have done many good deeds in your presence which the Father gave me to do; for which one of these do you want to stone me?'

33 They replied, 'We do not want to stone you because of any good deeds, but because of your blasphemy! You are only a man, but you are trying to make yourself God!'

34 Jesus answered, 'It is written in your own Law that God said, "You are gods". 35We know that what the scripture says is true for ever; and God called those people gods, the people to whom his message was given. 36As for me, the Father chose me and sent me into the world. How, then, can you say that I blaspheme because I said that I am the Son of God? 37Do not believe me, then, if I am not doing the things my Father wants me to do. 38But if I do them, even though you do not believe me, you should at least believe my deeds, in order that you may know once and for all that the Father is in me and that I am in the Father.'

39 Once more they tried to seize Jesus, but he slipped out of their hands.

40 Jesus then went back again across the River Jordan to the place where John had been baptizing, and he stayed there. 41Many people came to him. 'John performed no miracles,' they said, 'but everything he said about this man was true.' 42And many people there believed in him.

There is a certain dramatic irony in this next part of John's story.

It was a time of national thanksgiving. The 'Festival of the Dedication of the Temple' (verse 22) commemorated the epic victory of the freedom fighters under Judas Maccabaeus in 164 BC. The temple had been desecrated by the enemies of the Jews, but in 164 BC it was ceremonially cleansed and purified, and Judas Maccabaeus ordered that 'the days of the dedication of the altar should be kept in their season from year to year, by the space of eight days, from the five and twentieth day of the month of Chislev, with gladness and joy' (1 Maccabees 4:59).

This Festival was also called the Festival of Lights, and illuminations would be seen in the temple and in every Jewish home, as a reminder that the light of freedom had come back to Israel.

Yet the irony of it was this. While they celebrated freedom, they were in fact slaves. Slaves to the Roman occupation army, and slaves, many of them, to their own prejudices, fears and passions.

Jesus was offering them 'freedom', but as he walked in the temple, in the place (Solomon's Porch) where rabbis would often talk with their students, it is doubtful whether the Jews really wanted to learn from him. We wave our flags for freedom too. But how much inner freedom have we discovered? This incident shows Jesus' patience with his enemies as well as his love for his disciples.

114

a. His patience with his enemies

The Jewish leaders ask for plain speaking, but are probably trying
to trap Jesus in his speech so that they can arrest him (verse 39).
Jesus is amazingly patient with them, and continues to give them
evidence for his claims. Once again he urges them to consider
his works (verse 25) and *his words* (verse 27). When they argue
that his words are blasphemous, for he claims to be God (verse
33), Jesus tries to help them take a more reasonable attitude. He
argues from the Old Testament Scriptures in a way that would be
familiar to them. The Jews believed, as Jesus did, that the Scriptures (Old Testament) were completely reliable (verse 35). Yet in
the Old Testament the writer of Psalm 82 had called some unjust
judges 'gods'. For a judge is commissioned by God to bring God's
help and justice to men. He is God to men (see Psalm 82). Jesus
argues that if Scripture can speak like that about men who are set
apart for a special task by God, how much more should they be
willing to call Jesus God, who has so obviously been sent by God
into this world for a unique purpose, as his words and works bear
witness.

Furthermore, even if they cannot accept this verbal argument,
surely the life of Jesus and his works are clear enough evidence of
his unique relationship to his Father? Surely only the Son of God,
someone equal with God, could do such mighty works?

Some men will not listen to Jesus, however patiently and logic-
ally he states his case. The Jews did not belong to Jesus and so
would not believe him. They had no arguments against his case,
no real reasons to reject him. So they tried force (verse 39). But
some believed, some realized that Jesus practised what he preached.
John the Baptist had done no 'miracles' (Greek: *signs*, verse 41).
Jesus had done many. Some began to realize that everything that
the Baptist said about Jesus was true. But they could only be sure
of this when they came to Jesus (verse 41) and believed in him
(verse 42).

b. His love for his disciples (verses 27–30)

Yet again Jesus uses the picture of the shepherd's love for the sheep
in describing his relationship with believers. Once a believer has
come to the good shepherd, he is able to recognize the voice of

Jesus, and to know that his words are reliable. He enters into a relationship with Jesus. Jesus can say 'I know him', and he is able to follow Jesus. Jesus gives his disciples eternal life and promises them eternal security. This security is based on his Father's love as well as his own (verses 28, 29).

Some people go through life never knowing whether they have eternal life or not, and uncertain of their future destiny. Jesus says that those who believe on him may be certain of eternal security—'I give them eternal life, and they shall never die. No one can snatch them away from me.'

It is interesting to compare these sure promises of Jesus with the uncertainties of many of our modern thinkers. In *A Writer's Notebook*, Somerset Maugham comments on Bertrand Russell's philosophy.* 'It may be that, as he (Russell) says, philosophy doesn't offer or attempt to offer a solution of the problems of human destiny; it may be that it mustn't hope to find an answer to the practical problems of life; for philosophers have other fish to fry. But who then will tell us whether there is any sense in living, and whether human existence is anything but a tragic—no, tragic is too noble a word—whether human existence is anything but a grotesque mischance?' One can only wish that Maugham had pondered the words of Jesus as much as the philosophy of Russell. There is nothing aimless or uncertain for those who follow the good shepherd throughout their life.

Questions for discussion

1. What do we learn in these verses about the true followers of Jesus? Contrast this with the attitude of those who wanted to get Jesus out of the way (verse 39).
2. How do we answer from this passage those who say that we can never be sure whether or not we belong to God?
3. 'We know that what the scripture says is true for ever' (verse 35). What do we learn here about Jesus' attitude to the Old Testament and his interpretation of it?

*W. Somerset Maugham, *A Writer's Notebook*, p. 313.

25 The raising of Lazarus

11:1-53

A man named Lazarus, who lived in Bethany, was ill. Bethany was the town where Mary and her sister Martha lived. ([2]This Mary was the one who poured the perfume on the Lord's feet and wiped them with her hair; it was her brother Lazarus who was ill.) [3]The sisters sent Jesus a message: 'Lord, your dear friend is ill.'

4 When Jesus heard it, he said, 'The final result of this illness will not be the death of Lazarus; this has happened in order to bring glory to God, and it will be the means by which the Son of God will receive glory.'

5 Jesus loved Martha and her sister and Lazarus. [6]Yet when he received the news that Lazarus was ill, he stayed where he was for two more days. [7]Then he said to the disciples, 'Let us go back to Judaea.'

8 'Teacher,' the disciples answered, 'just a short time ago the people there wanted to stone you; and are you planning to go back?'

9 Jesus said, 'A day has twelve hours, hasn't it? So whoever walks in broad daylight does not stumble, for he sees the light of this world. [10]But if he walks during the night he stumbles, because he has no light.' [11]Jesus said this and then added, 'Our friend Lazarus has fallen asleep, but I will go and wake him up.'

12 The disciples answered, 'If he is asleep, Lord, he will get well.'

13 Jesus meant that Lazarus had died, but they thought he meant natural sleep. [14]So Jesus told them plainly, 'Lazarus is dead, [15]but for your sake I am glad that I was not with him, so that you will believe. Let us go to him.'

16 Thomas (called the Twin) said to his fellow-disciples, 'Let us all go with the Teacher, so that we may die with him!'

17 When Jesus arrived, he found that Lazarus had been buried four days before. [18]Bethany was less than three kilometres from Jerusalem, [19]and many Judaeans had come to see Martha and Mary to comfort them over their brother's death.

20 When Martha heard that Jesus was coming, she went out to meet him, but Mary stayed in the house. [21]Martha said to Jesus, 'If you had been here, Lord, my brother would not have died! ²²*But I know that even now God will give you whatever you ask him for.'*

23 *'Your brother will rise to life,' Jesus told her.*

24 *'I know,' she replied, 'that he will rise to life on the last day.'*

25 *Jesus said to her, 'I am the resurrection and the life. Whoever believes in me will live, even though he dies;* ²⁶*and whoever lives and believes in me will never die. Do you believe this?'*

27 *'Yes, Lord!' she answered. 'I do believe that you are the Messiah, the Son of God, who was to come into the world.'*

28 *After Martha said this, she went back and called her sister Mary privately. 'The Teacher is here,' she told her, 'and is asking for you.'* ²⁹*When Mary heard this, she got up and hurried out to meet him.* (³⁰*Jesus had not yet arrived in the village, but was still in the place where Martha had met him.*) ³¹*The people who were in the house with Mary, comforting her, followed her when they saw her get up and hurry out. They thought that she was going to the grave to weep there.*

32 *Mary arrived where Jesus was, and as soon as she saw him, she fell at his feet. 'Lord,' she said, 'if you had been here, my brother would not have died!'*

33 *Jesus saw her weeping, and he saw how the people who were with her were weeping also; his heart was touched, and he was deeply moved.* ³⁴*'Where have you buried him?' he asked them.*

'Come and see, Lord,' they answered.

35 *Jesus wept.* ³⁶*'See how much he loved him!' the people said.*

37 *But some of them said, 'He gave sight to the blind man, didn't he? Could he not have kept Lazarus from dying?'*

38 *Deeply moved once more, Jesus went to the tomb, which was a cave with a stone placed at the entrance.* ³⁹*'Take the stone away!' Jesus ordered.*

Martha, the dead man's sister, answered, 'There will be a bad smell, Lord. He has been buried four days!'

40 *Jesus said to her, 'Didn't I tell you that you would see God's glory if you believed?'* ⁴¹*They took the stone away. Jesus looked up and said, 'I thank you, Father, that you listen to me.* ⁴²*I know that you always listen to me, but I say this for the sake of the people here, so that they will believe that you sent me.'* ⁴³*After he had said this, he called out in a loud voice, 'Lazarus, come out!'* ⁴⁴*He came out, his hands and feet wrapped in grave clothes, and with a cloth round his face. 'Untie him,' Jesus told them, 'and let him go.'*

45 *Many of the people who had come to visit Mary saw what Jesus*

did, and they believed in him. ⁴⁶But some of them returned to the Pharisees and told them what Jesus had done. ⁴⁷So the Pharisees and the chief priests met with the Council and said, 'What shall we do? Look at all the miracles this man is performing! ⁴⁸If we let him go on in this way, everyone will believe in him, and the Roman authorities will take action and destroy our Temple and our nation!'

49 One of them, named Caiaphas, who was High Priest that year, said, 'What fools you are! ⁵⁰Don't you realize that it is better for you to let one man die for the people, instead of having the whole nation destroyed?' ⁵¹Actually, he did not say this of his own accord; rather, as he was High Priest that year, he was prophesying that Jesus was going to die for the Jewish people, ⁵²and not only for them, but also to bring together into one body all the scattered people of God.

53 From that day on the Jewish authorities made plans to kill Jesus.

The attitude of Jesus Christ and his followers to death is one of the most distinctive marks of Christianity.

The Greek philosopher Aristotle once said: 'Death is a dreadful thing, for it is the end.' In more modern times Rousseau said: 'He who pretends to face death without fear is a liar! And more recently still Aldous Huxley wrote: 'If you're a busy film-going, newspaper-reading, chocolate-eating modern, then death is hell!' Quite recently someone said to me something like this: 'When you die, you die, and that's the end of it!'

How different is the Christian view! The Christian martyr Stephen could say as the stones began to fly: 'Look! . . . I see heaven opened and the Son of Man standing at the right-hand side of God!' (Acts 7:56). That great Christian, the apostle Paul, could write: 'For what is life? To me, it is Christ. *Death, then, will bring more*' (Philippians 1:21); and the American evangelist D. L. Moody could say before his death: 'Some fine morning you will see in the newspapers, D. L. Moody is dead. Don't you believe it. I shall be more alive that morning than ever before!' I have stood by the bedside of a dying Christian and heard her say without fear, 'I'm longing to see Jesus.'

What is the basis for such a positive attitude towards death? The story of the raising of Lazarus gives us some answers to that question.

Lazarus was a great friend of Jesus, and lived with his two sisters in the village of Bethany. His serious illness, followed by death, was the occasion of one of the most astonishing signs in the ministry of Jesus. Bethany was only a few miles out from Jerusalem, not far from where opposition to Jesus' ministry was increasing.

In this story we learn how 'unanswered' prayer, sickness, death and bereavement can be used to uphold the reputation of God, strengthen the faith of disciples and make possible a positive attitude to death.

The chief purpose behind this event is expressed in the words of Jesus himself. 'This has happened in order to bring glory to God, and it will be the means by which the Son of God will receive glory.' Later, he adds: 'Lazarus is dead, but for your sake I am glad that I was not with him, so that you will believe.' We shall notice how these apparently calamitous events strengthened the faith of those involved.

a. The disciples' faith in the wisdom of Jesus

When the message comes to Jesus that Lazarus is seriously ill, we read the unlikely comment, 'When he received the news that Lazarus was ill, he stayed where he was for two more days' (verse 6). By the time, therefore, that Jesus reached Bethany, Lazarus had died. At first the disciples could not understand this at all. Furthermore, when Jesus announced that he was going to Bethany, the disciples believed that they would be walking into further trouble (verse 8). Sometimes God's actions are baffling even to the believer.

> 'God moves in a mysterious way,
> His wonders to perform.'

But the disciples learnt that day at Bethany that even when a request is not immediately answered (verse 6), and when the way seems unnecessarily difficult and dangerous (verse 8), Jesus knows what he is doing. When we follow him, we walk in the light and not in the darkness (verses 9–10). He has a plan and a purpose even when sickness and death and bereavement afflict his friends. At first Thomas expresses only brave but pessimistic loyalty (verse 16). Later the faith of the disciples is strengthened as they discover the loving wisdom of Jesus Christ in all his actions. Christians can say, with the apostle Paul, that 'we know that in all things God works for good with those who love him, those whom he has called according to his purpose' (Romans 8:28).

b. Martha's faith in the authority of Jesus (verses 17–27)

Martha was shattered by the failure of Jesus to do what she asked. She could not resist reproaching Jesus: 'If you had been here, Lord, my brother would not have died' (verse 21). No doubt she felt the same as others who have prayed desperately that God would save a relative or a friend from death, only to find that God has not answered in that way. Martha, I imagine, is a busy, practical woman, who is not much given to deep thought or meditation. Her faith in Jesus is such that she still believes he can help them (verse 22). She can trot out the orthodox Jewish belief about the resurrection at the last day (verse 24). But there was no doubt a hollow sound about those words while the loss of her brother was so close. But Jesus is concerned to strengthen the faith of ordinary, practical men and women. Bereavement has caused her to think about life and death in a deeper way. She has yet to understand that Jesus can not only heal the sick, but he can also raise the dead. Indeed, to believe in Jesus is to experience spiritual life now and for ever. 'Whoever *lives* and *believes* in me will never die.' At that moment of grief and sorrow Martha's faith in the authority and uniqueness of Jesus came to life. ' "I do believe," she said, "that you are the Messiah, the Son of God, who was to come into the world." '

c. Mary's faith in the love of Jesus (verses 28–37)

Mary was of a very different temperament from Martha. She preferred to stay at home, consoled by her friends, until Jesus called her. She, too, could not understand why Jesus had not come to Bethany sooner (verse 32). But if Jesus had not delayed his coming, Mary would not have seen that day how much Jesus understands human sorrow and suffering. For 'Jesus wept' (verse 35). No doubt his tears were in sorrow at the sense of desolation and loss that death brought to those who were still in the dark about the future life. No doubt he wept out of sympathy for his friends. This story assures the Christian that Jesus understands and cares about human sorrow. Like Mary, our faith in the love of Jesus can be strengthened in times of bereavement.

d. The crowd's faith in the power of Jesus (verses 38–57)

It is hard to imagine how men could begin to understand the

power of Jesus over death and the grave unless he demonstrated this power in a sign of this kind. The other Gospels speak of Jesus raising people from the dead (see Matthew 9:18-26; Luke 7:11-17), but they do not in fact mention this remarkable story, which involves restoration—for the body had begun to decompose (verse 39). Jairus's daughter and the widow of Nain's son were raised soon after death. If Peter was not with the disciples at Bethany and if Peter's sermons and memoirs are one of the chief sources for Mark's Gospel, then this may explain the absence of this story from the Synoptic Gospels, for Matthew and Luke depend to some extent on Mark's record. Also, John is writing at a later date, when Lazarus is probably no longer alive. The story might have embarrassed Lazarus if he had been still alive. Certainly this description of the raising of Lazarus, simple and restrained as it is, has all the marks of an eyewitness account.

Jesus prayed (verses 41, 42) that people might know that God had sent him—and then he demonstrated the power of God over death and the grave by summoning Lazarus back to life again (verses 43, 44). Jesus had thus authenticated his claim to be 'the resurrection and the life' (verse 25), which he proved conclusively by his own resurrection from the dead.

But if many believed in the power of Jesus that day at Bethany (verse 45), there were others who would not believe. Indeed a sign of this kind only increased their jealousy and fear and hatred (verses 46-53). John, however, reminds us again that God's purpose was being worked out in this, so that even a casual comment from the high priest, Caiaphas, has a deeper significance than he himself realized. Jesus was still moving forward to that hour when his death would be the means of uniting all believers (verses 50-52).

Questions for discussion

1. Discuss non-Christian attitudes to illness and death. What does this story tell us about distinctively Christian attitudes?

2. 'When he received the news that Lazarus was ill, he stayed where he was for two more days'. How does this story help us to understand why God does not always answer our prayers as we expect?

3. Why did Martha's belief in the final resurrection (verse 24) fail to have much effect upon her at the time of Lazarus' death? Should

someone who follows Christ have a different attitude to bereavement compared to other people?

4. How would you use this story to help someone face up to death?

26 Reactions to Jesus

11:54 – 12:26

54 So Jesus did not travel openly in Judaea, but left and went to a place near the desert, to a town named Ephraim, where he stayed with the disciples.

55 The time for the Passover Festival was near, and many people went up from the country to Jerusalem to perform the ritual of purification before the festival. ⁵⁶They were looking for Jesus, and as they gathered in the temple, they asked one another, 'What do you think? Surely he will not come to the festival, will he?' ⁵⁷The chief priests and the Pharisees had given orders that if anyone knew where Jesus was, he must report it, so that they could arrest him.

12 Six days before the Passover, Jesus went to Bethany, the home of Lazarus, the man he had raised from death. ²They prepared a dinner for him there, which Martha helped to serve; Lazarus was one of those who were sitting at the table with Jesus. ³Then Mary took half a litre of a very expensive perfume made of pure nard, poured it on Jesus' feet, and wiped them with her hair. The sweet smell of the perfume filled the whole house. ⁴One of Jesus' disciples, Judas Iscariot—the one who was going to betray him—said, ⁵'Why wasn't this perfume sold for three hundred silver coins and the money given to the poor?' ⁶He said this, not because he cared about the poor, but because he was a thief. He carried the money bag and would help himself from it.

7 But Jesus said, 'Leave her alone! Let her keep what she has for the day of my burial. ⁸You will always have poor people with you, but you will not always have me.'

9 A large number of people heard that Jesus was in Bethany, so they went there, not only because of Jesus but also to see Lazarus, whom Jesus had raised from death. ¹⁰So the chief priests made plans to kill

Lazarus too, [11]because on his account many Jews were rejecting them and believing in Jesus.

12 The next day the large crowd that had come to the Passover Festival heard that Jesus was coming to Jerusalem. [13]So they took branches of palm-trees and went out to meet him, shouting, 'Praise God! God bless him who comes in the name of the Lord! God bless the King of Israel!'

14 Jesus found a donkey and rode on it, just as the scripture says, [15]'Do not be afraid, city of Zion! Here comes your king, riding on a young donkey.'

16 His disciples did not understand this at the time; but when Jesus had been raised to glory, they remembered that the scripture said this about him and that they had done this for him.

17 The people who had been with Jesus when he called Lazarus out of the grave and raised him from death had reported what had happened. [18]That was why the crowd met him—because they heard that he had performed this miracle. [19]The Pharisees then said to one another, 'You see, we are not succeeding at all! Look, the whole world is following him!'

20 Some Greeks were among those who had gone to Jerusalem to worship during the festival. [21]They went to Philip (he was from Bethsaida in Galilee) and said, 'Sir, we want to see Jesus.'

22 Philip went and told Andrew, and the two of them went and told Jesus. [23]Jesus answered them, 'The hour has now come for the Son of Man to receive great glory. [24]I am telling you the truth: a grain of wheat remains no more than a single grain unless it is dropped into the ground and dies. If it does die, then it produces many grains. [25]Whoever loves his own life will lose it; whoever hates his own life in this world will keep it for life eternal. [26]Whoever wants to serve me must follow me, so that my servant will be with me where I am. And my Father will honour anyone who serves me.'

Although the story of Jesus is big business today—films, musicals, books, stickers and even tee-shirts and jeans have advertised his name—it is still true that there are as many different reactions to him and his teaching today as there were amongst his contemporaries.

When Jesus stayed with his friends, first at Ephraim, in the mountainous country north-east of Jerusalem, and then at Bethany with Lazarus, Martha and Mary, it became increasingly clear that people had to take sides for or against him. The raising of Lazarus from the dead was either an act of God or magic. Lazarus was there for all to see, and many came to see him, curious about the strange event of his resurrection.

Jesus did not immediately walk into danger (verse 54), but it is clear that he was quite prepared to declare himself as Messiah when the right moment came, whatever his enemies might say or do (see verses 12–18). Again we notice that the reactions to Jesus nearly 2,000 years ago were very similar to typical reactions to him today.

a. Some were curious about Jesus (verses 55, 56)

Before a Jew attended a feast he was obliged to be ceremonially clean. Many Jewish pilgrims arrived in Jerusalem several days before the Passover, so that they could attend to the various cere-monial and religious obligations. By this time Jerusalem was re-sounding with the name of Jesus. His reputation as a miracle-worker and his clash with the religious authorities made him an exciting topic of conversation. But it is not sufficient merely to talk about Jesus, if we would really know him. For many in the crowd curiosity did not lead to concern for the truth.

b. Mary lavished her love on Jesus (verses 1–3, 7–8)

At Bethany, only six days before the Passover, Jesus was invited back there for a meal, we may believe, prepared specially in his honour. Martha, as always, was busy serving the meal. Lazarus sat at table and talked with Jesus. Then Mary, quieter than her sister, but capable of greater depths of love and loyalty, makes an extravagant gesture of gratitude. She takes a pound of very costly ointment and anoints Jesus with it. It is a spontaneous gesture which receives the commendation of Jesus, for he sees that her heart has been touched and her motives are the best. Love and loyalty to Jesus should never be cold and calculating. We love him because he first loved us. The church of God needs more of those who will love Jesus with reckless and extravagant love.

c. Judas loved money more than Jesus (verses 4–6)

The contrast between Judas and Mary is striking. It is the contrast between belief and unbelief. We have here one of the clearest statements in the Gospels about the motives of Judas Iscariot, who later betrayed Jesus (verse 6). The writer of this Gospel is quite clear that Judas has used his position as treasurer in the band of disciples to make money for himself. His disgruntled comment about Mary's extravagance was therefore both hypocritical and deceitful. Maybe Judas's dissatisfaction was partly because Jesus gave no indication the he was prepared to bring off a political coup which would have suited Judas's materialistic attitude better. But his words (verse 5) about giving 'to the poor' warn us that it is easy enough to excuse our lack of love for Jesus by pretending we want to give to some good cause. We cannot buy off our responsibility to Jesus Christ by acts of charity. Neither can we serve both Christ *and* money.

d. The chief priests threatened to kill Jesus (verses 9–11)

Their motives too are clear. They are jealous of the influence that Jesus has over the crowds (verses 10, 11, 19), and they have no answer to the claims that Jesus makes. There are always men who will utterly oppose Christianity through jealousy and resentment.

e. The crowds are prepared to shout for Jesus (verses 12–19)

In describing the entry of Jesus into Jerusalem, John does not mention the way in which the disciples first went to prepare for the Passover meal, which the other Gospels describe. John's interest is in the response of the crowds. 'Hosanna' (RSV verse 13) means 'save, we pray'; and the shouting of this word and the quotation from Psalm 118, which was one of the Psalms sung at the Passover in anticipation of the coming of the Messiah, show that many people were prepared to accept Jesus as the Messiah. We cannot be sure whether their ideas about the Messiah were still only political and materialistic; but Jesus goes out of his way to emphasize that he comes to Jerusalem as a king of peace in fulfilment of the Old Testament Scriptures. Judges and kings usually rode on donkeys (verses 14–15) on errands of peace, and on horseback in time of war.

It is easier to shout for a Christ who brings material and political improvements than for a king who suffers in order to establish a spiritual kingdom. But the New Testament constantly reminds us that there can be no peace and prosperity among men unless there is first peace with God. The disciples understood the full significance of this only after the death and resurrection of Jesus (verse 16).

f. The Greeks wanted to see Jesus (verses 20–26)

The Greeks who came to Jerusalem were probably Jewish proselytes, or converts to Judaism. They found the revealed religion of the Jews more satisfying than pagan superstitions. But the appeal of Jesus is more satisfying still. One of the disciples, Philip, had a Greek name, and was probably born in a Greek-speaking community. Perhaps it was for this reason that the Greeks first approached Philip, who then cautiously asks Andrew's advice. Together they go to Jesus, and we assume that they introduced the enquiring Greeks to him. Certainly Jesus was concerned for Greeks as well as Jews. But he was also concerned that those who sought to follow him should understand the nature of his mission and the cost of discipleship. So Jesus emphasizes two important principles.

1. *For Jesus—the way of life is through death* (verses 23–24). The moment when Jesus will be most honoured will not be when Jews and Gentiles flock to see him, but when, like a grain of wheat, he dies as a prelude to rising again and giving life to many. Nature is a constant reminder to us that death is a necessary prelude to life (verse 24). It was necessary for Jesus to die, if we are to live.

2. *For the disciple—the way of life is through death* (verses 25–26). The disciple of Jesus Christ is called to die to self and to live for Christ. If his love for Christ is such that in comparison his love for himself is like hatred, then he will enjoy God's gift of eternal life. Negatively, he must hate self-centred living and, positively, he must serve Christ. The rewards of such unselfish service will be the presence of Christ and the honour of God (verse 26).

The story of Jim Vaus, a notorious criminal wire-tapper in America, converted under the preaching of Dr. Billy Graham a few years ago, illustrates this change of attitude from self-centredness to unselfish service. After Vaus had begun to follow Christ, a man came to him willing to pay $10,000 for information that would settle a case of libel. Jim Vaus speaks: 'Evidently you haven't heard.' 'Haven't heard what?' the man replies. Jim Vaus answers,

'Jim Vaus is dead.' Vaus describes the man's reactions: 'The man's eyes bulged, his chin dropped, and he looked as if I'd lost my mind.' 'That's right', said Vaus, 'the man you are looking for, who used to tap wires, make recordings and sell them to the highest bidder, is dead. I'm a new man, because the Bible says, "If any man be in Christ he is a new creation".'* Jesus Christ calls his disciples to die to the old self-centred sinful life, and to live for him in daily sacrificial service.

Questions for discussion
1. Which of the various reactions to Jesus in chapter 12 are nearest to our own reactions today?
2. 'The church of God needs more of those who will love Jesus with reckless and extravagant love.' What does this mean in practice? How do we apply Mary's act of love to the church's love for Jesus today—or *yours*? (See 12:1-8.)
3. What is the significance of Jesus' entry into Jerusalem—for him, and for the crowds, and for us (verses 12-19)?
4. What do we mean when we talk of the cost of discipleship? How far should we emphasize the cost when we talk to people about Christianity and 'becoming a Christian' (verses 20-26)?

27 A time for decision

12:27-50
27 '*Now my heart is troubled—and what shall I say? Shall I say, "Father, do not let this hour come upon me"? But that is why I came—so that I might go through this hour of suffering. 28Father, bring glory to your name!*'

Then a voice spoke from heaven, 'I have brought glory to it, and I will do so again.'

29 *The crowd standing there heard the voice, and some of them said it was thunder, while others said, 'An angel spoke to him!'*

*Jim Vaus, Why I quit syndicated crime.

30 But Jesus said to them, 'It was not for my sake that this voice spoke, but for yours. *31*Now is the time for this world to be judged; now the ruler of this world will be overthrown. *32*When I am lifted up from the earth, I will draw everyone to me.' (*33*In saying this he indicated the kind of death he was going to suffer.)

34 The crowd answered, 'Our Law tells us that the Messiah will live for ever. How, then, can you say that the Son of Man must be lifted up? Who is this Son of Man?'

35 Jesus answered, 'The light will be among you a little longer. Continue on your way while you have the light, so that the darkness will not come upon you; for the one who walks in the dark does not know where he is going. *36*Believe in the light, then, while you have it, so that you will be the people of the light.'

After Jesus said this, he went off and hid himself from them. *37*Even though he had performed all these miracles in their presence, they did not believe in him, *38*so that what the prophet Isaiah had said might come true:

> 'Lord, who believed the message we told?
> To whom did the Lord reveal his power?'

39 And so they were not able to believe, because Isaiah also said,
> *40*'God has blinded their eyes and closed their minds,
> so that their eyes would not see,
> and their minds would not understand,
> and they would not turn to me, says God,
> for me to heal them.'

41 Isaiah said this because he saw Jesus' glory and spoke about him.

42 Even then, many of the Jewish authorities believed in Jesus; but because of the Pharisees they did not talk about it openly, so as not to be expelled from the synagogue. *43*They loved the approval of men rather than the approval of God.

44 Jesus said in a loud voice, 'Whoever believes in me believes not only in me but also in him who sent me. *45*Whoever sees me sees also him who sent me. *46*I have come into the world as light, so that everyone who believes in me should not remain in the darkness. *47*If anyone hears my message and does not obey it, I will not judge him. I came, not to judge the world, but to save it. *48*Whoever rejects me and does not accept my message has one who will judge him. The words I have spoken will be his judge on the last day! *49*This is true, because I have not spoken on my own authority, but the Father who sent me has commanded me what I must say and speak. *50*And I know that his *command brings eternal life. What I say, then, is what the Father has told me to say.'*

Sometimes people are surprised and even offended that the death of Jesus is so central and important in Christianity. The symbol of Christianity is a cross. The story of the death of Jesus in the Gospels takes up a disproportionate amount of space compared with other biographies. Some modern thinkers would even like to dismiss this teaching about the death of Christ, with its emphasis upon blood and sacrifice, as 'a hangover from a primitive blood ritual'. But the visit of the Greeks to Jesus provides an occasion for Jesus himself to tell us how central in his own thinking is his death.

a. The importance of his death (verse 27)

In his real humanity, Jesus naturally shrinks from the prospect of physical suffering and death. 'Now my heart is troubled—and what shall I say? Shall I say, "Father do not let this hour come upon me"?' Jesus is one of us. He understands and has shared this instinctive reaction to suffering. But he also acknowledges that he has come into this world to die. This is the chief purpose of his coming. This is 'the hour' which is to be the climax of his life and ministry.

b. The glory of his death (verses 28–29)

There is little doubt that the disciples of Jesus as well as others would regard his death as shameful and a terrible disgrace. Jesus knows it will be the moment when God is honoured and glorified. For Jesus, the glory of God matters. It is doing God's will, even if it leads to death on a Roman gibbet, that brings glory to God. The voice from heaven, which appears to be no more than a clap of thunder to those whose ears are not attuned to God, assures the crowds and Jesus himself that such a life of obedience has already brought honour to God, and will do so again.

c. The victory of his death (verses 30–31)

In the eyes of the world the death of Christ appeared to be a tragic failure, a defeat. Jesus knew that in the plan of God it was to be a

130

great victory. The 'ruler of this world', a title emphasizing the great power of the devil, would be cast out, and the selfishness and sin of the world would be judged.

Men sometimes ask why evil is so rampant today. In the last World War the victory at Normandy was decisive in the eventual victory of the Allies. However, there was much further fighting and mopping up that needed to be completed before final victory came. The death of Christ was decisive in the overthrow of Satan. We must wait until Jesus Christ comes again at the end of the world for the complete victory to be accomplished and enjoyed.

d. The power of his death (verses 32–33)

For some people the death of Christ seems to be nonsense, and because of man's pride it is sometimes a stumbling-block (see 1 Corinthians 1:23–24). For it tells us that God has had to do something about man's rebellion and sin, and that man cannot save himself. However, the Christian knows that his sins are forgiven and that God accepts him because of the death of Christ. It is the love of God revealed supremely in Christ's death for sinners that draws a man to God. Jesus here predicts that it will be as a consequence of his being 'lifted up' to die on the cross that men will be drawn to him.

This was the experience of a man who served as a pilot and commissioned flying instructor during World War II and who then went up to Cambridge to take his degree. He was invited to a mission service that was being held under the auspices of the Cambridge Inter-Collegiate Christian Union. He writes, 'One evening the address was on Isaiah 53, and then for the first time I realized that Christ's death on the cross affected me personally. "He was wounded for *my* transgressions, he was bruised for *my* iniquities ... with his stripes *I* am healed." I certainly had no overwhelming sense of sin, and I reckoned that I had lived a normal, decent sort of life. But I knew, too, that I had never really thanked Christ for what He had done for me on the cross, and that ingratitude was just a form of sin. As I thanked Him that night, and offered Him my life in gratitude, a sense of assurance came to me, based not on any feelings, and certainly not on any sense of worthiness, but on the written Word of God. I knew that I was now saved, not because of anything that I had done, but because Jesus Christ had done all that was necessary for my salvation.'* The message of the death of Christ still draws people today.

e. Reactions to the message of his death (verse 34–43)

There is more than one way to react to the message of Christ's death, as these next verses make clear.

1. *Some did not understand* (verses 34–36). Some could not believe in a *Messiah* that would have to die (verse 33). Should not the Messiah live for ever? Again, the 'Son of man' described in Daniel 7:13 would come in glory 'surrounded by clouds'. Who, then, is this 'Son of Man' who speaks of this glory of death by crucifixion? Jesus implies that if only they were willing, he would give them understanding and take away their ignorance. '*Believe* in the light, then, while you have it, so that you will be the *people of the light.*' We shall never fully understand the meaning of the death of Christ with our finite minds. But if we look to Christ and listen to him we shall find sufficient light to walk by.

2. *Some would not believe* (verses 37–41). In spite of the miracles and signs of Jesus many reacted to Jesus in the same way as many had reacted earlier to the prophet Isaiah. Indeed, Isaiah had foreseen that when the Messiah came many would be too blind to see him, and too hardened to respond to him. The writers in the Bible sometimes spoke of *God* hardening men's hearts. When the Pharaoh of Egypt had repeatedly rejected the message from God which he heard from the lips of Moses, it was finally said, 'The Lord made the king stubborn' (see Exodus 7–11). There comes a moment when persistent rejection of God's Word leads to such hardness of heart that God is not willing to speak any more. Paul uses the phrase, '*God . . . has given them over* to corrupted minds' (Romans 1:28). The more we reject God's Word the harder our hearts become. That is why there is often a note of urgency in the Bible, when men are exhorted to turn from their sins to God. 'Listen! This is the hour to receive God's favour; today is the day to be saved' (2 Corinthians 6:2).

3. *Some believed in secret* (verses 42–43). Jesus once said that if we were to be ashamed of him in this life, he would be ashamed of us in the next life (Mark 8:38). John tells us that many people, even those in important and responsible positions in society, did not reject Christ but were ashamed to acknowledge him publicly. Why should men want to be only secret disciples? John's answer

*W. F. Batt (editor), *Facing the Facts*, p. 60.

is: (i) *They feared men's opinions.* These men were afraid of the Pharisees. Fear of what others will think often keeps a man from confessing he is a Christian. (ii) *They loved men's praise.* These men were not prepared to be thrown out of the synagogue, isolated from their group in society. They did not want to lose their friends or their comfortable niche in society. John sums up their position by saying of them what, sadly, can often be said of us: 'They loved the approval of men rather than the approval of God.'

f. What is our response to Jesus and his message? (verses 44–50)

In the last verses of this chapter Jesus once again makes the issue clear. To believe in Jesus is to believe in God. To see Jesus as the Son of God and Saviour of sinners is to see God. To believe on him is to walk in the knowledge of God and not in ignorance. It is to walk in the light and not darkness. But what if we hear this message and reject it ? Jesus told the Pharisees that his coming into this world was primarily for salvation and not judgment (verse 47). But one day he will come to judge the world, and on that day our salvation, our acceptance with God, will depend on our attitude and response to the divine and authoritative words of Jesus Christ, which God has commanded him to speak (verses 49–50). To reject Christ and his teaching is to reject God (verse 48). To believe on him is to receive One who has come as light into the world (verse 46).

In St. Paul's Cathedral and in the Chapel at Keble College, Oxford, there are two well-known and almost identical paintings by Holman Hunt. They show Jesus as the Light of the world. Part of John Ruskin's letter to *The Times* on 5 May 1854, describing the paintings, reads as follows: 'The legend beneath it (the painting) is the beautiful verse—"Behold I stand at the door and knock. If any man hear my voice and open the door, I will come in to him, and will sup with him, and he with me" (Revelation 3:20). On the left hand side of the picture is seen this door of the human soul. It is fast barred; its bars and nails are rusty; it is knitted and bound to its stanchions by creeping tendrils of ivy, showing that it has never been opened . . . Christ approaches it in the night time . . .'

So Jesus Christ may approach us. If we believe that he is the Son of God and the Saviour of sinners, and if we are ready to receive him as personal Saviour, Master and God, then we could open the door of our lives and ask him to come in and abide with us for ever. Here is a prayer we could use.

'Lord Jesus, I admit I am a sinner, living a self-centred life, and I confess my sins to you, especially those on my conscience.
I believe that you are the Son of God and the Saviour of sinners and that you died for *my* sins on the cross, bearing the judgment I deserved.
I have counted the cost and I am willing to die to self and live for you, with your help, and to serve you in the fellowship of your church. So I come to you and receive you into my life as my Saviour, Master and God, now and for ever. Amen'

Jesus said, 'Listen! I stand at the door and knock; if anyone hears my voice and opens the door, *I will come in*' (see Revelation 3:20).

Questions for discussion

1. What do we learn about Jesus' own view of the importance and meaning of his death in this passage?
2. What do we learn in this passage about the nature of unbelief? What reasons can we offer for unbelief? Does unbelief matter?
3. Why are some people ashamed of their belief in Jesus Christ?
4. How does a man believe in Christ and become a Christian today?

28   The humility of Jesus

13:1-17
13 It was now the day before the Passover Festival. Jesus knew that the hour had come for him to leave this world and go to the Father. He had always loved those in the world who were his own, and he loved them to the very end.

2 Jesus and his disciples were at supper. The Devil had already put the thought of betraying Jesus into the heart of Judas, the son of Simon Iscariot. ³Jesus knew that the Father had given him complete power;

he knew that he had come from God and was going to God. ⁴So he rose from the table, took off his outer garment, and tied a towel round his waist. ⁵Then he poured some water into a basin and began to wash the disciples' feet and dry them with the towel round his waist. ⁶He came to Simon Peter, who said to him, 'Are you going to wash my feet, Lord?'

7 Jesus answered him, 'You do not understand now what I am doing, but you will understand later.'

8 Peter declared, 'Never at any time will you wash my feet!'

'If I do not wash your feet,' Jesus answered, 'you will no longer be my disciple.'

9 Simon Peter answered, 'Lord, do not wash only my feet, then! Wash my hands and head, too!'

10 Jesus said, 'Anyone who has had a bath is completely clean and does not have to wash himself, except for his feet. All of you are clean—all except one.' (¹¹Jesus already knew who was going to betray him; that is why he said, 'All of you, except one, are clean.')

12 After Jesus had washed their feet, he put his outer garment back on and returned to his place at the table. 'Do you understand what I have just done to you?' he asked. ¹³'You call me Teacher and Lord, and it is right that you do so, because that is what I am. ¹⁴I, your Lord and Teacher, have just washed your feet. You, then, should wash one another's feet. ¹⁵I have set an example for you, so that you will do just what I have done for you. ¹⁶I am telling you the truth: no slave is greater than his master, and no messenger is greater than the one who sent him. ¹⁷Now that you know this truth, how happy you will be if you put it into practice!'

It is not always appreciated that Christians have been the pioneers of a great deal of the social, educational and medical welfare that we so easily take for granted in this country. Indeed this would also be true to a large extent throughout our Western civilization and in many of the developing countries. Our next story gives us a clue to some of the reasons for this impressive fact of history.

The scene is the upper room in Jerusalem. The twelve disciples have met with Jesus to eat the passover meal.* It is clear that a new

*See R. V. G. Tasker, *The Gospel according to St. John*, p. 153, where it is suggested that verse 1 of this chapter is the heading for the next five chapters and should be taken separately. In this way it does not imply that the Last Supper could not be the passover meal.

stage in the ministry of Jesus has begun. His public ministry is over. Now he must concentrate on teaching and training the disciples to face up to the future.

John does not give us all the information about the Last Supper that can be found in the other Gospels. Presumably it would be well known to the early Christians. He does not mention the preparation of the room for the meal (Matthew 26:17-19; Mark 14:12-16; Luke 22:7-13) or the quarrelling of the disciples over rival claims to greatness (Matthew 20:25-28; Mark 10:42-45; Luke 22:24-27). There is no mention of the symbolic taking of bread and wine which is central in the other Gospels (Matthew 26:26-29; Mark 14:22-25; Luke 22:17-19). But he does recount another equally symbolic action.

In Palestine, the roads were often inches deep in dust in dry weather, and turned to liquid mud in wet weather. Normally therefore a slave would take water and a towel and wash the feet of the guests, whose sandals were not designed to keep out the dust. It seems that on this occasion no slave was available, and the disciples were more interested in arguing about the best seats in the kingdom than in doing the work of a slave. No-one volunteered. But during supper Jesus rose, laid aside his garments, put on a slave's apron, and taking a basin and water began to wash the disciples' feet. In recording this symbolic action of Jesus, John emphasizes two things.

a. An example of humility (verses 1-5)

'Jesus knew that the hour had come for him to leave this world and go to the Father', yet he deliberately and symbolically illustrated by this action how he was laying aside his Father's glory. He became like a slave, and humbled himself even to the death of the cross (see Philippians 2:5-11). 'Jesus knew that *the Father had given him complete power'* (verse 3), yet later he was prepared to submit to the insignificant authority of the cruel and vacillating Pontius Pilate. Jesus knew that *'he had come from God and was going to God'* (verse 3), yet, although he was conscious of his own majesty and authority, he deliberately put on the apron of a slave, and washed the disciples' feet as a sign that, like the ideal servant of Old Testament prophecy, he was willing to 'pour out his soul to death' (Isaiah 53:12, RSV).

b. A call for humility (verses 6–17)

It is not enough to *call* Jesus 'Teacher' and 'Lord'. It is not enough to admire his example of humility. He calls us to follow his example and to 'put on the apron of humility' (*cf.* 1 Peter 5:5). This story underlines two aspects of humility in particular.

1. *The humility of receiving* (verses 6–11). It is often a deeper mark of humility to receive something from a friend than to do something for him. Most of us, like Simon Peter, instinctively prefer to do something for God than to receive something from him. 'Are *you* going to wash *my* feet, Lord?' Jesus explains that Peter will not fully understand the significance of what he is doing until later, but insists, 'If *I* do not wash *your* feet . . . you will no longer be my disciple.' Peter then, true to form, blurts out impulsively, 'Lord, do not wash only my feet, then! Wash my hands and head, too!'

We can now understand what Jesus means. The washing of Peter's feet is symbolic of the cleansing from sin which Peter must receive from Christ, if he is to have fellowship with him. Such initial cleansing, symbolized by baptism, symbolic of forgiveness and new life, is once and for all and cannot be repeated. But it must be humbly received from Christ himself. Some commentators make much of the different Greek words used: 'Anyone who has had a bath' (*louō*) is completely clean and does not have to wash (*niptō*) himself, except for his feet.' A man normally bathed (*louō*) before he went out for a meal. When he reached the house where he would feast, he did not need to bathe again, but his feet would need to be washed (*niptō*) once more. It is certainly true that a Christian receives new life once he is washed and accepted by God. He is brought into a new relationship which cannot be altered. But he also needs daily to confess his sins and he needs daily forgiveness. He needs to have the dirt of each day washed away. For sin cannot break our relationship with Jesus Christ, but it can spoil our fellowship with him. In a letter to Christians, John assures us that 'if we confess our sins to God, he will keep his promise and do what is right: he will forgive us our sins and purify us from all wrongdoing' (1 John 1:9).

2. *The humility of serving* (verses 12–17). 'I, your Lord and Teacher, have just washed your feet. You, then, should wash one another's feet.' Jesus calls his disciples not only to *receive* his cleansing but to *serve* other people.

There are sections of the Christian church which still observe the ritual of feet-washing as carefully as the Lord's Supper and baptism. But Jesus chiefly intends us to follow his example of humble service in our daily lives. We fail to see the force of what he is saying if we are not willing, for example, to do a menial task for his sake; if we stand on our dignity or insist on our rights; and there are many opportunities for Christians today to exercise such menial service.

Countless Christians have done this down the centuries; and that is why they have pioneered in so many areas of human need. Today, the modern Welfare State, which cares so much for the material and physical needs of men, often fails to meet the needs of loneliness, fear and depression which affect the less fortunate members of society. So, one of the tasks of the Christian church is to help create a community where Christians love one another, care for one another and accept one another—and at the same time show their love for all men including those outside their own fellowship.

This will mean, for example, that a Christian may help to re-decorate the room of an elderly couple, mend a fuse, help with the shopping, dig the garden, or simply lend a sympathetic ear to a neighbour. It will mean that Christians in the local church will think out ways of 'serving the community'.

If Jesus could do the task of a slave and wash the disciples' feet, there is no task too menial for his disciples. 'Now that you know this truth, how happy you will be if you put it into practice!' (verse 16).

Questions for discussion
1. In what way did Jesus express his 'service' of others in his life on earth?
2. How should we follow his example today?
3. What was wrong with Peter's attitude to Jesus in this story (verses 6–10)?
4. What do people mean by 'the servant church'? Is it a true description of the church you know best? If not, how would you set about putting things right?

29 The love of Jesus

13:18–35

18 'I am not talking about all of you; I know those I have chosen. But the scripture must come true that says, "The man who shared my food turned against me." ¹⁹I tell you this now before it happens, so that when it does happen, you will believe that "I Am Who I Am." ²⁰I am telling you the truth: whoever receives anyone I send receives me also; and whoever receives me receives him who sent me.'

21 After Jesus had said this, he was deeply troubled and declared openly, 'I am telling you the truth: one of you is going to betray me.'

22 The disciples looked at one another, completely puzzled about whom he meant. ²³One of the disciples, the one whom Jesus loved, was sitting next to Jesus. ²⁴Simon Peter motioned to him and said, 'Ask him whom he is talking about.'

25 So that disciple moved closer to Jesus' side and asked, 'Who is it, Lord?'

26 Jesus answered, 'I will dip some bread in the sauce and give it to him; he is the man.' So he took a piece of bread, dipped it, and gave it to Judas, the son of Simon Iscariot. ²⁷As soon as Judas took the bread, Satan entered him. Jesus said to him, 'Be quick about what you are doing!' ²⁸None of the others at the table understood why Jesus said this to him. ²⁹Since Judas was in charge of the money bag, some of the disciples thought that Jesus had told him to go and buy what they needed for the festival, or to give something to the poor.

30 Judas accepted the bread and went out at once. It was night.

31 After Judas had left, Jesus said, 'Now the Son of Man's glory is revealed; now God's glory is revealed through him. ³²And if God's glory is revealed through him, then God will reveal the glory of the Son of Man in himself, and he will do so at once. ³³My children, I shall not be with you very much longer. You will look for me; but I tell you now what I told the Jewish authorities, "You cannot go where I am going." ³⁴And now I give you a new commandment: love one another. As I have loved you, so you must love one another. ³⁵If you have love for one another, then everyone will know that you are my disciples.'

Church history teaches us that Judas Iscariot is not the only person in a privileged position who has betrayed Jesus. Judas was probably the treasurer of the inner band of Jesus' disciples (verse 29). Yet he was not immune to the temptation to betray him. So, whatever our position in the church, or however much we may appear to be a disciple of Jesus, we presumably are not immune to that temptation either.

In the previous passage the humility of Jesus is contrasted with the pride of the disciples. Here the love of Jesus is contrasted with the treachery of Judas.

a. The treachery of Judas (verses 18–20)

Some writers have tried to whitewash the character of Judas, who is perhaps the most tragic figure in history. They have suggested that perhaps he was trying to force the hand of Jesus by this betrayal, in order that he might declare himself to be the Messiah. But it is important to note all the evidence about Judas. In this Gospel, Judas is described as 'a devil' (6:70), as 'a thief' (12:4–6), as tempted by the devil (13:12), and finally as possessed by Satan, for 'Satan entered him' (13:27). The fact that the other disciples did not apparently suspect that Judas would betray Jesus (verses 27–29) shows that Judas must have been a clever hypocrite as well. When Jesus revealed that there was one of them who would betray him, and that he knew who it would be, he emphasized the extent of his treachery by quoting the Old Testament scripture, 'The man who shared my food turned against me.' A close friend would deal brutally with him.

Jesus gave this information to the disciples so that later they would understand that Jesus had divine foreknowledge of the events that led to his death, and would be strengthened to acknowledge him as God's Messiah (verse 19). At the same time he emphasizes the high calling of those who represent Christ in the world, so that they can understand that a man whose heart is not right could not remain with them (verse 20).

b. The love of Jesus (verses 21–35)

In spite of Judas' treachery Jesus loved him 'to the very end'. John records that Jesus 'was deeply troubled' (verse 21). He was in great distress at the enormity of Judas's betrayal. Yet he continued to love him. It is probable that Judas sat on the left of Jesus at supper, as it appears that Jesus could carry on a conversation with him without moving from his place. Simon Peter had to beckon to John when he wanted to put a question to Jesus, so he could not have been in that position. John was clearly on the right of Jesus (verse 25). If Judas did sit on the left of Jesus he was of course sitting in the place of highest honour, usually kept for the host's intimate friend. The bread or 'morsel' (RSV) was probably a choice piece of the dish, and was offered to Judas as an expression of special friendship (verse 26).*

Judas's rejection of this final appeal by Jesus is the moment when Satan and darkness fill his soul. There comes a time when the love of Jesus is so often rejected that he has to leave us to settle our own destiny. Jesus says, 'Be quick about what you are doing!' It was night: not only in the streets of Jerusalem but also in the soul of Judas.

The factors involved in man's choice or rejection of Jesus Christ are not simple ones. Nor is it possible for the finite mind of man to understand perfectly the relationship between God's plan and man's responsibility. The narrative had made plain that Jesus loved Judas to the end, and that Judas was responsible for his own actions. Yet when Judas had finally rejected Christ's appeal of love, Jesus could say, 'Now the Son of Man's glory is revealed; now God's glory is revealed through him!' God was going to overrule the wickedness and treachery of men in accordance with his own plan and foreknowledge (see Acts 2:23). The death of Christ was to be the moment of glory to be followed by the victory of the resurrection and ascension (verse 32). The disciples could not yet share in that glory (verse 33), but they could glorify God by loving one another in the same kind of selfless, humble, patient and sacrificial way that Jesus loved them. This was to be the badge of their discipleship whereby people would know they belonged to Jesus Christ (verses 34–35).

Modern man often feels he is part of a machine, that life is absurd or pre-determined, that there is no loving or logical purpose at all.

*It is also believed to have been common practice for the 'morsel' to be used when two people were making a bargain. Rather than shaking hands or signing a contract, a morsel dipped in wine was given and received and this pledge was absolutely binding on both parties. So Judas took the morsel knowing full well that he would be breaking a contract with Jesus.

As a result he often blames his environment or even his hormones for his own predicament. Arthur Koestler actually suggests that if man is to be prevented from blowing himself up, he may have to receive injections of some synthetic hormones to change his character. In Sartre's novels the same pessimistic view of man is depicted, and someone has called Sartre's world a 'world without grace'. The story of Judas reminds us, however, that man is responsible for his actions, and that the world is not without grace or a loving purpose. But when grace and love are persistently spurned then man, like Judas, 'goes to his own place' and settles his own destiny.

Questions for discussion
1. What do we learn from this passage about the reasons for Judas' treachery, and the enormity of it?
2. What part does Satan play in this story? Are the other disciples in any way responsible for Judas' failure?
3. How can we help someone who is set upon a wrong course of action? (Consider Jesus' attitude to Judas.)

30 Jesus answers questions

13:36 – 14:11
36 'Where are you going, Lord?' Simon Peter asked him.

'You cannot follow me now where I am going,' answered Jesus; 'but later you will follow me.'

37 'Lord, why can't I follow you now?' asked Peter. 'I am ready to die for you!'

38 Jesus answered, 'Are you really ready to die for me? I am telling you the truth: before the cock crows you will say three times that you do not know me.

14 'Do not be worried and upset,' Jesus told them. 'Believe in God and believe also in me. ²There are many rooms in my Father's house, and I am going to prepare a place for you. I would not tell you this if it were not so. ³And after I go and prepare a place for you, I will come back and take you to myself, so that you will be where I am. ⁴You know the way that leads to the place where I am going.'

5 Thomas said to him, 'Lord, we do not know where you are going; so how can we know the way to get there?'

6 Jesus answered him, 'I am the way, the truth, and the life; no one goes to the Father except by me. ⁷Now that you have known me,' he said to them, 'you will know my Father also, and from now on you do know him and you have seen him.'

8 Philip said to him, 'Lord, show us the Father; that is all we need.'

9 Jesus answered, 'For a long time I have been with you all; yet you do not know me, Philip? Whoever has seen me has seen the Father. Why, then, do you say, "Show us the Father"? ¹⁰Do you not believe, Philip, that I am in the Father and the Father is in me? The words that I have spoken to you,' Jesus said to his disciples, 'do not come from me. The Father, who remains in me, does his own work. ¹¹Believe me when I say that I am in the Father and the Father is in me. If not, believe because of the things I do.'

Every parent knows that children discover a great deal about life by asking questions. Sometimes they never stop! But it is one of the best ways of learning and understanding what we really want to know. Jesus taught a great deal in answer to questions. In this next passage the disciples ask him some questions that are as relevant and important today as they were then.

Judas had left the room. Jesus had told them that he was soon to go where they could not come. So, perplexed and no doubt a little afraid, the disciples began to question Jesus. Simon Peter asks the first question.

a. 'Where are you going, Lord?' (13:36 – 14:4)

Was it to die? Then Simon Peter wanted to die too. 'Lord, why can't I follow you now? . . . I am ready to die for you!' These were brave words and typical of the warm-hearted, impulsive Peter. But they promised more than they achieved. As Jesus pointed out, for all his self-confidence, Simon Peter would in fact deny that he ever knew Jesus. Jesus knew Peter through and through. But it is typical of his graciousness that, although he knew how weak Peter was, he saw in him nonetheless the stuff that martyrs are made of. 'You cannot follow me now where I am going . . . but later you will follow me' (*cf.* John 21:18, 19).

Jesus then turned to all the disciples (verses 1–4) and answers Peter's question. He is going to his Father's house (heaven) to prepare a place for his disciples. He then promises to come again to receive them and welcome them and be with them for ever.

Heaven is where Jesus is. It is a place of rest. It is a place prepared for those who have trusted in Jesus Christ. When Jesus says, 'Believe in God and believe also in me', he is encouraging the disciples to turn their thoughts from fears of the immediate future on earth to thoughts of their ultimate destiny in heaven. It is such confidence that enables Christians to keep present anxieties in perspective, just as the apostle Paul was able to write later, 'I consider that what we suffer at this present time cannot be compared at all with the glory that is going to be revealed to us' (Romans 8:18). Bertrand Russell* once wrote: 'The belief that we survive death seems to me . . . to have no scientific basis. I do not think it would ever have arisen except as an emotional reaction to the fear of death.' Professor Hoyle† wrote: 'While our intelligences are powerful enough to penetrate deeply into the evolution of this quite incredible universe, we still have not the smallest clue to our fate.' In contrast to these Jesus said, 'Do not be worried and upset . . . Believe in God and believe also in me. There are many rooms in my Father's house, and I am going to prepare a place for you. I would not tell you this if it were not so.'

Jesus concludes, 'You know the way that leads to the place where I am going.' At this Thomas, somewhat sceptical and pessimistic, interrupts with another question.

b. 'Lord, we do not know where you are going; so how can we know the way to get there?' (verses 5–7)

How can anyone know the way who does not know the destination? We must be grateful to Thomas for pressing the point. It is a solemn and sad thing to be unsure of our future destiny. Jesus' answer is both simple and profound. 'I am the way, the truth, and the life.' The way to heaven is through Jesus himself. Man has

*From an article in *The Times* later published in a book containing a series of articles entitled *The Great Mystery of Life Hereafter*.
†F. Hoyle, *The Nature of the Universe*.

often made the way to God and to heaven complicated and difficult. Many directions are given, often to our bewilderment. Truths and propositions are presented to us in difficult theological language. Taboos and prohibitions sometimes make the way unwelcome. But Jesus cuts through all this. *He* is the way to God. If you asked a man in the East to show you the way to a certain place, he might well say 'I am the way', by which he would mean, 'Follow me and I will bring you to your destination.' Jesus makes this claim concerning man's ultimate destiny. He claims, moreover, that he is the *only* way to the Father, that he alone embodies truth, and that he alone is the source of eternal life. When a man is introduced to Jesus Christ, he is introduced to God. Jesus is the way to the Father, the full truth about the Father, the very life of the Father. Other systems and philosophies have tried to bridge the gap between man and God. Jesus *is* the bridge between man and God.

Now it is Philip's turn to ask a question.

c. 'Lord, show us the Father; that is all we need' (verses 8–11)

Philip was a practical man who did not understand theological or mystical language. He would be satisfied if he could see God with his own eyes as clearly as he could see Jesus. Jesus gently rebukes him for not understanding and then says, 'Whoever has seen me has seen the Father.'

There was a day when death had darkened the home of the Scottish author, Thomas Carlyle. Someone, taking a New Testament, opened it at the Gospel of John and read the familiar words, 'Let not your heart be troubled . . . In my Father's house are many mansions.' 'Aye,' muttered the bereaved man. 'If you were God you had a right to say that, but if you were only a man, what do you know any more than the rest of us ?' Carlyle's query is answered in these words, 'Whoever has seen me has seen the Father.' The evidence that Jesus gives to substantiate this claim is threefold.

1. *His personality* (verse 10). Surely the intimate relationship between Jesus and his Father must have been apparent to the disciples. He always did those things that pleased the Father (see John 8:29).

2. *His words.* No-one ever spoke like Jesus (John 7:46). 'The one whom God has sent speaks God's words' (3:34).

3. *His works.* His miracles and mighty deeds all authenticated

his message and his claims. No-one could do the things that Jesus did unless he was God.

Questions for discussion
1. Christianity is 'all pie in the sky when you die'. How would you describe the significance of Jesus' teaching on heaven in this passage?
2. 'No one goes to the Father except by me' (14:6). How do you understand these words in the light of John 1:9 and other religions?
3. What do we learn about God from 'seeing Jesus'?
4. 'All roads lead to God.' Would that be a fair comment on all religions in the light of this passage?
5. Ghandi once said: 'The soul of religions is one, but it is encased in a multitude of forms. Truth is the exclusive property of no single scripture . . . I cannot ascribe exclusive divinity to Jesus. He is as divine as Krishna, or Rama, or Mohammed or Zoroaster.' Discuss in the light of this passage.

31 A new relationship

14:12–17
12 'I am telling you the truth: whoever believes in me will do what I do —yes, he will do even greater things, because I am going to the Father. 13And I will do whatever you ask for in my name, so that the Father's glory will be shown through the Son. 14If you ask me for anything in my name, I will do it.

15 'If you love me, you will obey my commandments. 16I will ask the Father, and he will give you another Helper, who will stay with you for ever. 17He is the Spirit who reveals the truth about God. The world cannot receive him, because it cannot see him or know him. But you know him, because he remains with you and is in you.'

'Does it work?' That is what many people ask about Christianity.

146

In this next section we learn what Jesus has to say. He tells the disciples some of the exciting privileges, responsibilities and consequences that follow personal commitment to him.

a. A new relationship (verses 12–14)

They will experience this when he leaves them and returns to his Father in heaven. The privileges of this relationship will be so great that they should be rejoicing at the prospect of his leaving them (see verse 28). 'For (the Father) is greater than I.' Jesus here acknowledges both the limitations and the voluntary subordination of his earthly ministry in relation to his heavenly Father. But once he has returned to share once again the glory of his Father, the resources available to the disciples will be limitless.

b. A new power in prayer (verses 12–13)

Once Jesus has ascended, his ministry will no longer be confined to Palestine. Through the power of prayer the believer will see greater works done in the name of Jesus than in his earthly ministry. These works will be greater in the sense that they will not be confined to one place at a time. Greater also because the full experience of the new birth and the knowledge of God in Jesus was possible only after the death, resurrection and ascension of Jesus. The secret of power is prayer *in the name of Jesus*. This must mean prayer in accordance with his will (no man will lend his name for a cause that is contrary to his own purposes and wishes). It must also mean prayer 'counting on the authority and power of Jesus'—as a man may use the name of an influential friend to gain access into normally inaccessible places. It also clearly means prayer that is concerned not with selfish desires but with the glory of God. The practical apostle James once wrote: 'You do not have what you want because you do not ask God for it. And when you ask, you do not receive it, because your motives are bad; you ask for things to use for your own pleasures' (James 4:2–3). The great cricketer and missionary, C. T. Studd, at the end of his resources in China, proved the power of prayer. 'My family in England knew nothing of our circumstances,' he wrote. 'The last of our supplies was finished. The mail came once a fortnight. If the postman brought no relief, starvation stared us in the face.' So C. T. Studd and his wife prayed to God in the name of Jesus. The mail arrived. The last letter was from a stranger, Frank Crossley. It said this: 'I have for some reason received the command of God to send you £100. I have never met you. I have only heard of you, and that not often, but God has prevented me from sleeping tonight by this command. Why He should command me to send you this, you will know better than I.'* There is power in prayer.

c. A new strength to obey (verses 15–17)

'If you love me, you will obey my commandments.' The teaching of the new moralists suggests that love removes the necessity for law. 'Nothing can of itself always be labelled as "wrong". One cannot, for instance, start from the position "sex relations before marriage" or "divorce" are wrong or sinful in themselves. They may be in 99 cases or even 100 out of 100, but they are not intrinsically so, for the only intrinsic evil is lack of love.'† Jesus contradicts this view of law: love is blind without the law. Love for Christ will be demonstrated by obedience to the law. The new element in Christ's teaching is that the disciple of Christ will discover that he *wants* to keep God's law and that he will have *power* to do so. This is because, in fulfilment of Old Testament promises that God would write his law on our hearts and take away the heart of stone (Jeremiah 31:33; Ezekiel 36:26), Jesus promises that he will come and dwell in our hearts by his Spirit, so that we may have both the power and the desire to keep his commandments.

Who is the 'Spirit who reveals the truth' (verse 17)? He is described as '*another* Helper'. The Greek word (*allon*) means 'another of the same kind as'. He is not a vague influence or power. He is *divine* like Jesus, yet a different person.‡ Indeed Jesus can speak of him interchangeably with himself and with his Father. Jesus tells us in this passage that the Helper will dwell with us and in us (verse 17). At the same time he says that he himself will come to the disciples and dwell in them (verse 20). Later he says that the Father would come and make his home in the lives and personalities of his followers. In the New Testament letters we find the

---

*Norman P. Grubb, *C. T. Studd: Cricketer and Pioneer*, pp. 98, 99.
†J. A. T. Robinson, *Honest to God*, p. 118.
‡See R. V. G. Tasker, *The Gospel according to St. John*, p. 172.

same kind of language. The early Christians could speak of God dwelling in them (1 Corinthians 3:16), Christ dwelling in them (Colossians 1:27) and the Spirit possessing their lives (Romans 8:14–16). The doctrine of the Trinity (God as three persons in one) was never formally worked out in the New Testament; but it was implicit in the teaching of Jesus, and inevitably arose out of the experience of the early Christians. The disciples believed in one God. Yet they were compelled by the evidence to believe that God became man in Jesus, and that Jesus continued with them in the power of the indwelling Spirit. In Christian experience it is not difficult to believe in one God in three persons. The unity of God is not a mathematical unity, any more than the unity of the atom. There is such a thing as organic unity.

He is *personal*, too, for Jesus speaks of him as 'teaching' and 'making you remember' (verse 26). Jesus also calls the Spirit '*Helper*' (*paraklētos*), which literally means 'someone called alongside to help'. Sometimes the Greeks used this word to describe an advocate in a court of law, or an expert called in to advise, or even someone called in to raise the morale of dispirited soldiers. As Dr. Leon Morris has said, 'the significance of the word is not so much "there, there, little one!" as "up guards and at 'em!" It is not soothing syrup but a clarion call.' It is the Spirit who gives us strength to obey God.

Questions for discussion

1. In what sense do Christians today 'do even greater things' through the Holy Spirit than Jesus did in his earthly ministry? (See verse 12.)

2. What does it mean to pray 'in the name of Jesus'? Should we ever pray 'if it be your will', or is that lack of faith?

3. Nothing can of itself always be labelled as 'wrong'. How does the teaching of Jesus here and in the rest of John's Gospel (*e.g.* John 8) contradict this view? How do we avoid being legalistic if we believe it is still important to keep God's commandments?

4. How would you explain the doctrine of the Trinity to an unbeliever?

32 A new assurance

14:18–31

18 'When I go, you will not be left all alone; I will come back to you. ¹⁹In a little while the world will see me no more, but you will see me; and because I live, you also will live. ²⁰When that day comes, you will know that I am in my Father and that you are in me, just as I am in you.

21 'Whoever accepts my commandments and obeys them is the one who loves me. My Father will love whoever loves me; I too will love him and reveal myself to him.'

22 Judas (not Judas Iscariot) said, 'Lord, how can it be that you will reveal yourself to us and not to the world?'

23 Jesus answered him, 'Whoever loves me will obey my teaching. My Father will love him, and my Father and I will come to him and live with him. ²⁴Whoever does not love me does not obey my teaching. And the teaching you have heard is not mine, but comes from the Father, who sent me.

25 'I have told you this while I am still with you. ²⁶The Helper, the Holy Spirit, whom the Father will send in my name, will teach you everything and make you remember all that I have told you.

27 'Peace is what I leave with you; it is my own peace that I give you. I do not give it as the world does. Do not be worried and upset; do not be afraid. ²⁸You heard me say to you, "I am leaving, but I will come back to you." If you loved me, you would be glad that I am going to the Father; for he is greater than I. ²⁹I have told you this now before it all happens, so that when it does happen, you will believe. ³⁰I cannot talk with you much longer, because the ruler of this world is coming. He has no power over me, ³¹but the world must know that I love the Father; that is why I do everything as he commands me.

'Come, let us go from this place.'

There is an old Arab proverb that says:
    'He that knows not, and knows not that he knows not, is a fool—
    shun him.

He that knows not, and knows that he knows not, is simple —
  teach him.
He that knows, and knows not that he knows, is asleep —
  wake him.
He that knows, and knows that he knows, is a wise man —
  follow him.

But can a man *know* that he is a Christian, that he has eternal life,
and that he belongs to God? Jesus teaches that he can and should.
'You *know* him (the Holy Spirit), for he remains with you and is in
you' (verse 17). 'You will *know* that I am in my Father and that
you are in me, just as I am in you' (verse 20).

This passage teaches that once the Spirit has made his home in
the personality of the believer, he experiences life and the assurance
that God lives in him (verses 16–23).

Jesus promises the disciples that he will not leave them desolate
(or like orphans, verse 18), but that the Spirit will enable them to
know that they belong to God. The Spirit gives certainty to believers
through inner conviction, the Word of God and a deep inner peace.

a. Inner conviction (verse 20)

'When that day comes (after the resurrection and ascension of
Jesus), you will *know* that I am in my Father and that you are in
me, just as I am in you.'

The apostle Paul obviously experienced that when he wrote in a
letter to Timothy: 'I *know* whom I have trusted . . .' Elsewhere he
tells us the reason for this inner certainty: 'God's Spirit joins
himself to our spirits to declare that we are God's children' (Romans
8:16).

b. The Word of God (verses 21–26)

Jesus calls the Helper the Spirit who reveals the *truth* (verse
17). He is given to teach the disciples all things, and bring to their
remembrance all that Jesus had said to them (verse 26). What Jesus
said, God said (verse 24). This is the basis of the Christian belief
that the New Testament writers as well as the Old were 'inspired
by God' as they wrote. The apostle Paul claimed: 'We have not
received this world's spirit; instead, we have received the Spirit
sent by God, so that we may know all that God has given us. So
then, we do not speak in words taught by human wisdom, but in

words taught by the Spirit, as we explain spiritual truths to those who have the Spirit' (1 Corinthians 2:12–13).

Jesus teaches in this passage that it is in keeping God's Word (that is, what we call the Old and New Testaments) that God makes himself known to the believer. This is his answer to Judas's question, 'Lord, how can it be that you will reveal yourself to us and not to the world?' We show our love to God by reading, receiving and obeying God's Word. He shows his love to us in revealing himself to us as we read, by the work of the Holy Spirit (see verses 21–26). If the Bible is coming alive to us, this is an assurance that God is with us. If we neglect to read the Bible or disobey its commands, then we prove that we do not love God (verse 24).

In his fascinating book, *Miracle on the River Kwai*, Ernest Gordon tells of the way in which the reading of the Gospels came alive to desperate men in a prisoner-of-war camp. They searched the New Testament to find whether Jesus was real and relevant to them in their situation. 'Through our readings and discussions we gradually came to *know Jesus*. He was one of us. He would understand our problems because they were the kind of problems He had faced Himself . . . As we read and talked He became flesh and blood . . . What He was, what He did, what He said all made sense to us.'

c. The peace of God (verses 27–31)

Whatever the circumstances the disciples would be given the assurance of God's presence by the gift of peace. This too would be a fruit of the Spirit, which would become theirs after Jesus had returned to his Father. Satan, or the ruler of this world, may be powerful; but he has no power over Jesus (verse 30). He might do all he could to divert Jesus from his path to the cross. But Jesus Christ knew that peace is to be found in loving God and doing his will whatever it costs (verse 31).

On 23 January 1964 Pastor Yona Kanamuzayi was martyred in the Ruanda riots. He was carried off from his home, shot in the back and then pushed into the river. Before he died he prayed for his executioners, and then, according to an eyewitness, went to his death joyfully singing a hymn. The soldiers were all amazed. They had never before seen a man walking calmly and unafraid to meet his murderers as he did, 'like a man just taking a stroll'.* But when Jesus said to the disciples, 'Peace is what I leave with you; it is my own peace that I give you', he meant it to be true for all believers, whatever the circumstances. When he said to the disciples 'Come let *us* go from this place', he made it clear that future crises and difficulties would be faced together with him.

Questions for discussion

1. 'When that day comes, you will *know* . . . that you are in me, just as I am in you' (verse 20). How do we answer the objection that Christian certainty of this kind breeds complacency, and is the height of presumption?

2. 'Whoever *accepts* my commandments and *obeys* them is the one who loves me' (verse 21). What grounds are there for *accepting* the commands of Jesus as we find them in the New Testament? Do these words teach us anything about our attitude to the Bible as a whole?

3. 'Jesus Christ knew that *peace* is to be found in loving God and doing his will whatever it costs.' Do we know that to be true, for us? Does it always exclude fear and worry (verse 27)? How is inner peace maintained?

33   A new community

15:1-17

15 *'I am the real vine, and my Father is the gardener.* ²*He breaks off every branch in me that does not bear fruit, and he prunes every branch that does bear fruit, so that it will be clean and bear more fruit.* ³*You have been made clean already by the teaching I have given you.* ⁴*Remain united to me, and I will remain united to you. A branch cannot bear fruit by itself; it can do so only if it remains in the vine. In the same way you cannot bear fruit unless you remain in me.*

5 *'I am the vine, and you are the branches. Whoever remains in me,*

*J. E. Church, *Forgive them*, p. 15.

and I in him, will bear much fruit; for you can do nothing without me. *⁶Whoever does not remain in me is thrown out like a branch and dries up; such branches are gathered up and thrown into the fire, where they are burnt. ⁷If you remain in me and my words remain in you, then you will ask for anything you wish, and you shall have it. ⁸My Father's glory is shown by your bearing much fruit; and in this way you become my disciples. ⁹I love you just as the Father loves me; remain in my love. ¹⁰If you obey my commands, you will remain in my love, just as I have obeyed my Father's commands and remain in his love.*

11 'I have told you this so that my joy may be in you and that your joy may be complete. ¹²My commandment is this: love one another, just as I love you. ¹³The greatest love a person can have for his friends is to give his life for them. ¹⁴And you are my friends if you do what I command you. ¹⁵I do not call you servants any longer, because a servant does not know what his master is doing. Instead, I call you friends, because I have told you everything I have heard from my Father. ¹⁶You did not choose me; I chose you and appointed you to go and bear much fruit, the kind of fruit that endures. And so the Father will give you whatever you ask of him in my name. ¹⁷This, then, is what I command you: love one another.'

I have often heard it said, 'Surely I can be a Christian without going to church!' Sometimes these words are no more than a cover up for laziness; sometimes they express a genuine disenchantment with the church and 'organized religion'. But certainly they express a view that is far removed from New Testament Christianity and the teaching of Jesus.

In this chapter Jesus makes it clear that it is God's purpose to do his work in the world through his people, not only as individuals, but as members of a divine community—as branches in a vine. If we belong to Christ, as one branch sharing the very sap or life of the Vine, then we also belong to his church. There are other branches in the Vine, even as there are many members of a body (to use Paul's metaphor for the church), or stones in a building, or members of a family, or citizens of a kingdom. God's purpose is that once we belong to him, we belong to his people.

In the Old Testament the vine was often used as a picture of God's relationship to his people. God planted the vine, and cared for it. Israel was the vine itself. Sadly, Israel failed in many ways to fulfil God's purposes (Isaiah 5:1–7). She was described as a 'rotten worthless vine' (Jeremiah 2:21) or 'empty vine' (Hosea 10:1, AV). In Jesus, however, the people of God will fulfil God's purposes. 'I am the *real* vine,' said Jesus. Fruitfulness of life and character (*cf.* Galatians 5:22, 23) and effective service and prayer (verse 16) are part of God's purpose for his people. They depend on '*remaining*' (or 'abiding', RSV) in Jesus, in fellowship with other believers. To 'remain' in Christ means at least four things for the individual and the church.

a. To be united to Christ

A Christian is not only someone who believes certain facts about Christ, or who follows the Christian ethic. He is someone as vitally in touch with Christ by faith as a fruit-bearing branch is vitally in touch with the vine. As the branch shares the sap, the life of the vine, and so bears fruit, so the Christian, united by faith to Christ, shares his life. He produces the fruit of the Spirit—love, joy, peace, patience, kindness, goodness, faithfulness, humility, self-control (Galatians 5:22, 23).

The tragedy of Judas is that, although he associated with the disciples and with Jesus, he was like a branch apparently attached to the vine, but in fact dead and fruitless. So he did not really share in the 'life' of Christ. He was not 'clean' (verse 3) like the other disciples. He had not believed in Christ in his heart, or obeyed him in his life. So, tragically, he was cast forth as a dead branch and withered. When vine wood is dead it is useless for anything but burning. A dead, nominal Christian, even though he may be a church member or office-bearer, is as useless in the service of God as a dead branch. He must likewise expect the judgment of God unless he is cleansed and united by faith to Christ.

b. To be dependent on Christ

To 'remain' in Christ is to depend on Christ (verses 4–5). 'For you can do nothing without me.' How do we learn daily dependence upon Jesus Christ? The clearest answer is in verse 7: 'If you remain in me and my words remain in you, then you will ask for anything you wish, and you shall have it.' In the same way that we need daily bread to sustain us physically, so we need spiritual food, the words of Jesus and of the Bible, to sustain us spiritually. For as Jesus himself quoted, 'Man cannot live on bread alone, but needs every word that God speaks' (Matthew 4:4). Jesus goes on to say that if his words take root in our lives by daily meditation upon them, and by daily obedience, we shall also learn dependence on him through prayer. When we are dependent upon Christ our prayers become more confident (verse 7) and our lives become more Christlike (note 'much fruit' in verse 8). In this way we bring glory to God and demonstrate the genuineness of our own discipleship (verse 8).

There is one other way that God teaches us dependence upon Jesus. 'He *prunes* every branch that does bear fruit, so that it will be clean and bear more fruit.' There is dead wood (sins of pride, independence, selfishness, impatience, covetousness and so on) that needs to be cut away from our lives if we are to become more Christlike. So God's word to us is sometimes like a pruning-knife. It hurts, it rebukes us, it humbles us. Sometimes he speaks to us through the circumstances of our lives, and chastens and humbles us through suffering, disappointment, or bereavement. If he does it is *always* for our good—that we might be more Christlike. The divine Gardener is a God of love.

c. To be obedient to Christ

To 'remain' in Christ involves *obedience*. It is not enough to believe—and then to sit back for 'God to do it all'. Jesus commands us to 'remain in my love' in response to his great love for us (verse 9). Indeed we can abide in his love only as we keep his commandments. The Christian is not saved by keeping God's law—for he cannot perfectly fulfil the demands of God's law. Only Jesus Christ has done that. But once the Christian has been saved from the guilt and judgment he deserves by the free and undeserved love of God in Christ, he responds to that love by keeping God's law. That is the way he shows his love to Christ. That is also the only way to discover the joy that Jesus gives (verse 11).

Jesus commands us not only to love him, but also to *love one another* (verse 12). Here again, he does not ask from us slavish obedience, or make unreasonable demands. Jesus' love for us was such that he gave his life for us. He gave his life that we might become his friends. He reveals his Father's secrets to his friends as they obey him. He chose us to be his friends that we might go into the world to be effective (fruitful) in our lives and witness. All the strength, love, patience, endurance and tolerance needed to love one another can be ours as we ask God to give this to us in the name of Jesus. I once asked a young woman, who had left a good secretarial job in this country to serve God overseas, to tell me the difference Jesus Christ had made to her life since she personally began to follow him. She said: 'I found that God gave me the power to love those I would not normally like.' When certain pagans in the first century said 'See how these Christians love one another', it was a tribute to the life and love of Jesus in the personalities of Christian disciples, as they obeyed his command to 'remain in his love'.

d. To continue with Christ

To 'remain' in Christ means literally to continue in dependence and obedience all our lives. It is not enough to begin with Christ, we must *continue* with him. Jesus said elsewhere, 'Whoever holds out to the end will be saved' (Matthew 10:22). Paul, putting it from God's point of view, said, 'I am sure that God, who began this good work in you, will carry it on until it is finished on the Day of Christ Jesus' (Philippians 1:6). We must 'keep on working with fear and trembling to complete (our) salvation, because God is always at work in (us) to make (us) willing and able to obey his own purpose' (Philippians 2:12). As we continue to trust and obey, so his life and power will sustain us to the end, and so we prove to be his disciples indeed.

To read the Bible, to pray and to have fellowship with other Christians is far more than a religious duty. It is the God-appointed way to trust and obey the risen Lord and to receive his life and grace and power for effective Christlike living.

Questions for discussion

1. How do you answer the person who says, 'Surely I can be a Christian without going to church'? Make use of the teaching from this passage.
2. What does the passage tell us about the difference between a 'nominal' and a 'real' Christian?
3. What does 'bearing fruit' really mean in John 15?
4. Does the teaching of this passage support the view that the

secret of growing in the Christian life is 'to let go and let God'?
If not, why not?

5. What does it mean to 'keep on working with fear and trembling
to complete (our) salvation' (Philippians 2:12)? How is that
thought supported in this passage?

34   A new responsibility

15:18 – 16:11

18 *'If the world hates you, just remember that it has hated me first.*
¹⁹If you belonged to the world, then the world would love you as its
own. But I chose you from this world, and you do not belong to it; that
is why the world hates you. ²⁰Remember what I told you: "No slave
is greater than his master." If they persecuted me, they will persecute
you too; if they obeyed my teaching, they will obey yours too. ²¹But
they will do all this to you because you are mine; for they do not know
the one who sent me. ²²They would not have been guilty of sin if I
had not come and spoken to them; as it is, they no longer have any
excuse for their sin. ²³Whoever hates me hates my Father also. ²⁴They
would not have been guilty of sin if I had not done among them the
things that no one else ever did; as it is, they have seen what I did, and
they hate both me and my Father. ²⁵This, however, was bound to
happen so that what is written in their Law may come true: "They
hated me for no reason at all."

26 *'The Helper will come—the Spirit, who reveals the truth about*
God and who comes from the Father. I will send him to you from the
Father, and he will speak about me. ²⁷And you, too, will speak about
me, because you have been with me from the very beginning.

16 *'I have told you this, so that you will not give up your faith. ²You*
will be expelled from the synagogues, and the time will come when any-
one who kills you will think that by doing this he is serving God. ³People
will do these things to you because they have not known either the
Father or me. ⁴But I have told you this, so that when the time comes
for them to do these things, you will remember that I told you.

'I did not tell you these things at the beginning, for I was with you.
⁵*But now I am going to him who sent me, yet none of you asks me
where I am going.* ⁶*And now that I have told you, your hearts are full
of sadness.* ⁷*But I am telling you the truth: it is better for you that I
go away, because if I do not go, the Helper will not come to you. But
if I do go away, then I will send him to you.* ⁸*And when he comes, he
will prove to the people of the world that they are wrong about sin
and about what is right and about God's judgment.* ⁹*They are wrong
about sin, because they do not believe in me;* ¹⁰*they are wrong about
what is right, because I am going to the Father and you will not see
me any more;* ¹¹*and they are wrong about judgment, because the
ruler of this world has already been judged.'*

Archbishop Temple once said that 'the Church of Jesus Christ is
the only society that exists for the benefit of its non-members'.
Christian fellowship is important. But so is Christian witness. Jesus
has called and chosen his church 'to *go* and bear much fruit' in the
world. As Jesus taught elsewhere, his disciples are called to be *salt*
in society (Matthew 5:13). Salt was rubbed into meat to prevent it
from going bad. They were to be *light*, so that men would see their
good works and glorify their Father in heaven (Matthew 5:16).

Here Jesus reminds the disciples of the difficulties and dangers
of speaking (literally, 'witnessing') for him in a hostile world. A
witness is someone who gives evidence of what he knows and has
seen. 'You, too, will speak about me, because you have been with
me from the very beginning.' We also ought to be witnesses to
Jesus Christ by our lives, by our actions, and by our words. This
passage reminds us of two important facts that we need to bear in
mind as we witness for Christ in the world.

a. The strength of the opposition

When John speaks about 'the world' he does not refer to the
physical universe which God has created. He speaks of 'society
organized without reference to God'. He speaks of the hearts and
minds of men which are still controlled by the 'ruler of this world'
(John 14:30), who is elsewhere called Satan, or 'the adversary'.
Jesus did not think of Satan as an impersonal force, but as a personal adversary. '*He* has no power over me' (John 14:30). A
Christian is someone who has handed over his life to the control of

159

Jesus Christ, so he no longer belongs to 'the world' in the sense that we have defined the term (verse 19). Jesus Christ has chosen us 'from this world' and freed us from its grip and its anti-Christian pressures. Now this brings us in conflict with society, even as it brought Jesus into conflict with the society of his own day. So the Christian may well face the hatred of the world, as Jesus did (verses 18–19). He may well suffer persecution for his loyalty to the teaching of Jesus, for the words of Jesus expose man's lack of knowledge of God, and his rebellion against God (verses 21–23), and his refusal to accept the evidence of the life and works of Jesus. A minister friend of mine was talking for hours to an argumentative student who would not accept the message that my friend was explaining to him. The student rejected the message repeatedly. At last the minister said, 'It is time to go now: but I hope you realize that it is not me you are fighting against, but God.' The student's face suddenly changed. 'I'd never thought of it like that before', he said.

There is no real cause to hate Christ and his words (verse 25). But men in their stubbornness and pride will sometimes do so, and in doing so will hate and persecute his followers too. 'Remember what I told you: "No slave is greater than his master." '

In some parts of the world today men suffer physically for their loyalty to Christ.* For many of us, however, persecution may come with a raised eyebrow, a sneer, a supercilious smile, a taunt about 'religious mania', a deliberate cold-shouldering by some of our friends, a quite irrational outburst of annoyance from our parents or even from a minister of religion. The disciple of Jesus Christ should never underestimate the strength of the opposition.

b. The power of the Spirit (15:26 – 16:11)

'The Helper *will* come—the Spirit' (verse 26). Yet again the disciples are reminded of the resources of God to help them face and overcome the opposition of the world. Jesus could say that the ruler of this world has no *power* over him (14:30). The Christian can say that 'the Spirit who is in you is more powerful than the spirit in those who belong to the world' (1 John 4:4). The Helper bears witness to the truth through the disciples' witness to Christ. He will keep them from falling away under persecution by re-

*See, *e.g.*, Pastor Richard Wurmbrand, *Tortured for Christ*.

minding them of Jesus' words (16:3–4). Indeed, Jesus' own departure to his Father will be an advantage to the disciples, because the Helper can do his work through them only after Jesus' death, resurrection and ascension.

What is the work that the Holy Spirit will do? The Greek word for 'to prove' (verse 8: RSV 'convince') that John uses means both to *convict*—that is, to show that something is wrong—as well as to *convince*—that is, to demonstrate the truth of something. The weakness of our witness in the world lies precisely along these lines. We fail to convince people of their need of Christ, and we fail to convince them of the truth about Christ. The Holy Spirit is given to God's people to do precisely these two things.

We notice too that man's greatest 'sin' is to fail to believe in Jesus (verse 9). The Holy Spirit alone can show men the seriousness of unbelief. The world needs to be convinced also that the death of Jesus was not the end nor the failure of his mission (verse 10). It was in fact the righteous act of a loving God, who thereby is able to declare sinners 'righteous', 'accepted' or 'in the right', because of Christ's death for sin on the cross. Finally, the world needs to see that by Christ's death Satan is judged and defeated and will eventually be destroyed (verse 11). How will men today believe such astonishing truths? Jesus encourages the disciples to believe that when the Spirit comes upon them, he will both convict and convince the unbeliever. There is a great deal of evidence that the Spirit does the same work today through the witness of ordinary Christians.

Questions for discussion

1. 'The Church of Jesus Christ is the only society that exists for the benefit of its non-members.' If we assume that to be true, does the church we know best organize its structures and its life as if it believes that statement? In the light of Jesus' teaching ought it to be doing so, and if so, how?

2. Jesus spoke of the difficulties of 'witnessing' to a hostile world. What does Christian witness mean in our situation, and what are the difficulties that we face?

3. How does the teaching of Jesus about the Holy Spirit (15:26 – 16:11) help us to go about the task of 'witnessing' for Christ? What are the vital factors for effective witness today?

161

35 Jesus encourages the disciples

16:12–33

12 'I have much more to tell you, but now it would be too much for you to bear. ¹³When, however, the Spirit comes, who reveals the truth about God, he will lead you into all the truth. He will not speak on his own authority, but he will speak of what he hears, and will tell you of things to come. ¹⁴He will give me glory, because he will take what I say and tell it to you. ¹⁵All that my Father has is mine; that is why I said that the Spirit will take what I give him and tell it to you.

16 'In a little while you will not see me any more, and then a little while later you will see me.'

17 Some of his disciples asked among themselves, 'What does this mean? He tells us that in a little while we will not see him, and then a little while later we will see him; and he also says, "It is because I am going to the Father." ¹⁸What does this "a little while" mean? We don't know what he is talking about!'

19 Jesus knew that they wanted to question him, so he said to them, 'I said, "In a little while you will not see me, and then a little while later you will see me." Is this what you are asking about among yourselves? ²⁰I am telling you the truth: you will cry and weep, but the world will be glad; you will be sad, but your sadness will turn into gladness. ²¹When a woman is about to give birth, she is sad because her hour of suffering has come; but when the baby is born, she forgets her suffering, because she is happy that a baby has been born into the world. ²²That is how it is with you: now you are sad, but I will see you again, and your hearts will be filled with gladness, the kind of gladness that no one can take away from you.

23 'When that day comes, you will not ask me for anything. I am telling you the truth: the Father will give you whatever you ask him for in my name. ²⁴Until now you have not asked for anything in my name; ask and you will receive, so that your happiness may be complete.

25 'I have used figures of speech to tell you these things. But the time will come when I will not use figures of speech, but will speak to you plainly about the Father. ²⁶When that day comes, you will ask

him in my name; and I do not say that I will ask him on your behalf, ²⁷*for the Father himself loves you. He loves you because you love me and have believed that I came from God.* ²⁸*I did come from the Father, and I came into the world; and now I am leaving the world and going to the Father.'*

29 Then his disciples said to him, 'Now you are speaking plainly, without using figures of speech. ³⁰*We know now that you know everything; you do not need someone to ask you questions. This makes us believe that you came from God.'*

31 Jesus answered them, 'Do you believe now? ³²*The time is coming, and is already here, when all of you will be scattered, each one to his own home, and I will be left all alone. But I am not really alone, because the Father is with me.* ³³*I have told you this so that you will have peace by being united to me. The world will make you suffer. But be brave! I have defeated the world!'*

There is a delightful legend told of the Angel Gabriel. It is said that he asked Jesus after he had returned to heaven, how his mission on earth would now be accomplished. Jesus replied that he had left the mission in the hands of his eleven disciples. 'But what if they fail?' asked Gabriel. According to the legend, Jesus replied, '*I have no other plans*'. That is only a legend. But the *fact* was that Jesus did leave the task of spreading his message throughout the world to a small company of very ordinary men and women. All were very liable to fail in their task, if left to themselves. It was as they began to realize that Jesus was soon to die, that Jesus gave them specific encouragement to prepare them for the immediate crisis, and the future responsibilities.

First he acknowledged that there were some things that he could not tell them yet, for they would not be able to understand (verse 12). It is good for all of us to recognize that there are some truths and doctrines which we cannot fully understand until we know more about Christ and his purposes. However, Jesus promises certain things for the future.

a. The guidance of the Spirit, who reveals the truth (verses 12–15)

Here is another assurance to the Christian church that Jesus Christ foresaw the importance of leaving a record of the events and teaching of his life marked with the authority of God. So he promises the Spirit, who reveals the truth, to the disciples to lead them into truth, to reveal the things of God to them and to make Jesus real to them (see 14:25–26). Elsewhere in the Gospels Jesus assumes the authority of the Old Testament. What the Scripture said, God said (compare Genesis 2:24 with Matthew 19:4–6).

Here he promises to the disciples, and later promises to Paul (compare Galatians 1:11–17 with 1 Corinthians 2:12, 13), that his Spirit would guide their writing and inspire their words.

The corollary for us is that we should approach the whole Bible humbly as revealing the truth of God, and ask for the guidance of God the Holy Spirit in seeking to understand and interpret it. A sun-dial is a useless object while the clouds obscure the sun. Once the sun shines on it, it fulfils its purpose. So the reading of the Bible can be a pointless exercise without the illumination of the Spirit who reveals the truth.

b. The joy of a personal relationship (verses 16–28)

When Jesus spoke about leaving the disciples, they naturally thought that their personal relationship with him would be broken and lost for ever. In saying that in 'a little while' they would see him no more, he obviously referred to his impending death. What did he mean, then, when he said 'then a little while later you will see me' and 'because I am going to the Father'? Jesus seems to be referring to both his resurrection and ascension. At his death they would be sad. But at his resurrection their sorrow would turn into joy, for they would see him again (verses 19–22).

But Jesus promises still more to the disciples. 'Your hearts will be filled with gladness, the kind of gladness that no one can take away from you' (verse 22). Even after the resurrection and ascension the disciples will continue to enjoy a personal relationship with Jesus Christ, and then they will understand more easily some of the more enigmatic sayings of Jesus which as yet they cannot grasp. The joy of that personal relationship will be fostered and will grow as they learn to have increasing confidence in prayer to the Father in the name of Jesus. Clearly, the coming of Jesus Christ into the world and his return to his Father is part of the Father's loving plan to deepen our relationship with himself (verses 23–24).

164

Jesus' clear claims to come from the Father and to return to him strengthen the faith of the disciples (verses 29–30). But he continues to warn them of their own moment of failure when they will all forsake him and only his Father will remain faithful. Nevertheless, in their relationship with Jesus Christ there will be peace and joy and victory in the midst of trouble and difficulty. Jesus does not save us from tribulation, but he saves us *in* it. He gives us the strength to have victory in spite of it.

Questions for discussion

1. 'Christians make the Bible mean whatever they want it to mean.' How does the teaching of Jesus in this passage help Christians to answer that criticism? How do we know that our understanding of the Bible is under the guidance of the Holy Spirit?

2. How does the teaching of this passage help us to understand what Christians mean by the inspiration and the authority of the New Testament?

3. 'Jesus does not save us from tribulation, but he saves us *in* it.' What does this mean in your own experience? Does it mean that a Christian should never feel sorrow or depression?

36 Jesus prays for his disciples

17:1–19

17 *After Jesus finished saying this, he looked up to heaven and said, 'Father, the hour has come. Give glory to your Son, so that the Son may give glory to you.* ²*For you gave him authority over all mankind, so that he might give eternal life to all those you gave him.* ³*And eternal life means knowing you, the only true God, and knowing Jesus Christ, whom you sent.* ⁴*I have shown your glory on earth; I have finished the work you gave me to do.* ⁵*Father! Give me glory in your presence now, the same glory I had with you before the world was made.*

6 *'I have made you known to those you gave me out of the world.*

They belonged to you, and you gave them to me. They have obeyed your word, [7]*and now they know that everything you gave me comes from you.* [8]*I gave them the message that you gave me, and they received it; they know that it is true that I came from you, and they believe that you sent me.*

9 '*I pray for them. I do not pray for the world but for those you gave me, for they belong to you.* [10]*All I have is yours, and all you have is mine; and my glory is shown through them.* [11]*And now I am coming to you; I am no longer in the world, but they are in the world. Holy Father! Keep them safe by the power of your name, the name you gave me, so that they may be one just as you and I are one.* [12]*While I was with them, I kept them safe by the power of your name, the name you gave me. I protected them, and not one of them was lost, except the man who was bound to be lost—so that the scripture might come true.* [13]*And now I am coming to you, and I say these things in the world so that they might have my joy in their hearts in all its fullness.* [14]*I gave them your message, and the world hated them, because they do not belong to the world, just as I do not belong to the world.* [15]*I do not ask you to take them out of the world, but I do ask you to keep them safe from the Evil One.* [16]*Just as I do not belong to the world, they do not belong to the world.* [17]*Dedicate them to yourself by means of the truth; your word is truth.* [18]*I sent them into the world, just as you sent me into the world.* [19]*And for their sake I dedicate myself to you, in order that they, too, may be truly dedicated to you.*'

It has been said that you can learn much about a man if you hear him pray. Certainly that is true of this prayer of Jesus. There are a number of references in the Gospels to Jesus praying. We read that Jesus prayed all night before he chose his disciples. It is important to make time for unhurried prayer before making a big decision. On another occasion the disciples asked him to teach them to pray; and he gave them the model prayer, 'The Lord's Prayer' (Luke 11:1). Jesus prayed in the wilderness before he began his public ministry (Matthew 4 and Luke 4), and in the Garden of Gethsemane before he was arrested and crucified (Matthew 26:36–44). Peter, James and John may well have overheard some of his prayer on that occasion. No doubt he prayed privately at home or in the Galilean and the Judean hills, as well as publicly in the synagogue and temple. He lived his whole life in perfect fellowship with his Father.

In John's Gospel this is the only account of a long prayer by Jesus. Did they take it down at the time? Did Jesus remind them of it afterwards? Was this one of those occasions when the Holy Spirit 'brought things to their remembrance'? We do not know. But we catch a glimpse in this prayer of the unique and intimate relationship that Jesus had with his heavenly Father; we also learn something of the deep concerns of his heart for his own mission and for his disciples.

Sometimes this prayer is called 'the high priestly prayer' because in the Old Testament the high priest would go once a year into the Holiest of Holies and pray for the people before he offered a sacrifice for their sins. So Jesus prays, before he lays down his own life as a sacrifice for the sins of the whole world. We stand on holy ground.

The prayer divides naturally into three sections: (a) A prayer concerning his own mission (verses 1–5); (b) a prayer for the eleven disciples (verses 6–19); (c) a prayer for those who would believe in Christ through the teaching of the disciples—that is, a prayer for the church throughout all ages (verses 20–26).

a. A prayer for himself (verses 1–5)

This is expressed in the words, 'Give glory to your Son, so that the Son may give glory to you.' Jesus knows that God's moment has come, 'the hour' to which all the ministry of Jesus has been moving. The climax of his life-work is upon him. It will be a moment of glory for Jesus and his heavenly Father. That is what he confidently prays for. He has glorified God by his obedience to God's will, and now in accomplishing the work which God had given him to do, he could already say 'I have shown your glory on earth'.

Stop and think for a moment. In what way do you think Jesus most honoured God? By his matchless teaching? 'No man ever spoke like this man!' By his miraculous signs? 'Surely God was with him' in those. Yet, astonishingly, the hour of glory is clearly *his death*. It was by his death that he made possible eternal life. It is by knowing God and Jesus Christ as Sin-bearer, Saviour and King, that we enjoy eternal life.

Of course the death of Jesus Christ is only the moment of glory because it led on to the resurrection and ascension. The resurrection demonstrated God's acceptance of the death of Christ as a

167

sufficient sacrifice for sins. So Jesus also prays that the Father would honour him with the sharing of the Father's glory once more (verse 5).

b. A prayer for the disciples (verses 6–19)

We notice that when Jesus described his disciples in this prayer, he does not regard them as men who had become camp-followers and only vaguely believed in him. A disciple then, as a disciple now, knows something of the person and character of God (verse 6). God is not a remote and impersonal power or 'an old man in the sky'. He is a heavenly Father revealed in flesh and blood in Jesus Christ. It is impossible to be a Christian unless in some measure God has revealed himself to us in the Person of Jesus Christ. A disciple belongs to Christ. A disciple obeys God's word (so he must read it), for the very words of God have been given to us by Jesus (verse 8). The disciple has a definite view of Jesus Christ. He knows he is not merely a man. He comes from God, and the disciple believes God has sent him (verse 8). Christian discipleship has nothing to do with vague beliefs about God. There are certain objective truths which a Christian must believe if he is to experience eternal life. Furthermore, a Christian disciple is not only someone who belongs to God but in whom in some measure the power and love of Jesus is exhibited. As Jesus put it, 'My glory is shown through them' (verse 10).

c. What does Jesus pray for his disciples?

1. *Keep them safe by the power of your name, the name you gave me, so that they may be one just as you and I are one* (verse 11). Jesus was concerned that his disciples should be kept in *unity*; he was concerned that no-one should *fall away* (verse 12). (Judas was already judged and lost.) He was concerned that they should experience the joy of Jesus in all their circumstances (verse 13) and that they should be kept from the evil one (verse 15).

2. *Dedicate them to yourself by means of the truth* (verses 14–19). Christians are 'in the world' but not 'of the world' (verses 14, 15, 18). Furthermore, Jesus sends them into the world, and has consecrated himself in obedience even unto death so that they might similarly dedicate themselves to the task of doing God's will in the

168

world. How are Christians to be kept true to Christ in their involvement in the world? It is not easy. For we have to avoid two extremes. As Dr. Leighton Ford has expressed it: the two extremes are 'isolation from the world and imitation of the world. God does not want us to be either holier-than-thou or worldlier-than-thou. He wants us to be like Jesus, who came into the world to save the world. And this demands an attitude both of separation from the world in its sin, and identification with the world in its need. Without separation—the difference Christ makes—we have an audience but nothing to say. Without identification, we have something to say but no audience.'*

So the only way for the Christian to walk wisely in such a situation is by being 'dedicated (to God) by means of the truth', with mind and life moulded by the truth of the Bible and example of Jesus.

Questions for discussion

1. Jesus regarded prayer as important. What practical steps could we take to make certain we give prayer the same priority in our lives?
2. 'I have finished the work you gave me to do.' Jesus had a clear sense of a mission accomplished as he drew near to 'the hour' of his death. Should we have a similar sense of mission, and personal goals for our own individual lives? What motivated Jesus?
3. 'Christian discipleship has nothing to do with vague beliefs about God.' What essential truths ought a Christian to believe according to this passage?
4. What principles help us to be 'in the world' but not 'of it'? What are the chief dangers to avoid?

37 Jesus prays for the church

17:20–26
20 *'I pray not only for them, but also for those who believe in me because of their message.* 21*I pray that they may all be one. Father!*
  *Leighton Ford, The Christian Persuader.

May they be in us, just as you are in me and I am in you. May they be one, so that the world will believe that you sent me. ²²*I gave them the same glory you gave me, so that they may be one, just as you and I are one:* ²³*I in them and you in me, so that they may be completely one, in order that the world may know that you sent me and that you love them as you love me.*

24 'Father! You have given them to me, and I want them to be with me where I am, so that they may see my glory, the glory you gave me; for you loved me before the world was made. ²⁵*Righteous Father! The world does not know you, but I know you, and these know that you sent me.* ²⁶*I made you known to them, and I will continue to do so, in order that the love you have for me may be in them, and so that I also may be in them.'*

The twentieth century has seen a growing concern among Christians to get together and to demonstrate a greater degree of visible unity. For the many different Christian denominations and sects today present a confusing and divided church to the unbelieving world. The German philosopher Nietzsche may well have had this partly in mind when he said 'I will not believe in the Redeemer of these Christians until I see that they are redeemed.'

It is all the more striking, therefore, to realize that when Jesus began to pray for those who would later come to believe in him through the word of the disciples (verse 20) he was praying as much for the church in the twentieth century as in the first.

It seems as if Jesus knew well what would spoil the witness of the church more easily than anything else. In spite of the commands of Jesus that we love one another, only too often the church has been split and divided and disunited. So he prays for the Christian church in every generation when he says 'that they may all be one, Father! May they be in us, just as you are in me and I am in you. May they be one, so that the world will believe that you sent me' (verse 21).

But what kind of unity did Jesus have in mind? This prayer emphasizes two essential factors.

a. It was a unity of spirit

'I pray that they may all be one. Father! May they be in us, just as you are in me and I am in you. May they be one, so that the world will believe that you sent me' (verse 21). The unity between Christians should be like the spiritual unity between God the Father and God the Son. Now this is possible only as we share in the glory of Christ—his living presence and power (verse 22). This is possible through the gift of the Holy Spirit, whom God gives to those who believe in Christ, as we have noticed in an earlier passage (14:16).

So there is a spiritual unity between all Christians, between all those who possess the Spirit of Christ. We are then 'all one in Christ Jesus', and it is important that we recognize that fact. Different denominations cannot break that unity. The church is an organism, not an organization, and all those 'in Christ' are in the *one* family.

If, then, there is already a spiritual unity between Christians, for what is Jesus praying? The answer lies in verse 23. Jesus prays that Christians may become '*completely* one'. Writing to the Christians at Ephesus, Paul exhorted them, 'Do your best to *preserve* the unity which the Spirit gives by means of the peace that binds you together' (Ephesians 4:3). A spiritual unity between real Christians is already there, but it needs to be recognized, maintained and wherever possible *visibly* demonstrated, so that the world may know that the coming of Jesus Christ has really broken down man-made barriers. Paul gives a wonderful picture of Christians growing together in love and friendship with one another and with Christ, exercising their gifts for the good of the church and the glory of God, 'reaching to the very height of Christ's full stature' (Ephesians 4:13). Perfect love and unity will of course be fully achieved only when we share in the glory of Christ in heaven. Jesus prays that we may enjoy that experience one day, and promises until then a progressively deeper revelation and experience of the love of God in our lives (verses 24–25). It is 'Christ in us' (verse 26) which is the basis of our spiritual unity with other Christians. This is something that all Christians can experience.

b. It was a unity of truth (verses 6, 8, 17–26)

Why is work towards visible unity in the church so slow and difficult? Undoubtedly it is partly a lack of love between Christians. It is also, and this is much more difficult, disagreement about the essential truths upon which Jesus clearly assumed that we would be united when he prayed that we might become perfectly one. The words of Paul again confirm the teaching of Jesus in this prayer. We are not to be like children 'carried by the waves and blown about by every shifting wind of the teaching of deceitful men, ... Instead, by *speaking the truth* in a spirit of love, we must grow up in every way to Christ, who is the head' (see Ephesians 4:14–16). The church of Jesus Christ is not only built on love, but upon the foundation of the apostles and prophets and Jesus Christ, the chief corner-stone (Ephesians 2:20). Unity must therefore be based upon the truth of Christ and his apostles. Jesus confirms this when he prays that the disciples might be *consecrated in the truth* (RSV), and adds *'your word is truth'* (verse 17). He has already stated that the disciples have kept God's word (verse 6) and received the words of Christ as God's words, and that they know *in truth* that Jesus comes from God. There can be no real unity therefore if a fellow Christian denies that Jesus comes from God, or claims that his teaching is not authoritative. That is why there is a place for contending for the truth of the gospel in the church of God. But if God calls us to do this, we must 'speak the truth in love'. The old maxim is still helpful today in these matters: 'In necessary things, unity; in doubtful things, liberty; in all things, charity.'

Questions for discussion

1. What causes disunity between Christians in the local church? In what way should we seek to be more 'completely one' with those with whom we differ in our own church?

2. If Christians are already 'one in the spirit' is it necessary for different Christian churches to seek more 'visible' unity? If so, what is the relevant teaching in this passage? What are the chief difficulties? What is the best way forward?

3. What attitude should we take towards those within the church who deny the deity of Jesus and the authority of his and the apostles' teaching? How far should we co-operate with 'un-orthodox' Christians? What principles should guide us?

4. What are your hopes, fears and realistic expectations about any current schemes for church unity? How does this passage help us to determine our attitude towards them?

38   The arrest and trial

18:1–11

18 After Jesus had said this prayer, he left with his disciples and went across the brook called Kidron. There was a garden in that place, and Jesus and his disciples went in. ²Judas, the traitor, knew where it was, because many times Jesus had met there with his disciples. ³So Judas went to the garden, taking with him a group of Roman soldiers, and some temple guards sent by the chief priests and the Pharisees; they were armed and carried lanterns and torches. ⁴Jesus knew everything that was going to happen to him, so he stepped forward and asked them, 'Who is it you are looking for?'

5 'Jesus of Nazareth,' they answered. 'I am he,' he said.

Judas, the traitor, was standing there with them. ⁶When Jesus said to them, 'I am he,' they moved back and fell to the ground. ⁷Again Jesus asked them, 'Who is it you are looking for?'

'Jesus of Nazareth,' they said.

8 'I have already told you that I am he,' Jesus said. 'If, then, you are looking for me, let these others go.' (⁹He said this so that what he had said might come true: 'Father, I have not lost even one of those you gave me.')

10 Simon Peter, who had a sword, drew it and struck the High Priest's slave, cutting off his right ear. The name of the slave was Malchus. ¹¹Jesus said to Peter, 'Put your sword back in its place! Do you think that I will not drink the cup of suffering which my Father has given me?'

The story is told of a visitor to a military hospital during the Second World War. Seeing a soldier with only one arm, the visitor said sympathetically, 'I'm sorry you had to lose your arm.' The soldier replied, 'I didn't lose it. I gave it.'

As Jesus moved steadily towards his death it becomes increasingly clear that his attitude, reflected in some measure by the soldier, is one of total self-giving. According to the other Gospels (see

Matthew 26:36–46, Mark 14:32–42, Luke 22:39–46) it was in the garden (verse 1) that Jesus prayed, 'Father . . . all things are possible for you. Take this cup of suffering away from me. Yet not what I want, but what you want.' Jesus then went on to give his life voluntarily according to the will of his Father.

The garden where Jesus prayed lay just across the Kidron Valley. It was a favourite meeting place for Jesus and his disciples. While Jesus was praying, the disciples, worn out by the emotional excitement of the preceding hours, fell fast asleep. Suddenly, they were rudely awakened by the shining of torches and the clatter of weapons. Judas had betrayed his Master. How little Judas understood Jesus! Was it necessary to bring torches, when the Passover new moon shone so brightly? Did Judas really think he needed not only the temple police ('guards') but a *speira* (band) of soldiers as well, which could mean as many as 200–600 men? The world has always overestimated the strength of force of arms.

It is at this point that we are very much aware that we are following an eyewitness account. The mention of guards as well as soldiers; the careful description of Jesus' conversation with these men (verses 4–8); the mention of Malchus by name (verse 10): even the careful note that it was the *right* ear which was affected by Peter's blow (verse 10). But note, too, the contrasts outlined here.

We have already noticed *the treachery of Judas* (see chapter 13). This is contrasted here with *the majesty of Jesus*. Jesus is the master of this situation, not Judas. It is Jesus who takes the initiative and steps forward to reveal his identity. It is Jesus whose words, 'I am he' (the divine name), and whose manner caused the soldiers to fall to the ground. How puny man is before Jesus Christ! These men came brandishing their weapons, confident in their resources, cocksure about success. 'We'll soon silence this crazy preacher with his hopeless idealism,' they seem to say. Then a look. A word. The divine name; and they shrink from his presence, afraid to lift a finger to touch him. We sometimes swagger into Christ's presence like that. We come to demolish him with our clever arguments. We come to put him where we want him, out of the way, locked up. He is too disturbing. But if we really met him we too would fall to the ground. We would learn that no man could take his life from him. He laid it down of his own free will.

The second contrast is between Jesus and Peter, and it reveals again *the impulsiveness of Peter* contrasted with *the steadiness of*

Jesus. Peter makes a brave but misguided attempt to resist the
arrest of his Master (verse 10). But it shows us only too clearly that
he still has not understood that Jesus must suffer. Jesus, on the
other hand, steadily moves to his death, determined to fulfil the
promises of God (verse 9) and to do the will of God (verse 11).
The cup which Jesus must drink is the cup of suffering. Sometimes
in the Old Testament the prophets refer to the cup of God's
wrath and judgment upon sin (see Isaiah 51:17, 22). In a real sense
Jesus knew he must drink such a cup if man is to be saved from the
judgment he deserves. In full knowledge of what he was doing,
Jesus majestically and steadily moves forward to the cross.

Questions for discussion
1. What do we learn in this passage from the attitude in the garden
of (a) Judas (b) the soldiers (c) the disciples ?
2. How does the example of Jesus in this story help us to face up
to suffering and the demands of Christian discipleship ?
3. In Matthew's account of verses 10 and 11 (*cf.* Matthew 26:50–56)
Jesus also said to Peter, 'All who take the sword will die by the
sword.' What does this teach us about the Christian's attitude to
violence ? (Compare Romans 13.)

39 Jesus is tried by the ecclesiastical leaders

18:12–27
*12 Then the Roman soldiers with their commanding officer and the
Jewish guards arrested Jesus, bound him, 13and took him first to Annas.
He was the father-in-law of Caiaphas, who was High Priest that
year. 14It was Caiaphas who had advised the Jewish authorities that it
was better that one man should die for all the people.*

*15 Simon Peter and another disciple followed Jesus. That other
disciple was well known to the High Priest, so he went with Jesus into
the courtyard of the High Priest's house, 16while Peter stayed outside*

by the gate. Then the other disciple went back out, spoke to the girl at the gate, and brought Peter inside. [17]The girl at the gate said to Peter, 'Aren't you also one of the disciples of that man?'

'No, I am not,' answered Peter.

18 It was cold, so the servants and guards had built a charcoal fire and were standing round it, warming themselves. So Peter went over and stood with them, warming himself.

19 The High Priest questioned Jesus about his disciples and about his teaching. [20]Jesus answered, 'I have always spoken publicly to everyone; all my teaching was done in the synagogues and in the Temple, where all the people come together. I have never said anything in secret. [21]Why, then, do you question me? Question the people who heard me. Ask them what I told them—they know what I said.'

22 When Jesus said this, one of the guards there slapped him and said, 'How dare you talk like that to the High Priest!'

23 Jesus answered him, 'If I have said anything wrong, tell everyone here what it was. But if I am right in what I have said, why do you hit me?'

24 Then Annas sent him, still bound, to Caiaphas the High Priest.

25 Peter was still standing there keeping himself warm. So the others said to him, 'Aren't you also one of the disciples of that man?'

But Peter denied it. 'No, I am not,' he said.

26 One of the High Priest's slaves, a relative of the man whose ear Peter had cut off, spoke up. 'Didn't I see you with him in the garden?' he asked.

27 Again Peter said 'No'—and at once a cock crowed.

It is a sad commentary on the twentieth century that we know only too much about rigged trials and miscarriages of justice. In the early sixties a British lawyer, Peter Benenson wrote: 'Every day, opening your paper in the morning, you read that somewhere in the world human beings are being thrown into prison, tortured or killed because their political or religious views are at variance with those of their government.' Since these words were written, millions of people have been persecuted; there have been countless victims of injustice and incredible cruelty; and still in many countries violent suppression of religious and political opposition is the established procedure.

The trial, or more accurately, *trials* of Jesus, therefore, have a familiar ring about them to modern ears. It is in the garden that the temple police and the Roman soldiers bind Jesus, as Judas looks on, and take him to the residence of the Jewish high priest. First, Jesus is brought to Annas, who had been high priest from AD 6 to 15, and was now high priest emeritus (verse 13). Later he is taken to Caiaphas (possibly in another room in the same house), who is the son-in-law of Annas, and the high priest at the time (verse 24). It was Caiaphas, John reminds us, who had callously said: 'It is better for you to let one man die for the people.' The high priests under the Romans were always more concerned with expediency than principle. They were the arch-collaborators with the hated enemy, Rome. The office of high priest was a matter of intrigue and bribery. The fact that four of the sons of Annas became high priest and that Caiaphas was his son-in-law speaks for itself.

At the same time that Jesus was being questioned, Simon Peter was able to use the influence of a friend, another disciple, to gain admittance to the servants' quarters of the high priest's residence. The trial of Jesus and Peter's denial take place at the same time. As Jesus calmly and majestically moves forward to his 'hour' of destiny, we notice both injustice and inconsistency towards him.

a. Injustice (verses 19–24)

There is no doubt that the so-called trial by Annas and Caiaphas was thoroughly rigged. In Jewish law a prisoner could be condemned only by witnesses. That is why Jesus refuses to answer the high priest's questions (verse 19), and insists that he has spoken clearly enough on a number of public occasions for witnesses to give their evidence. The other Gospels make it clear that when Caiaphas produced witnesses to speak against Jesus, even though they were 'planted' to discredit Jesus, they still could not agree (Mark 14:53–59). The action of one of the temple police (verse 22) is only too typical of those who have already made up their mind about Jesus, and who do not care for truth or justice. A brainwashing session in a totalitarian state is not far removed from this scene. Jesus understands only too well those who suffer injustice at the hands of unscrupulous men.

There is a passage in the Jewish Talmud which reads: 'Woe to the house of Annas: woe to their serpents hiss: they are High Priests: their sons are keepers of the treasury: their sons-in-law are guardians of the Temple and their servants beat the people with staves.' Annas was as notorious as he was unscrupulous. He and his family had made a pile of money. The temple stalls which Jesus overturned because of the shameful exploitation of the poor were probably part of what was called 'the bazaars of Annas'. Jesus therefore had attacked the vested interests of Annas. When a man's financial interests are affected, he is sometimes only too ready to resist truth and to stoop to injustice.

b. Inconsistency (verses 15–18, 25–27)

If there is injustice among the enemies of Jesus, there is also inconsistency and failure among his friends. The other disciples have already deserted Jesus. Peter at least has the courage to stay as near as he can. But Peter now finds himself cut off from his friends and open to the curiosity, ridicule and possible hostility of the world. The words of the waitress, 'Aren't you also one of the disciples of that man ?', could read, 'Surely *you* are not another of this man's disciples ?' It is not easy to remain loyal to Christ in such situations. Peter had boasted so much, but was as weak as any of us when he was tested. Twice more he was questioned. Each time he denied that he belonged to Jesus, the other Gospels recording that he did this with oaths and curses (see Mark 14:71).

If we wonder how Peter could be so inconsistent, perhaps the other Gospels give us the clue. In the Garden of Gethsemane Jesus had encouraged the disciples to 'keep watch, and pray' in readiness for the hours of crisis which were before them. Peter like the others slept rather than prayed. Jesus understands. 'The spirit is willing, but the flesh is weak' (Mark 14:38). But there is no short cut to consistent Christian living. As Richard Trench expressed it:

> 'Lord, what a change within us one short hour
> Spent in Thy presence will avail to make!
> What heavy burdens from our bosoms take!
> What parched ground refresh us with a shower!
> We kneel, how weak! We rise, how full of power!
> Why therefore should we do ourselves this wrong
> Or others, that we are not always strong,
> That we are sometimes overborne with care,
> That we should ever weak or heartless be,

Anxious or troubled—when with us is prayer
And joy and strength and courage are with Thee?'

Questions for discussion
1. 'The high priests under the Romans were always more concerned with expediency than principle.' In what matters of daily life do we find ourselves most liable to the same temptation?
2. Jesus knew what it was to suffer injustice and to be denied *human* rights—yet alone the rights of the Son of God. What would he have us do about the injustices in our own community and in the wider world? What should our attitude be if we ourselves suffer unjustly? (Compare 1 Peter 2:18ff.)
3. What reasons would we give for Peter's denial of Jesus? How can we avoid failing Jesus in the same way?

40 Jesus is brought before the Roman governor-general

18:28 – 19:16
28 *Early in the morning Jesus was taken from Caiaphas' house to the governor's palace. The Jewish authorities did not go inside the palace, for they wanted to keep themselves ritually clean, in order to be able to eat the Passover meal.* 29*So Pilate went outside to them and asked, 'What do you accuse this man of?'*

30 Their answer was, 'We would not have brought him to you if he had not committed a crime.'

31 Pilate said to them, 'Then you yourself take him and try him according to your own law.'

They replied. 'We are not allowed to put anyone to death.' (32*This happened in order to make the words of Jesus come true, the words he used when he indicated the kind of death he would die.)*

33 Pilate went back into the palace and called Jesus. 'Are you the King of the Jews?' he asked him.

34 Jesus answered, 'Does this question come from you or have others told you about me?'

179

35 Pilate replied, 'Do you think I am a Jew? It was your own people and the chief priests who handed you over to me. What have you done?'

36 Jesus said, 'My kingdom does not belong to this world; if my kingdom belonged to this world, my followers would fight to keep me from being handed over to the Jewish authorities. No, my kingdom does not belong here!'

37 So Pilate asked him, 'Are you a king, then?'

Jesus answered, 'You say that I am a king. I was born and came into the world for this one purpose, to speak about the truth. Whoever belongs to the truth listens to me.'

38 'And what is truth?' Pilate asked.

Then Pilate went back outside to the people and said to them, 'I cannot find any reason to condemn him. 39But according to the custom you have, I always set free a prisoner for you during the Passover. Do you want me to set free for you the King of the Jews?'

40 They answered him with a shout, 'No, not him! We want Barabbas! (Barabbas was a bandit.)

19 Then Pilate took Jesus and had him whipped. 2The soldiers made a crown out of thorny branches and put it on his head; then they put a purple robe on him 3and came to him and said, 'Long live the King of the Jews!' And they went up and slapped him.

4 Pilate went out once more and said to the crowd, 'Look, I will bring him out here to you to let you see that I cannot find any reason to condemn him.' 5So Jesus came out, wearing the crown of thorns and the purple robe. Pilate said to them, 'Look! Here is the man!'

6 When the chief priests and the temple guards saw him, they shouted, 'Crucify him! Crucify him!'

Pilate said to them, 'You take him, then, and crucify him. I find no reason to condemn him.'

7 The crowd answered back, 'We have a law that says he ought to die, because he claimed to be the Son of God.'

8 When Pilate heard this, he was even more afraid. 9He went back into the palace and asked Jesus, 'Where do you come from?'

But Jesus did not answer. 10Pilate said to him, 'You will not speak to me? Remember, I have the authority to set you free and also to have you crucified.'

11 Jesus answered, 'You have authority over me only because it was given to you by God. So the man who handed me over to you is guilty of a worse sin.'

12 When Pilate heard this, he tried to find a way to set Jesus free.

But the crowd shouted back, 'If you set him free, that means that you are not the Emperor's friend! Anyone who claims to be a king is a rebel against the Emperor!'

13 When Pilate heard these words, he took Jesus outside and sat down on the judge's seat in the place called 'The Stone Pavement.' (In Hebrew the name is 'Gabbatha'.) ¹⁴*It was then almost noon of the day before the Passover. Pilate said to the people, 'Here is your king!'*

15 They shouted back, 'Kill him! Kill him! Crucify him!'

Pilate asked them, 'Do you want me to crucify your king?'

The chief priests answered, 'The only king we have is the Emperor!'

16 Then Pilate handed Jesus over to them to be crucified.

All of us at some time or another are called upon to make some important decisions in life. It may be decisions over examination subjects, or marriage, or a job, or where we're going to live. There will also be decisions about God, and our relationship to Jesus Christ. The results of these decisions usually affect many other people as well as ourselves. I cannot imagine a more important decision, with such far-reaching consequences, than that which faced Pontius Pilate, the governor of Judea, when Jesus was brought before him.

Under the Roman occupation, the Jews had no legal right to put any man to death (verse 31). This was why they were prepared to call Pilate, the Roman governor in Jerusalem, in the small hours of the morning, to ratify their decision to sentence Jesus to death. In the plan of God they also strangely fulfilled Jesus' own insistence that he would be 'lifted up' to die (verse 32 and John 12:32) Jesus died on a cross not only at the hands of wicked men, but in accordance with God's 'own plan' (Acts 2:23). There is a sad comment here on the motives of the Jewish leaders in bringing Jesus to Pilate (verse 28).* They were so blind and full of hatred for Jesus that they could see no inconsistency in carefully avoiding ceremonial defilement (verse 28) and at the same time setting aside justice and truth, and planning a calculated political murder.

Such is the awful plight of men, religious or otherwise, who 'strain a fly out of (their) drink, but swallow a camel!' (Matthew

---

*The Jew believed that 'the dwelling places of Gentiles are unclean'. This was particularly true at Passover time when in a Gentile home leaven might be found, whereas it was banished from every Jewish home as part of the Passover festival (see Exodus 12:15, 18–20). Leaven was a symbol of wickedness and corruption.

23:24); who make ritual more important than honesty in business, faithfulness in marriage, truthfulness in speech, love for their neighbour, and openness to Jesus Christ and his truth.

The conversation between the Jews and Pilate shows that there was no love lost between them (verses 29–32; cf. John 18:35; 19:6, 12, 14–16, 20–22). Pilate must have been an able administrator to have been offered such a difficult job in the civil service of Rome. But history records that he handled the Jews in Palestine with little sympathy or understanding. He had nothing but contempt for them and was often cruel and brutal. Already the Jews in Palestine had threatened to report him to the Emperor Tiberius for his mishandling of civilian affairs. Pilate then was not too happy in his job or sure of his position. This may help us to understand the overwhelming impression in this story of the indecision of Pilate and, in contrast, the resolution of Jesus.

a. The indecision of Pilate

At first Pilate speaks contemptuously to Jesus. 'Are *you* (emphatic word in the Greek) the King of the Jews?' Clearly the Jews have dropped the charge of blasphemy in coming to Pilate, and concentrated on the supposed political offence. Jesus answers quietly and authoritatively (verses 34, 36) and explains that his kingdom is not of this world, and that he has come to witness to truth, not to reign by force. If Pilate cared about truth, he would acknowledge Jesus. Pilate's question 'And what is truth?' might have been jesting or wistful. Certainly he knows Jesus is innocent (verse 38). But Pilate is like many of us. If truth is inconvenient and demands recognition and commitment, we hesitate.

Pilate hoped first that the Jews would make the decision for him and release Jesus (verses 39, 40). Then he compromised and arranged that Jesus should be flogged, hoping this would satisfy the Jews (verses 1–4). Flogging was severe and brutal. The back of Jesus would have been exposed to the lash of a long leather thong studded at intervals with pellets of lead and sharp pieces of bone. Few remained conscious under such treatment. Some died. Some went mad. In addition to this, there is the mocking of the soldiers (verse 3). The words 'Here is the man!' (verse 5) are clearly meant to arouse pity for the helpless victim.

But Pilate must still make a decision. 'Crucify him! Crucify him!'

(verse 6). The crowds are stirred up by their leaders and are thirsty for his blood. Pilate still tries to avoid a decision. He is frightened, probably for superstitious reasons, when the Jews bring forward the blasphemy charge again (verse 7); but the real issue that settles the matter for Pilate is threat of the loss of his own personal position and standing as Governor. 'If you set him free, that means that you are not the Emperor's friend!' (verse 12). Men today will still sell their soul because of fear of men, or fear that they will lose position or prestige. However much Pilate wanted 'to wash his hands' (see Matthew 27:24) of the whole affair, the moment came when he had to take sides for or against Christ. He tried feebly once more to get the Jews to make the decision for him (verses 14–15). Then he handed him over to them to be crucified.

There is one dramatic postscript of the trial that must have left Pilate cynical and astonished. When Pilate said 'Do you want me to crucify your king?' the chief priests, successors of those who acknowledged God as the only real King, could say, 'The only king we have is the Emperor.' Continued indecision and rejection of Jesus Christ leads not only to the abandonment of justice and truth, but of *God himself*.

b. The resolution of Jesus

Here again we have one of the great contrasts in this Gospel. Pilate, weak and indecisive: Jesus, strong and resolute, It is clear that Pilate is far more 'on trial' than Jesus. It is Jesus, too, in spite of the flogging and the mocking, who has the greater authority. Only once in this narrative does Jesus refuse to answer one of Pilate's questions. Jesus always knows whether we really want to know the answer to our theological and intellectual questions. He once refused to answer Herod's questions (Luke 23:9). Jesus has no time for triflers, or those who show curiosity without concern. Pilate thought that he had the life of Jesus in his hands. Jesus knew that what authority Pilate had as Governor was given him by God. 'You have authority over me only because it was given to you by God' (verse 11). In the knowledge that God was working out his purpose through Pilate and the chief priests and the Jews, Jesus, 'when he was insulted, he did not answer back with an insult; when he suffered, he did not threaten, but placed his hopes in God, the righteous Judge' (1 Peter 2:23).

183

We, too, stand on trial as we consider this story. There is real danger in continually trying to avoid making any decision about Jesus Christ. Anatole France, in the book *Mother of Pearl*, attempts to draw an imaginary picture of Pilate near the end of his life. He depicts him living in lust and luxury in a villa on the shores of Italy. Many years had passed when one day a visitor from Rome, conversing with him, said, 'By the way, Pilate, were you not a procurator in Judea when they put to death that man Jesus?' Pilate, looking at his visitor through bleary eyes, said, 'Jesus, Jesus, I don't remember the name!' This is an imaginary conversation without historical foundation. But it is true philosophically. We can even forget Jesus if we avoid his claims often enough.

Questions for discussion
1. What differences are there in the attitude to Jesus of (a) the Jewish leaders (b) Pilate (c) the soldiers (d) the crowds? Do I find these same attitudes to Jesus in me?
2. What does Jesus mean when he says, 'My kingdom does not belong to this world?' Should the followers of Jesus say the same thing? If so, how does it apply to everyday life and our earthly 'citizenship'?
3. How do we answer Pilate's question, 'And what is truth' (18:38)?
4. 'You have authority over me only because it was given to you by God' (verse 11). What do these words, and this passage, tell us about the relationship between God's sovereign plan and man's responsibility? How should these two truths affect our lives?

41 The death of Jesus

19:17–30
So they took charge of Jesus. [17]*He went out, carrying his cross, and came to 'The Place of the Skull,' as it is called. (In Hebrew it is called 'Golgotha.')* [18]*There they crucified him; and they also crucified two other men, one on each side, with Jesus between them.* [19]*Pilate wrote a*

notice and had it put on the cross. 'Jesus of Nazareth, the King of the Jews,' is what he wrote. [20]Many people read it, because the place where Jesus was crucified was not far from the city. The notice was written in Hebrew, Latin, and Greek. [21]The chief priests said to Pilate, 'Do not write "The King of the Jews," but rather, "This man said, I am the King of the Jews."'

22 Pilate answered, 'What I have written stays written.'

23 After the soldiers had crucified Jesus, they took his clothes and divided them into four parts, one part for each soldier. They also took the robe, which was made of one piece of woven cloth without any seams in it. [24]The soldiers said to one another, 'Let's not tear it; let's throw dice to see who will get it.' This happened in order to make the scripture come true:

> 'They divided my clothes among themselves
> and gambled for my robe.'

And this is what the soldiers did.

25 Standing close to Jesus' cross were his mother, his mother's sister, Mary the wife of Clopas, and Mary Magdalene. [26]Jesus saw his mother and the disciple he loved standing there; so he said to his mother, 'He is your son.'

27 Then he said to the disciple, 'She is your mother.' From that time the disciple took her to live in his home.

28 Jesus knew that by now everything had been completed; and in order to make the scripture come true, he said, 'I am thirsty.'

29 A bowl was there, full of cheap wine; so a sponge was soaked in the wine, put on a stalk of hyssop, and lifted up to his lips. [30]Jesus drank the wine and said, 'It is finished!'

Then he bowed his head and died.

There's a story which a well-known archbishop of Paris used to tell.

A number of youths were idling around the famous cathedral of Notre Dame, not knowing what to do with themselves. Someone suggested that it would be fun to go into the cathedral and make a bogus confession to the priest there, accusing himself of all the worst sins he could think of, just to see what the priest would say and do. One of the boys did just that. When he had finished, the old priest looked up and said to him: 'Go and kneel at the foot of that figure of Christ on a cross over there, and look at his face, and say deliberately and slowly, "I know you died for me; and I don't care a damn." Then come back and tell me.' The boy went, and was so moved by what he saw, that he found it impossible to say those words. 'I know that story's true,' the old archbishop would say, 'because *I* was that boy.'

Countless lives have been changed by a look at Jesus on the cross.

It was about the sixth hour, according to John's reckoning, when Pilate passed the death sentence on Jesus (verse 14). The Jewish custom was to reckon hours from 6 a.m. to 6 p.m. and 6 p.m. to 6 a.m. If John is consistent with Mark's Gospel, then he is probably following the western system of reckoning from midnight to noon and noon to midnight, a system which was in use in Asia Minor at the time this Gospel was written. So at 6 a.m. the death sentence was passed on Jesus. As was customary, Jesus began to carry his own cross, which, as the other Gospels tell us, proved too much for him. So Simon from Cyrene was press-ganged into carrying it for him (see Matthew 27:32). Golgotha was possibly so named because it was a hill outside the city walls which was similar in shape to a skull. Calvary is the Latin name for it. The story is told with breathless simplicity and great restraint.

a. The meaning of his death

1. *His physical and mental sufferings.* John does not not make much of this. 'There they crucified him; and they also crucified two other men, one on each side, with Jesus between them' (verse 18). Nothing could be more restrained. But we must remember that the horrors of crucifixion and the shame of such a death would be known well enough in the first century. Cicero talked about 'the most cruel and horrifying death' of crucifixion.

The shame of it may be seen in the fact that it was unthinkable that a Roman citizen should be crucified. Crucifixion was possible only for slaves and criminals. The Jew, for his part, believed that any man 'hanged on a tree' was under 'God's curse' (see Deuteronomy 21:23; Galatians 3:13).

It is hard for us to imagine the physical pain and mental sorrow that Jesus suffered. Crucifixion followed the long periods of cross-questioning, the flogging with the Roman cat-o'-nine-tails, the insults, blows, spitting and scorn of his enemies, the desertion, betrayal, denial of many of his friends. Jesus, whose thoughts were always for others first (see verses 26, 27), gave no expression of his own physical and mental anguish until the main purpose for his death was finished (verse 28). Then, and not until then, he cried 'I am thirsty'. The scripture he fulfilled here was probably Psalm 69:21, 'When I was thirsty, they offered me vinegar'.

If God became man in Christ, then God is concerned about the physical and mental sufferings of mankind. A lady whom I was visiting, and who was enduring great suffering, found great comfort in being able to say sincerely, 'I could never have suffered more than he did.' Bishop Stephen Neill has written:* 'There are times when we are so afflicted by the suffering in the world that we are inclined to shake our fists at the sky, and blaspheme whatever God allows such things to happen in His World. If we are concerned about the hundreds of thousands of refugees, who are homeless and workless and rotting in the cheerless camps that are all that civilization has been able to provide for them, we may be inclined to say to Him, "What is the use of telling these people about you? You know nothing of what it is really like to be a refugee, and therefore you are not in a position to help them." To which He might well answer, "Did you never read that it is written, the Son of man hath not where to lay his head?" Or watching some helpless and cruel suffering, we might resentfully say, "Why do you permit such suffering that you do not share?" and we might not immediately catch His answer, "Well, have you ever tried being crucified?"'

2. *His spiritual sufferings.* There is no doubt, however, that the soul of his sufferings was the sufferings of his soul. John has made it clear that Jesus deliberately laid down his life to drink the cup of God's judgment upon sin (verse 11). It was in this way that God would be glorified. This was the purpose of the hour to which he had come. John also makes it clear that Jesus is doing this consciously and deliberately in order to fulfil the Old Testament prophecies which explain God's plan of suffering for sin. Jesus was indeed king, but his throne was a cross. He was king not only of the Jews but of the world, as the placard in Hebrew, Greek and Latin script, which Pilate cynically wrote, ironically suggested. The seamless robe (verse 24) which the soldiers cast lots for, just as the Old Testament had suggested (Psalm 22), might well have reminded John of the high priest's robe, without seam, and woven

*S. C. Neill, *Christian Faith Today*, p. 262.

in one piece from top to bottom. For John's eye for symbolism would not fail to see that the great High Priest had now at last laid down his own life, a perfect sacrifice for sin, and had 'finished' (verse 30) the work which God had given him to do.

'It is finished' is one word in the Greek. The other Gospels say that Jesus died with a great shout (Matthew 27:50; Mark 15:37; Luke 23:46). 'Finished' was a shout of triumph, not a cry of resignation. It is left to the other Evangelists to describe the darkness, symbolic of the sin of the world which he bore in our place; Matthew speaks of the cry of desolation, 'My God, my God, why did you abandon me?' It was this spiritual agony that was now *finished*. It was the bearing of the sin of the world, your sin and mine, coming as a cloud between the Father and the Son, which had to be endured and which was now *finished*. God's judgment had fallen. God had 'condemned sin in (the) human nature' of Jesus (Romans 8:3). God had 'made the punishment fall on him' (Isaiah 53:6). 'God was in Christ reconciling the world to himself' (2 Corinthians 5:19, RSV). Jesus became 'a curse for us' that he might redeem us 'from the curse that the Law brings' (Galatians 3:13). Jesus was the Lamb of God, taking away the sin of the world (John 1:29). He had now finished that great work. The Father was satisfied. It was the moment of glory. 'For God loved the world so much that he gave his only Son, so that everyone who believes in him may not die but have eternal life' (John 3:16). He suffered judgment that we might escape judgment. He drank the cup of wrath that we might receive the cup of salvation. He died that we might live.

When the famous eighteenth-century preacher Charles Simeon was an undergraduate at King's College, Cambridge, he became conscious of his own lack of a real experience of forgiveness of sins and knowledge of God. He read a book in Passion week by a certain Bishop Wilson on the sacrifice of Christ. Simeon tells us, 'The thought came into my mind, What, may I transfer all my guilt to another? Has God provided an Offering for me, that I may lay my sins on His head? Then, God willing, I will not bear them on my own soul one moment longer. Accordingly I sought to lay my sins upon the sacred head of Jesus.'* That is what the cross makes possible. That is the basic meaning of the death of Christ.

*Handley C. G. Moule, *Charles Simeon*, pp. 25, 26.

b. The challenge of his death

It is impossible to remain neutral in the shadow of the cross. As John describes some of those who watched him die we find three attitudes to Jesus and his sufferings which we still find today.

1. *Rejection.* There are no signs that the Jewish leaders are at all repentant. They are furious that Pilate will not take down the placard 'Jesus of Nazareth, the King of the Jews'. Pilate is truculent. 'What I have written stays written' (verse 22). It is strange that he is so firm here, and so weak when it comes to deciding about Jesus. The Jewish leaders have made their decision. They have rejected Jesus. Many in the crowd had weakly followed the party line (verse 15). It was outright rejection, and weak acquiescence to the majority view, which led to the murder of Jesus Christ.

2. *Indifference.* One of the other Evangelists records Jesus' prayer at the crucifixion: 'Forgive them, Father! They don't know what they are doing' (Luke 23:34). The soldiers who nailed Jesus to the cross were in many respects ignorant of what they were doing. They were carrying out their duty in doing a very unpleasant task. But although, like Jesus, we can recognize their ignorance, it is hard to excuse their indifference. They gambled as he suffered. They stood at the feet of the Son of God, and simply passed another day without, it seems, a thought about him.

Studdart Kennedy expressed the indifference of twentieth-century man when he wrote:

'When Jesus came to Golgotha, they hanged Him on a tree,
They drove great nails through hands and feet and made a
      calvary.
They crowned Him with a crown of thorns, red were His wounds
      and deep,
For those were crude and cruel days, and human flesh was cheap.
When Jesus came to Birmingham, they simply passed Him by,
They never hurt a hair of Him, they only let Him die.
For men had grown more tender, and they would not give Him
      pain,
They only just passed down the street, and left Him in the rain.'

3. *Loyalty.* Jesus mentions four women who remained loyal to him through it all. John was with them, and that same day began to discover the fellowship and friendship that binds together those

who are loyal to the Saviour of the world (verses 26, 27). What is your attitude to Jesus Christ?

Questions for discussion
1. In what ways does the death of Jesus help us to face up to the fact of suffering today?
2. What had Jesus 'finished' by his death (verse 30)? How does his 'finished' work on the cross help us?
3. Describe the different responses to the crucifixion of Jesus in this passage? What should our response be?

42 The burial of Jesus

19:31–42
31 Then the Jewish authorities asked Pilate to allow them to break the legs of the men who had been crucified, and to take the bodies down from the crosses. They requested this because it was Friday, and they did not want the bodies to stay on the crosses on the Sabbath, since the coming Sabbath was especially holy. 32So the soldiers went and broke the legs of the first man and then of the other man who had been crucified with Jesus. 33But when they came to Jesus, they saw that he was already dead, so they did not break his legs. 34One of the soldiers, however, plunged his spear into Jesus' side, and at once blood and water poured out. (35The one who saw this happen has spoken of it, so that you also may believe. What he said is true, and he knows that he speaks the truth.) 36This was done to make the scripture come true: 'Not one of his bones will be broken.' 37And there is another scripture that says, 'People will look at him whom they pierced.'

38 After this, Joseph, who was from the town of Arimathea, asked Pilate if he could take Jesus' body. (Joseph was a follower of Jesus, but in secret, because he was afraid of the Jewish authorities.) Pilate told him he could have the body, so Joseph went and took it away. 39Nicodemus, who at first had gone to see Jesus at night, went with

Joseph, taking with him about thirty kilogrammes of spices, a mixture of myrrh and aloes. ⁴⁰The two men took Jesus' body and wrapped it in linen with the spices according to the Jewish custom of preparing a body for burial. ⁴¹There was a garden in the place where Jesus had been put to death, and in it there was a new tomb where no one had ever been buried. ⁴²Since it was the day before the Sabbath and because the tomb was close by, they placed Jesus' body there.

In his best seller, *The Ring of Truth*, the famous writer and translator J. B. Phillips sums up his years of study in the New Testament by saying, 'It is my serious conclusion that we have here in the New Testament, words that bear the hall-mark of reality and the ring of truth.' It is hard to escape that 'ring of truth' as we read the careful eyewitness account of the burial of Jesus.

In the Old Testament the Jews have a law which says: 'If a man has committed a crime punishable by death and he is put to death, and you hang him on a tree, his body shall not remain all night upon the tree, but you shall bury him the same day, for a hanged man is accursed by God' (Deuteronomy 21:22, 23 RSV). The Romans often left their criminals to die on the cross for days, and then refused to bury them. But these Jews, just as we would expect, took great pains to keep one part of the law (verse 31) while remaining blind to more important issues. It is not enough to be a correct, orthodox, religious enthusiast. Our attitude to Christ matters far more than our attitude to religion.

The rest of this chapter emphasizes, with the kind of detail that rings true, five further truths about the death of Christ.

a. It was real (verses 32, 34)

A few years ago considerable publicity was given to a book by Dr. Hugh Schonfield* which asserted that Jesus did not die on the cross, but was so drugged that he was able to survive crucifixion and the tomb. So it is important to notice the witness of John that Jesus was certainly dead when the soldiers came; and the piercing of his side was further confirmation for any who might wonder. It is hard to believe that Nicodemus and Joseph, in handling the body of Jesus, would not be certain of this fact too.

*H. J. Schonfield, *The Passover Pilot*.

b. It was costly (verses 35-36)

When John solemnly records the evidence of the witness who saw blood and water come from the pierced side of Jesus, it is clear that he regards this phenomenon as highly significant. In 1862 Sir James Simpson, writing from a medical point of view on the causes of the death of Christ, tried to account for the blood and water by suggesting that it was the sign of a ruptured heart. The blood of the heart mingled with the fluid of the pericardium which surrounds the heart. The spear pierced the pericardium and the mingled fluid and blood came forth. He believed that Jesus had died of a broken heart.

More recent medical knowledge tends to support the view that the spear had drawn water from a dilated stomach as well as blood from the heart.* This too could have been due to his distress in the garden, and the sufferings of mind and soul.†

Certainly his death was no ordinary death. It was costly. It involved the crushing sorrow of bearing the sin of the world.

c. It was life-giving (verse 34)

It is hard to believe that John did not see symbolism in the blood and water. The blood speaks of the forgiveness made possible by the death of Christ. An early Jewish Christian wrote, 'Without the shedding of blood there is no forgiveness of sins' (Hebrews 9:22, RSV). The water usually signifies in John the new life (see John 4:14; 7:38, 39). God offers us, on the grounds of the death of Christ, forgiveness and new life.

d. It was planned (verse 36)

John is quick to point out that, even in the small incidents connected with the death of Christ, God's hand is seen in it all: 'This was done to make the scripture come true: "Not one of his bones will be broken."'

---

*See R. V. G. Tasker, *The Gospel according to St. John*, pp. 212, 213.
†A. Rendle Short, *The Bible and Modern Medicine*, chapter 9 on 'The physical cause of the death of Christ'.

e. It was powerful (verses 38–42)

The death of Jesus Christ is already beginning to exercise its power in drawing men out to acknowledge him. Joseph of Arimathea and Nicodemus (see John 3) were two influential men in the Jewish Council, or Sanhedrin, who up to this point had remained as secret disciples. The fear of men had kept them from making known their secret allegiance to Jesus. But the death of Christ moves them not only to identify themselves with his cause, but to express generous though belated love for Jesus. Joseph unashamedly asks Pilate for permission to take away the body of Jesus (verse 38). Nicodemus, known for his retiring nature, brings vast quantities of costly spices for the burial (verse 39). Together they take the body down and bind it in the traditional way with linen cloths, placing the spices in between (verse 40). The tomb was a new tomb in a garden. Before the sabbath came they had reverently and lovingly laid the body of Jesus in the tomb and sealed up the entrance with a boulder (Mark 15:46).

The death of Jesus Christ still has power to call people from their fears and from their half-heartedness to unashamed service. C. T. Studd said about a turning-point in his own life: 'When I came to see that Jesus Christ had died for me, it didn't seem hard to give up all for him. It seemed just common, ordinary, honesty.'*

Questions for discussion
1. It has been argued that if we could be sure of the historical truths of the Gospels there would be no need for faith. So we can believe in Jesus, it is said, whether all the events in these Gospels are true or not. What grounds have we in this passage for believing that historical truth and personal faith are *both* important and should not be divorced one from the other?
2. What do we learn about the meaning of Jesus' death in this passage?
3. Nicodemus and Joseph were secret disciples (see also John 3:1–10 and 7:50–52) until this moment. Why do you think they 'sat on the fence' until the death of Jesus? Why do we? What is it about the death of Jesus that draws out whole-hearted discipleship?

*Norman P. Grubb, *C. T. Studd: Cricketer and Pioneer*.

43 Evidence for the resurrection

20:1-10

20 Early on Sunday Morning, while it was still dark, Mary Magdalene went to the tomb and saw the stone had been taken away from the entrance. ²She went running to Simon Peter and the other disciple, whom Jesus loved, and told them, 'They have taken the Lord from the tomb, and we don't know where they have put him!'

3 Then Peter and the other disciple went to the tomb. ⁴The two of them were running, but the other disciple ran faster than Peter and reached the tomb first. ⁵He bent over and saw the linen wrappings, but he did not go in. ⁶Behind him came Simon Peter, and he went straight into the tomb. He saw the linen wrappings lying there ⁷and the cloth which had been round Jesus' head. It was not lying with the linen wrappings but was rolled up by itself. ⁸Then the other disciple, who had reached the tomb first, also went in; he saw and believed. (⁹They still did not understand the scripture which said that he must rise from death.)

10 Then the disciples went back home.

Some years ago a young lawyer named Frank Morison decided to write a book to prove that Jesus never rose from the dead. He thought that it would be an easy thing to do. 'As a young man,' he tells us, 'when I first began seriously to study the life of Christ, I did so with a very definite feeling that, if I may so put it, His history rested upon very insecure foundations.' However, as he began to study critically all the evidence he discovered that 'slowly but very definitely the conviction grew that the drama of those unforgettable weeks of human history was stranger and deeper than it seemed.' In the end Frank Morison wrote one of the best books ever written on the evidence for the resurrection. The book that he originally intended to write became 'the book that was never written'. Convinced by the cumulative evidence of the New Testament records, he argued instead that Jesus must have risen from the dead!*

*Frank Morison, *Who moved the stone?*

John begins his evidence for the resurrection with the visit of Mary Magdalene to the garden tomb very early on the Sunday morning that followed the crucifixion. She was astonished to find that the heavy boulder, which had been placed in a groove and rolled in front of the entrance to the burial cave, had been rolled away. Hurriedly she fetched Peter and John, who came to examine the tomb and find out what had happened.

John came to the conclusion that morning that Jesus was not dead but risen (verse 8). But it was not the scriptures that convinced him then — though later Psalm 16:10* was often quoted as a foretelling of the resurrection. On that Sunday morning it was other evidence that convinced John. Evidence that he saw with his own eyes. '*He saw and believed.*'

What did John see that convinced him and Frank Morison and millions of others that Jesus was risen? We notice in this passage two lines of evidence.

a. The empty tomb (verses 1–2)

We must not isolate this evidence from the rest (see the next section, verses 11–31); but John certainly attaches importance to it. Later, when the Christians preached the resurrection, they knew that anyone could check up on this claim. The tomb was only a short distance from where they were preaching. Indeed the very fact that a rumour was spread that the disciples had stolen the body of Jesus at least emphasizes that the tomb *was* empty.

It is hard to believe that *the disciples stole the body*, because they would have no motive for doing so. It is not easy to believe that men would preach a doctrine which resulted in unpopularity with the authorities, persecution and even death, when they knew all the time that Jesus was not risen from the dead at all.

Some have argued that *his enemies stole the body*. Why did they not produce evidence of this when they tried to forbid the preaching of the early Christians? Others have said that *Jesus did not really die at all* (see above, p. 191). Long ago the historian, Strauss, answered this theory by saying, 'It is impossible that a being who had stolen half dead out of the sepulchre, who crept about weak

*Psalm 16:10 quoted in Acts 2:25–31 '(David) foresaw and spoke of the resurrection of the Christ, that he was not abandoned to Hades, nor did his flesh see corruption' (RSV).

195

and ill, wanting medical treatment, who required bandaging, strengthening and indulgence, and who still at last yielded to His sufferings, could have given the disciples the impression that He was a conqueror over death and the grave, the Prince of Life: an impression which lay at the bottom of their future ministry. Such a resuscitation could by no possibility have changed their sorrow into enthusiasm, have elevated their reverence into worship.' Furthermore, of course, on this explanation, Jesus himself would be party to dishonesty and deception.

John saw an empty tomb, and believed that Jesus had risen.

b. The grave-clothes (verses 4–8)

Strictly speaking the tomb was not completely empty. The body of Jesus was no longer there, but the grave-clothes were so placed that John saw these—and believed. The significance of the grave-clothes is that John describes them as 'lying undisturbed'. That is the force of the Greek word (*keimena*) in verse 5. 'Lying collapsed' is one translation. The heavy spices placed between the folds would collapse the burial cloths once the body had gone, but the cloths remained intact. Furthermore, the napkin, or turban head-cloth, was still 'rolled up' (verse 7) or 'twirled' (*entetuligmenon*). It kept its turban shape and was lying exactly where the head of Jesus would have been.*

On this evidence, it is clear that no-one could have stolen the body and left the grave-clothes like that. It is equally clear that Jesus could not have swooned, only to recover, remove the grave-clothes and escape. John saw, and believed.

Questions for discussion

1. What importance should we attach to the historical evidences for the resurrection in this passage and others? How do we relate the statement 'we saw and believed' to Jesus' words to Thomas (John 20:29), 'How happy are those who believe without seeing me!'?
2. What do we learn about Mary Magdalene, Peter and 'the other disciple, whom Jesus loved' (John) in this passage? How serious is their ignorance of Scripture? (Compare Luke 16:19–31 and Luke 24:25–27.)
3. Since Jesus had told the disciples he would rise again from the

*For further reading see Michael Green, *Man Alive!*, especially pp. 41, 42.

dead, why do you think that Mary and the other disciples (chapters 20 and 21) seemed to be so surprised that the tomb was empty? Has this anything to teach us?

44 More evidence for the resurrection

20:11–31

11 Mary stood crying outside the tomb. While she was still crying, she bent over and looked in the tomb [12]*and saw two angels there dressed in white, sitting where the body of Jesus had been, one at the head and the other at the feet.* [13]*"Woman, why are you crying?" they asked her.*

She answered, 'They have taken my Lord away, and I do not know where they have put him!'

14 Then she turned round and saw Jesus standing there; but she did not know that it was Jesus. [15]*"Woman, why are you crying?" Jesus asked her. 'Who is it that you are looking for?'*

She thought he was the gardener, so she said to him, 'If you took him away, sir, tell me where you have put him, and I will go and get him.'

16 Jesus said to her, 'Mary!'

She turned towards him and said in Hebrew, 'Rabboni!' (This means 'Teacher.')

17 'Do not hold on to me,' Jesus told her, 'because I have not yet gone back up to the Father. But go to my brothers and tell them that I am returning to him who is my Father and their Father, my God and their God.'

18 So Mary Magdalene went and told the disciples that she had seen the Lord and related to them what he had told her.

19 It was late that Sunday evening, and the disciples were gathered together behind locked doors, because they were afraid of the Jewish authorities. Then Jesus came and stood among them. 'Peace be with you,' he said. [20]*After saying this, he showed them his hands and his side. The disciples were filled with joy at seeing the Lord.* [21]*Jesus said to them again, 'Peace be with you. As the Father sent me, so I send you.'* [22]*Then he breathed on them and said, 'Receive the Holy Spirit.*

²³*If you forgive people's sins, they are forgiven; if you do not forgive them, they are not forgiven.'*

24 One of the twelve disciples, Thomas (called the Twin), was not with them when Jesus came. ²⁵*So the other disciples told him, 'We have seen the Lord!'*

Thomas said to them, 'Unless I see the scars of the nails in his hands and put my finger on those scars and my hand in his side, I will not believe.'

26 A week later the disciples were together again indoors, and Thomas was with them. The doors were locked, but Jesus came and stood among them and said, 'Peace be with you.' ²⁷*Then he said to Thomas, 'Put your finger here, and look at my hands; then stretch out your hand and put it in my side. Stop your doubting, and believe!'*

28 Thomas answered him, 'My Lord and my God!'

29 Jesus said to him, 'Do you believe because you see me? How happy are those who believe without seeing me!'

30 In his disciples' presence Jesus performed many other miracles which are not written down in this book. ³¹*But these have been written in order that you may believe that Jesus is the Messiah, the Son of God, and that through your faith in him you may have life.*

It was an Easter Sunday morning. My brother-in-law was speaking to a packed church of some five hundred or so people. Suddenly he produced a yellow daffodil and solemnly ate part of it before an astonished congregation. (Don't try it, it did him no good!) Then he made his point, somewhat like this; 'If someone says to a friend, "I hear the Vicar ate a daffodil in church this morning", they probably won't believe him! But if you say, "I and five hundred other people saw the Vicar eat a daffodil this morning, and you can ask anyone who was there!", then your evidence is not so easily dismissed.'

John does not speak of five hundred people seeing the risen Jesus in this chapter (though Paul did in 1 Corinthians 15:6, and added 'most of whom are still alive'); but he gives a number of examples of Jesus appearing to very different people at different times. He makes a strong case.

There was Mary, who remained by the tomb, weeping, after the other two disciples had returned to their homes. In the midst of her sorrow Jesus came to her (verses 14–18). Then Jesus came to a group of disciples in the upper room that same evening (verses 19–23). The following Sunday he came to the disciples again, this time when Thomas, a born sceptic, was with them (verses 26–29).

In these three dramatic stories the Evangelist emphasizes the reality and the effects of the resurrection appearances, which provide us with further evidence for the Christian claim that *Jesus is risen*.

a. The reality of the resurrection appearances

There is no doubt on the evidence here that the resurrection body of Jesus was real and not phantom. It was not identical with his earthly body, because it was not so limited. Jesus could appear among the disciples, even through closed doors (verse 19). He could appear and disappear at will, and in what must have been a startling manner. Furthermore, he obviously wanted to teach the disciples to depend less on his physical presence, and to prepare for a deeper and more spiritual relationship with him. This would be possible once he had ascended to his Father. This must be the . . . meaning of his words to Mary Magdalene, 'Do not hold on to me because I have not yet gone back up to the Father. But go to my brothers and tell them that I am returning to him who is my Father and their Father, my God and their God' (verse 17). These words also emphasize the uniqueness of his own relationship to his Father. He does not say 'to *our* Father'; but 'to my Father and their Father'.

Nevertheless, although his risen body was different in some sense from his earthly body, it is clear that the disciples can recognize Jesus (verses 16, 20, 28). Mary could touch him (verse 17). The disciples could see the marks of crucifixion in his hands and side (verse 20), and Thomas was invited to put his hands on them (verse 27). In the next chapter we read that Jesus could cook breakfast and eat it with the disciples (21:4–14). Jesus was no apparition.

Some have tried to explain away the appearances of Jesus as due to the disciples suffering hallucinations. Arnold Lunn describes an occasion when he himself suffered hallucinations when searching a mountain peak for the body of a friend of his who had been killed.* 'We had travelled all through the night from London, and

Arnold Lunn, *The Third Day*, pp. 74,75.

started on our search party within an hour or two of arriving at the little inn from which he (the friend) started for his last climb. We were out of training and tired, and the strain of the search gradually began to tell. Every time we turned a corner *we expected to see our friend*; again and again we thought we saw his body stretched out on the rocks, and heard the other members of the party shouting that they had found him . . . These hallucinations were vivid while they lasted, *but they never lasted for more than a second or two.*'

If Lunn's experience of hallucinations is at all typical, then we see that the resurrection appearances do not fit the hallucination theory at all. The disciples of Jesus were certainly not *expecting* to see Jesus, risen from the dead. When Mary saw Jesus, she thought it was the gardener (verse 15). When the disciples in the upper room saw Jesus, we are told in Luke's Gospel that their first re-action was that 'they were terrified, thinking that they were seeing a ghost' (Luke 24:37). When Thomas was told by the others, 'We have seen the Lord', he said, 'Unless I see the scars of the nails in his hands and put my finger on those scars and my hand in his side, I will not (in the Greek a double negative is used for emphasis: 'no never') believe' (verse 25). Furthermore, these appearances of Jesus clearly lasted for more than a few seconds, and far from the effects wearing off, the disciples became so convinced that Jesus was alive that they were prepared to suffer imprisonment, persecution and death rather than stop preaching the resurrection.

b. The effects of the resurrection appearances

Those who deny the resurrection of Jesus Christ have a difficult task to explain the changed lives of the disciples following the death of their leader. John hints at the effects of the resurrection in this chapter.

1. *Sorrow is turned into joy* (verses 11–16). Mary is overcome with grief at the death of Jesus (verses 11, 15). She starts the day by saying bitterly, 'They have taken my Lord away, and I do not know where they have put him!' She ends the day by joyfully telling the disciples, 'I have seen the Lord.' It is still true today that the Christian, who mourns the loss of a close relative or friend, can experience peace and joy in the knowledge of the risen Lord Jesus.

2. *Fear is turned into boldness* (verses 19–23). The disciples

skulked behind locked doors 'because they were afraid of the Jewish authorities', the Evangelist tells us. Their hopes and plans had been dashed to the ground by the death of Jesus. 'We had hoped that he would be the one who was going to set Israel free!', one of them said miserably (Luke 24:21).

Then Jesus came to them. He promised them peace instead of their fears (verses 19, 21) and power in place of their feebleness (verses 21–23). He would send them out into the world to bring the assurance of forgiveness to those who turned from their sins and trusted in the Lord Jesus Christ. 'As the Father sent me, so I send you.' Then he breathed on them, symbolically assuring them of the breath of God's Spirit who would come to them and strengthen them. A few weeks later these same men were witnessing with such boldness that thousands became Christians. They had such courage that they sang hymns in prison and prayed for their persecutors when stoned to death. They said of themselves, 'We cannot stop speaking of what we ourselves have seen and heard' (Acts 4:20).

3. *Doubt is turned into faith* (verses 24–26). Thomas wanted proof (verse 25). A week went by, and then Thomas saw the risen Lord. Jesus gently rebuked him, but offered him the evidence he wanted. 'Put your finger here, and look at my hands; then stretch out your hand and put it in my side. Stop your doubting, and believe!' Thomas's expression of personal faith and commitment comes as a climax to this Gospel, '*My* Lord and *my* God!'

When Jesus says 'How happy are those who believe without seeing me', it is a word for us. This assurance of faith is possible for all those who personally trust Jesus as Lord and God. Malcolm Muggeridge has told how he was filming in the Holy Land, and walking with a friend along the same road, the Emmaus Road, that Jesus had walked with two disciples on that first Easter morning. 'As my friend and I walked along like Cleopas and his friend, we recalled as they did the events of the crucifixion and its aftermath in the light of our utterly different and yet similar world. Nor was it a fancy that we too were joined by a third presence. And I tell you that wherever the walk, and whoever the wayfarers, there is always this third presence ready to emerge from the shadows and fall in step along the dusty, stony way.'* The risen Christ still turns doubt into faith.

*Malcolm Muggeridge, *Another King*, p. 14.

'These have been written in order that *you* may believe that Jesus is the Messiah, the Son of God, and that through your faith in him you may have life.'

Questions for discussion

1. How does this passage help us to answer the objection that the disciples only *imagined* that they saw Jesus alive, and that they were suffering from hallucinations?
2. What difference did Jesus make to the sorrows, fears and doubts of the disciples in this chapter? How far are his words to the disciples in this chapter helpful to us in similar situations today?
3. 'As the Father sent me, so I send you' (verse 21). How do these words and this passage help us to understand the mission of the church today?
4. What do we learn from this passage about the reasons for Thomas's doubts, and the way Jesus dealt with them? How can we help someone to face up to doubt?

45 The challenge of Christian discipleship

21:1–25

21 *After this, Jesus appeared once more to his disciples at Lake Tiberias. This is how it happened.* ²*Simon Peter, Thomas (called the Twin), Nathanael (the one from Cana in Galilee), the sons of Zebedee, and two other disciples of Jesus were all together.* ³*Simon Peter said to the others, 'I am going fishing.'*

'We will come with you,' they told him. So they went out in a boat, but all that night they did not catch a thing. ⁴*As the sun was rising, Jesus stood at the water's edge, but the disciples did not know that it was Jesus.* ⁵*Then he asked them, 'Young men, haven't you caught anything?'*

'Not a thing,' they answered.

6 He said to them, 'Throw your net out on the right side of the boat, and you will catch some.' So they threw the net out and could not pull it back in, because they had caught so many fish.

7 The disciple whom Jesus loved said to Peter, 'It is the Lord!' When Peter heard that it was the Lord, he wrapped his outer garment round him (for he had taken his clothes off) and jumped into the water. [8]*The other disciples came to shore in the boat, pulling the net full of fish. They were not very far from land, about a hundred metres away.* [9]*When they stepped ashore, they saw a charcoal fire there with fish on it and some bread.* [10]*Then Jesus said to them, 'Bring some of the fish you have just caught.'*

11 Simon Peter went aboard and dragged the net ashore full of big fish, a hundred and fifty-three in all; even though there were so many, still the net did not tear. [12]*Jesus said to them, 'Come and eat.' None of the disciples dared ask him, 'Who are you?' because they knew it was the Lord.* [13]*So Jesus went over, took the bread, and gave it to them; he did the same with the fish.*

14 This, then, was the third time Jesus appeared to the disciples after he was raised from death.

15 After they had eaten, Jesus said to Simon Peter, 'Simon son of John, do you love me more than these others do?'

'Yes, Lord,' he answered, 'you know that I love you.'

Jesus said to him, 'Take care of my lambs.' [16]*A second time Jesus said to him, 'Simon son of John, do you love me?'*

'Yes, Lord,' he answered, 'you know that I love you.'

Jesus said to him, 'Take care of my sheep.' [17]*A third time Jesus said, 'Simon son of John, do you love me?'*

Peter was sad because Jesus asked him the third time, 'Do you love me?' so he said to him, 'Lord, you know everything; you know that I love you!'

Jesus said to him, 'Take care of my sheep. [18]*I am telling you the truth: when you were young, you used to get ready and go anywhere you wanted to; but when you are old, you will stretch out your hands and someone else will bind you and take you where you don't want to go.'* [19]*(In saying this, Jesus was indicating the way in which Peter would die and bring glory to God.)* Then Jesus said to him, 'Follow me!'

20 Peter turned round and saw behind him that other disciple, whom Jesus loved—the one who had leaned close to Jesus at the meal and had asked, 'Lord, who is going to betray you?' [21]*When Peter saw him, he asked Jesus, 'Lord, what about this man?'*

22 Jesus answered him, 'If I want him to live until I come, what is that to you? Follow me!'

23 So a report spread among the followers of Jesus that this disciple would not die. But Jesus did not say that he would not die; he said, 'If I want him to live until I come, what is that to you?'

24 He is the disciple who spoke of these things, the one who also wrote them down; and we know that what he said is true.

25 Now, there are many other things that Jesus did. If they were all written down one by one, I suppose that the whole world could not hold the books that would be written.

On New Year's Day 1945, shortly before Dietrich Bonhoeffer was put to death in a Nazi concentration camp, he wrote these words,

'While all the powers of good, aid and attend us,
Boldly we'll face the future, be it what may.
At even, and at morn, God will befriend us,
And, oh most surely on each New Year's Day.'

As a disciple of Jesus Christ Bonhoeffer had learnt to face the future, however dark, in the knowledge that God was with him.

This last chapter of John's Gospel helps us to do the same. It may have been added to deal with a rumour that John, 'the disciple whom Jesus loved', would remain alive until Jesus came again at the end of the world (verse 23). John carefully records the incident when the words which give rise to this rumour were actually said, in order to correct a false impression (verse 24). His concern for sober truth is a characteristic of this Gospel.

But this third and last appearance of Jesus recorded in John's Gospel (verse 14) also moves us to consider the claims and demands of Christian discipleship, such as obedience, love and service, in the confidence that God has a loving plan for our lives even unto death.

a. Obedience

There is restlessness and perhaps impatience in the decision of Peter and some of the other disciples to go fishing (verse 3). The strain of recent events was no doubt beginning to tell. Maybe there was also a hankering for the old life. It was possibly an impulsive decision by Peter, which the others were only too glad to comply with. But, as so often happens to the Christian who acts impulsively, the fishing trip was a failure. That night they caught nothing (verse 3).

It was at this point of failure that Jesus once again revealed himself to these disciples. After a cold, wet and miserable night the dawn broke and the fishermen saw a stranger standing on the seashore. The question 'Young men, haven't you caught anything?' is met with an emphatic and impatient, 'Not a thing'. But when the stranger gives the authoritative command, 'Throw your net out of the right side of the boat, and you will catch some', they not only obey and make a great catch, but John recognizes the stranger as Jesus.

Once again in a fishing incident (*cf*. Luke 5) Jesus has revealed himself to the disciples. He has made it clear that obedience is better than impatience. If we want to become effective disciples of Jesus Christ we must also learn to wait and to listen and to obey Jesus. The net was full of large fish, and somebody even bothered to count them (verse 11). Indeed this comment by the writer, the description of Peter's impulsive rushing into the sea (verse 7), the careful noting that the net was full of fish and not broken, and that the boat was one hundred yards off the shore, are all evidences of an eyewitness account. When Jesus invites the disciples to bring some of the fish they have caught as a contribution to the breakfast he has begun to prepare for them (verses 9–10), we catch a glimpse of the love of Jesus for those who obey him. Sometimes he teaches us the importance of obedience in failure and difficult circumstances. But always he understands our human weakness, and cares for our physical as well as spiritual needs (verses 12–13). He also demonstrates to the disciples that he is no ghost or spirit—but the living, risen Lord.

b. Love

Simon Peter had denied Jesus three times in the courtyard of the high priest (see John 19). According to Luke's Gospel, Jesus had met Peter privately after the resurrection and probably he was then assured of forgiveness (Luke 24:34). Now he gives Peter the opportunity to wipe out the threefold denial with a threefold affirmation of love and loyalty.

When Jesus says to Peter, 'Simon, son of John, do you love me *more than these*?' (RSV) he may be referring to the other disciples or

205

to his fishing-nets. Peter had often boasted of his love for Jesus (see Mark 14:29). Did he now really love Jesus more than these others ? Was he learning humility with his love ? Was his love for Christ stronger than his love for his fishing ? Jesus requires us to love him with all our heart and soul and mind and strength. Love for our job, or our family, or friends, or pleasures must never count more than our love for him. Furthermore, love for Christ is the only motive that will keep the Christian disciple faithful to Christ whatever the circumstances. It is not enough to want to be successful, or to want to do good in the world, or to leave the world a better place. We can easily be disillusioned if that is our motive for Christian service. Jesus wants to make sure that we love him.*

c. Service

The Christian disciple has been saved to serve. Jesus is here commissioning Peter for service, which he describes in the familiar terms of doing the work of a shepherd. Jesus had previously implied (see Luke 5:1–11) that Peter would become a fisher of men, an evangelist. He now calls him also to the work of a shepherd, a pastor to the church of God. His responsibility would be for the young (the lambs) and the older, maturer Christians (the sheep). The lambs must be fed with appropriate food (verse 16); the sheep must be cared for, watched over and fed.

The test of our love for Jesus Christ will be seen in our willingness to serve him. He calls us to be fishers of men, seeking to introduce our friends to Jesus Christ. He may well call some of us to be shepherds, caring for young Christians, teaching the message of the gospel, supporting and encouraging the weak. But many people ask, how can I know what God wants me to do, and how can I best serve him ? Jesus implies that he has a different plan for each of us, and our part is to follow him.

*Many commentators point out that two different Greek words are used for 'love'. In verses 16 and 17 the verb for love employed by Jesus is *agapaō*, which speaks of the highest kind of love, God's love (see John 3:16). When Peter answers he uses the word *phileō*, which implies friendship or fondness. In the third question Jesus uses Peter's own word (*phileō*), which challenged Peter's sincerity. That may be the reason for Peter's sorrow (verse 17). However, this may be reading too much into the text, as these words are used synonymously in this Gospel and if Jesus was speaking in Aramaic there are no such distinctions.

d. Discipleship

For Peter this would mean a life-time of leadership in the Christian church, caring for the needs of God's people. It would not be an easy task, and as he grew older he would find himself more restricted (verse 18) and he would eventually die a martyr's death. Tradition tells us that Peter was crucified upside-down. Certainly Jesus indicated some such death; but the writer comments, 'In saying this, Jesus was indicating the way in which Peter would die and bring glory to God' (verse 19). A Christian may bring honour to God even in the way that he dies.

But not everyone is called by Christ to such a responsible task or to such a dramatic end. He has different plans for each of us. Like Peter, we are often curious about God's plan for another person. When Peter notices John following them he says, 'Lord, what about this man?' The reply that Jesus makes helps us to understand the importance of personally following Jesus, and not encouraging curiosity or even jealousy about God's plans for others. 'If I want him to live until I come, what is that to you? *Follow me!*'

In some ways John's life-work was less dramatic than Peter's. He became a man of reflection and deep thought, calling men and women in the pagan city of Ephesus to put their trust, not in vague religious experience or speculation, but in the historical Jesus. John must have lived to a very old age. Length of life is in God's hands.

Our task is to follow Jesus. He may call us to a position of responsibility or leadership in the church, or in business, or in one of the professions, or in industry, or in the local community or in the home. He may call us to stay at home or to go overseas. We follow him as we read his words to us in the Bible and obey them. We follow him as we talk to him in prayer and trust him to order the circumstances of our lives. For, as in the case of this Gospel, the witness of the Bible to God's dealings with men is a true witness (verse 24).

Much more could have been written in this Gospel and in the other Gospels (verse 25). But God has given us enough to know his will, so that we may follow him faithfully all the days of our life.

207

Questions for discussion

1. In what ways did Jesus help Simon Peter to face up to failure in this chapter? How do we apply this to ourselves?

2. What do we learn about the *motives*, *conditions* and *methods* of Christian service in this chapter?

3. In what sense can a Christian's *death* bring glory to God (verse 19)?

4. What do we learn about the love of Jesus for his disciples in this passage? What else do we learn from this chapter that helps us to face up to the future with confidence?

Where to go next

For more information about the Christian faith:

John Stott, *Basic Christianity* (IVP)
John White, *The fight* (IVP)

For more help in reading the Bible:

Peter Lee, Greg Scharf and Robert Willcox, *Food for Life* (IVP)
Clive Charlton (editor), *Learning to Live* (IVP)
Scripture Union, 47 Marylebone Lane, London W1M 6AX has a variety of material.